88 89 90 91 92 5 4 3 2 1

Douglas & McIntyre Ltd., 1615 Venables Street,
Vancouver, British Columbia V5L 2H1

Canadian Cataloguing in Publication Data
Schreiner, John, 1936–
The refiners

ISBN 0-88894-655-4

1. British Columbia Sugar Refining Company – History. 2. Sugar – Manufacture and refining – British Columbia – History. I. Title.
HD9114.C24B78 1989 338.7'6641'09711 C89-0913959-5

All photographs courtesy of BC Sugar Archives except where otherwise noted.
Jacket photography courtesy of Montizambert Photography
Design by Alexandra Hass
Typeset by The Typeworks
Printed and bound in Canada by John Deyell Company

THE REFINERS

A CENTURY OF BC SUGAR

JOHN SCHREINER

Douglas & McIntyre
Vancouver/Toronto

THE

CONTENTS

Preface

Some years ago when I was researching the history of the Canadian wine industry, I was distressed at the paucity of important records and documents. The little available material was stored carelessly, with no thought to turning it over to a professional archive. Far more material had been lost. As a result, many Canadian business people have been subjected to my standard lecture on the importance of preserving records that document Canadian achievement.

BC Sugar chairman Peter Cherniavsky was among those receiving that free advice, at a time when he had begun thinking about the events, including a book, to mark the 100th anniversary of the company. The advice, of course, was presumptuous since BC Sugar's records turned out to be unusually extensive. A large storage area in the head office basement contains approximately 120 legal-size file drawers crammed with records. The adjoining walk-in vault contains artifacts, letterbooks and hundreds of photographs. The refinery's museum, established in 1975, is one of the best corporate museums in the land. The richness of those records made this book possible.

The explanation for this historical treasure is apparent: throughout its history, the company's affairs have been directed by the founding Rogers family, and the company's records also are the family's records. This has given a continuity to the affairs of BC Sugar seldom encountered today in Canadian business. Because the company has gone about its business without especially seeking the public eye, there are details in this book which may surprise the reader.

Almost as soon as settlement began in British Columbia, schemes were promoted to develop the sugar industry. Research for the book turned up at least a dozen proposals either for sugar beet factories or for refineries. The citizens reasoned that, since sugar was a staple, a sugar refinery would become one of the foundations for long-term prosperity. In 1890, when $30,000 was a great deal of money, Vancouver's city councillors had the courage to float a bond issue for this sum and provide the inducement to secure finally a sugar refinery. And indeed, it did become a foundation of prosperity. BC Sugar, at 100, is one of Vancouver's oldest independent companies.

I am grateful for the support of BC Sugar and for the free access to BC Sugar's archives in the preparation of this book. Among the current company personnel, Peter Cherniavsky, Bill Brown and Martin Rogers have been especially generous with their help.

As well, gratitude is due the more than fifty other individuals who gave interviews and provided information. Their names are listed on page 263. A special acknowledgement goes to William Hetherington, who gave four extensive interviews and provided valuable advice on the manuscript.

Finally, I acknowledge the invaluable assistance of my wife, Marlene, in transcribing hours of taped interviews and providing counsel and encouragement; and my daughter Alison and son John, often pressed into service to run vital errands for me.

I

You Take Charge

IT BEGAN WITH A BRASH YOUNG MAN OF TWENTY-FOUR.

Constable J. H. Deacon was patrolling the corner of Vancouver's Granville and Hastings streets about eight o'clock on the warm Saturday evening of 22 June 1906 when a Pierce Arrow sedan whipped around the corner and accelerated southwards. A zealous policeman, he had earlier paced the distance—1347 feet—to the Granville and Georgia intersection. As he told the traffic court a week later, he was prepared for "just such an emergency." Since the automobile needed, according to Deacon's stopwatch, a mere fifty-three seconds to reach the farther intersection, where it swung west, it was travelling at seventeen miles an hour, a full seven miles above the urban speed limit.

Deacon did not stop the car to issue the ticket, for the vehicle and its driver, B. T. Rogers, were well known. Rogers had lived in Vancouver since 1890 when, as an ambitious twenty-four-year-old American impressively sponsored by New York and Montreal businessmen, he extracted a $30,000 subsidy from city council to build a sugar refinery. Vancouver's first major industry not based on logging or fishing, the refinery prospered to the extent that Rogers, at the turn of the century, was wealthy enough to erect the city's finest mansion and to violate traffic rules with one of the first three automobiles in the city, a vehicle described as "a one-cylinder puddle-jumper with a handlebar instead of a steering wheel." Its successor, the Pierce Arrow, the first of four such marques he was to own, and at about $4,500 one of the most expensive cars in its day, motored him into court several times. Constable Deacon's ticket yielded a $5 penalty. "Quite a number of automobilists have paid $5 to find out how fast they are going," the magistrate said sarcastically. "He was doing some fast time." A speeding infraction two years later cost $16 and brought the threat of jail the next time he was caught. In 1908, when a terrified horse bolted into the bush from a Vancouver Island road after Rogers passed, the horseman rejected an initial offer of $10 and threatened to sue until he received $35 compensation—the damaged harness alone having been valued at $22. Rogers's driving was entirely in character: determined, strong-willed and short-tempered, he was every bit as aggressive in business as he was at the wheel of his Pierce Arrow. He was always in a hurry.

◆

Benjamin Tingley Rogers (known throughout his life to business associates as B. T.) was born 21 October 1865 in Philadelphia, the second son of Samuel Blythe Rogers and Clara Augusta Dupuy. His grandfather Thomas Rogers was a farmer near Philadelphia. Samuel Rogers, a successful wholesale grocer in his youth, became president of the Columbia Steam Sugar Refinery in Philadelphia about 1866 and, with his brother-in-law, U.S. senator Henry Sanford, bought a Louisiana sugar plantation in 1869. After that partnership was dissolved in 1876, Samuel established and became president of the Planters refinery in New Orleans. His children were sent to good private schools, including Phillips Academy of Andover, Massachussetts. The older son, Blythe, took a law degree at Harvard but B. T. was too impatient to be a student. His mother, writing him at school in 1877, teased: "Also tell me if you can how long Canada has belonged to Spain?"[1] Having spent his school vacations in the laboratory at his father's refinery, he completed a technical course in sugar chemistry at the Standard Refinery Company in Boston and went to work for his father.

His father died suddenly in 1883. According to the 1958 memoir of the company written by B. T.'s widow Bella (Mary Isabella), Samuel Rogers died after being hit on the head by a brick thrown by a striker during a labour disturbance at the refinery. Samuel's widow moved the family north where B. T., at the age of eighteen, joined the Havemeyers and Elder sugar refinery in Brooklyn, then the largest and most modern refinery in the United States. Henry O. and Theodore Havemeyer, the most powerful figures in American sugar refining, and friends of his father, were impressed with the youth. Trim and energetic, Rogers had a bright, alert appearance: his jaw was firm, his nose long and straight, his forehead high and broad, and his eyes intense and direct. By 1887, when he was still only twenty-two, he had already become an assistant to the Brooklyn refinery's demanding chief superintendent, Ernst Gerbracht, indicating that Rogers had mastered the difficult art of sugar boiling. In a cane sugar refinery, raw sugar, which is dark brown and coarsely granulated, is dissolved in hot water. In several steps the impurities and the molasses, which give the colour, are removed and the remaining liquid is boiled under a partial vacuum to form uniform white sugar crystals. This process is now computer-controlled, but in B. T.'s day the sugar boiler periodically drew samples from the vacuum pan and judged by feeling the sugar and tasting it when the crystals had reached the correct size. This task, which determined the refinery's productivity and the quality of the sugar, was so exacting that Ernst Gerbracht was ordered by his doctor one day in 1887 to take a complete rest or face a nervous breakdown. Gerbracht tossed the keys to young Rogers, ordering: "You take charge. I'm off."[2] By the time the superintendent returned, Rogers had acquired the taste for running his own show.

He recognized his opportunity two years later when he was in Montreal installing Havemeyers and Elder filters in the Redpath refinery. Montreal's business community, then Canada's most influential, was alive with news about western Canada now that Canadian Pacific's transcontinental railway had been completed to Vancouver on the Pacific Ocean. Rogers discovered that the Montreal refinery was sending refined sugar by rail as far as Vancouver, comfortably shielded by tariffs which prevented San Francisco sugar refineries from grabbing the British Columbia market. The opportunity was obvious: a refinery in Vancouver would enjoy the same tariff protection, would buy raw sugar in the Pacific and, with lower freight costs, would displace Montreal sugar in western Canada.

The railway was the key to the refinery. As an American, Rogers would have surveyed available opportunities first in his native country for building refineries. There were none. The Havemeyers dominated the eastern United States and controlled one of two refineries in San Francisco. There were no refineries in the American Pacific Northwest at the time—but neither Seattle nor Portland was yet connected to the American railroad grid.[3] Vancouver's location was strategic, with the railroad accessing sugar markets on the Prairies, just opening to settlement, and as far east as Winnipeg.

Early in December 1889 Rogers outlined his ideas in a letter which still survives. The recipient is unknown: it likely was David Oppenheimer, the merchant and realtor who in 1888 had become the development-minded second mayor of Vancouver. Rogers was preparing the ground for a submission to city council late in January of the new year.

His credibility came from what he called his "associates." When the refining company was incorporated in March, with the shareholders subscribing for enough shares at $100 each to put $160,000 into the treasury, the *Vancouver Daily World* reported: "Most of the stock was taken up in Montreal and New York." The backers of the refinery included the Havemeyers; Theodore A. Havemeyer invested $25,000 in the Rogers venture on the understanding that he would sell the shares to Rogers when the young man could afford them.[4] In Rogers's December letter, he carefully named his American backers before describing the refinery he proposed: "I have already referred this matter to Mr. T. A. Havemeyer and Mr. Charles H. Senff, both of whom think well of the enterprise, and promise financial support." Senff was Havemeyer's cousin; he not only invested but also extended a personal loan that enabled the young Rogers to invest.

On 10 January 1890 Rogers had Lowell M. Palmer, a New York manufacturer of barrels for the sugar industry there and in Montreal, arrange an introduction to Canadian Pacific's president William C. Van Horne.[5] The aspiring refiner saw that the CPR was eager for economic development to anchor its western terminal. Palmer wrote that Rogers "has the capital and the experience necessary to make a success of an enterprise of this kind, if he can see his way clear to take hold of it, and the first point for him to establish is whether or not an arrangement can be made with the Canadian Pacific that shall protect him in rates that will warrant the establishing of this industry." In Montreal, he quickly got additional support. Van Horne and his associates were among the wealthiest men in Canada and had the best connections: CPR director R. B. Angus was general manager of the Bank of Montreal. He sat in on the meeting between Van Horne and Rogers and made a forceful recommendation on behalf of the young man. The Canadian Pacific directors, prepared to encourage any sensible industrial project at the Vancouver terminus, guaranteed the refinery—at least during its first five years—freight rates to Winnipeg as low as those the Montreal refiners were charged when they shipped sugar to the middle of the continent. Canadian Pacific even agreed that, when it had freight cars returning empty from Vancouver to Ontario, the refinery would be offered "especially low rates" should it need to market any surplus sugar beyond Western Canada.

By the time Rogers arrived from New York and checked into the CPR's Hotel Vancouver on 24 January 1890, influential opinion, including the city's newspapers, had been courted. The *Daily World* carried an editorial in its 27 January edition outlining what Rogers would put to council that evening. "It is hoped that the council will give these matters the consideration their importance demands," the newspaper urged. Earlier that day Rogers had drafted, in his clear, flowing longhand on hotel stationery, his two-and-a-half-page proposal. He and his associates would have a sugar refinery operating within nine months, he wrote, if the city was prepared to "bonus" the project with $40,000 worth of land and services, with a fifteen-year tax holiday and with ten years of free water. It was an audacious request, but Rogers had judged correctly the council's desire for business expansion. A sugar refinery, in particular, was identified with stability and prosperity.

Sugar consumption in the industrial world had increased dramatically in the latter half of the nineteenth century as improved refining techniques slashed the price of sugar, formerly a luxury. In Canada, annual per capita consumption had grown from fifteen pounds in 1868 to forty-four pounds in 1890.[6] Rogers, by researching Canadian Pacific's freight figures, learned that 5,150,000 pounds of sugar had been delivered to British Columbia in 1889, most of it from Montreal. The relatively high cost of the sugar had spurred Mayor Oppenheimer in 1888 to organize test plantings of sugar beets by farmers near Chilliwack in the Fraser Valley, a venture which died when the farmers were unable to produce beets with adequate sugar content.

Efforts to establish a sugar industry in British Columbia had begun at least twenty years earlier. In Victoria, the *Daily British Colonist* began a sustained editorial campaign in 1870 for a sugar industry, urging "legislative encouragement" after having noted the developing California's sugar beet industry. "Why should not British Columbia produce her own sugar?" the newspaper asked on 15 September. In New Westminster, a wine and spirits merchant named Ernst Picht asked himself the same question. Within two years he had planted twelve acres of beets and had produced both sugar and syrup from them. Early in 1873 Picht and several business associates formed the Fraser River Beet Sugar Company and secured access to more than one thousand acres on Annacis Island, downstream in the Fraser from New Westminster. Despite enthusiastic local support, Picht's venture vanished from the newspapers of the day as quickly as it had appeared. Annacis Island, with its severe drainage problems turned out to be a poor place for beet culture.

The *Colonist* continued to campaign for a sugar industry. "It is no secret," the paper declared on 15 July 1883, "that capitalists have had their attention drawn to Victoria as a profitable field for the establishment of a sugar refinery. . . . The Canadian tariff is especially favorable to the importation of raw sugars, and no other articles of Canadian manufacture enjoy so large a measure of protection as refined sugars." The stumbling block was the lack of subsidy. Two years earlier, for example, the legislature had passed a motion supporting a $20,000 subsidy for a beet sugar factory, but the premier was opposed, and the money was never made available.

It was absurd to ship refined sugar from distant Montreal. "This same sugar," Rogers noted in his solicitation to city council, "could be placed in Vancouver with 12,000 miles less ocean carriage; besides saving the extra expense of transshipment and rail haul from Halifax to Montreal, which the Montreal refineries have to undergo during several months of the year when navigation on the St. Lawrence is closed by ice."

Canadian Pacific's patronage gave Rogers invaluable contacts in Vancouver. One was CPR land commissioner in Vancouver, J. M. Browning, an alderman and chairman of the council's finance committee which received Rogers's 27 January draft. By the following Monday, Browning's committee had transformed the proposal into the Sugar Refinery Bonus by-law, shunting aside what the *Daily World* called "an endeavor . . . in some quarters to throw cold water on the bylaw simply because it emanated to a large degree from His Worship the Mayor, whose busy mind is hard at work inducing industries to establish themselves here."

Both Oppenheimer and Browning strongly backed Rogers at the 4 February council meeting when Alderman J. T. Carroll raised objections to the by-law. The city, Carroll noted, was proposing to give Rogers $30,000 worth of property but was only binding him to refine sugar on the site for five years. What was to stop Rogers from diverting his free property to other uses thereafter, he asked. The mayor, primed by Rogers's persuasive market research, replied that there was a ready demand in British Columbia for five million pounds of sugar a year. The refinery would produce eight million pounds, with the difference to be sold in the neighbouring western Canadian territories. Another alderman added that the Havemeyers of New York were "reliable." Vancouver council passed the by-law that evening. Mayor Oppenheimer, who left politics the next year, also invested in Rogers's company and bought the refinery's first sugar for Oppenheimer Brothers, the grocery wholesaling firm run by the mayor.

Council made only two significant changes to Rogers's draft proposal for the refinery. The bonus, to be used to buy and prepare a refinery site, was limited to $30,000; Rogers appears to have made no objection. Secondly, a condition was added to the bonus by-law at council's 10 February meeting insisting that the sugar company "shall not at any time employ Chinese labour in and about the said works." The city's xenophobic bias against Orientals—there were about one thousand Chinese then living amid Vancouver's twelve thousand citizens—had been deeply entrenched by the 1887 anti-Chinese riots. The *News-Advertiser* suggested on 4 February that no Chinese be hired for the proposed refinery. "The taxpayers of Vancouver will never vote any money that will, either directly or indirectly, foster Chinese labour," the newspaper warned. Alderman Carroll had stormed against the Chinese at the previous evening's council meeting. According to the *Daily World,* Carroll said that "it would be of no benefit to the city if Chinamen were employed. He did not want to see the money go to China. . . . He would rather let the factory go." William Fleming, the labour council's watchdog against the further penetration of Chinese labour beyond Vancouver's sawmills and fish canneries, appeared at city council when the refinery bonus was being debated. "I opposed any concessions to any industry unless white men were to be employed," he recalled in his memoirs. "Mr. Rogers protested he had no intention of employing any other." No Chinese names appear on a list of the refinery's employees published in the 1892 city directory nor were any hired for some years. An article in the June 1914 issue of *Industrial Progress,* a Vancouver business monthly, declared: "We may say that we are in a position to refute the statement that has been made in some quarters to the effect that Oriental labour is employed at the British Columbia Sugar Refinery. We have it direct from the management that since the start none but white labour has been employed."

With the bonus in place, Rogers in mid-February took Canadian Pacific's transcontinental train back to Montreal, spending the long journey on detailed planning. He worried about the waterfront site which the city had agreed to buy from the Vancouver Land Improvement Company, a real estate firm with headquarters in Victoria. At Brandon, he left the train to wire another of the aldermen: "Please find out what kind of bottom off refinery site Rock or Mud. Can piles be driven for wharf." The accommodating council passed the request to the city engineer, instructing that the results should be mailed as soon as possible to Rogers. In Montreal, he confirmed the necessary financial support from CPR president Van Horne and the other backers, for he needed capital both to order refinery equipment and for a $10,000 performance bond which Vancouver insisted be deposited with the Bank of British Columbia. He then went to New York, where he had been living and working, to order equipment, report to his New York backers and tie up loose ends. Moving fast—he faced a deadline to start refining sugar by early 1891—Rogers boarded the CPR in Montreal 14 March for Vancouver. The following day, while Rogers's train was clacking through northern Ontario, the Vancouver ratepayers approved a money by-law—the vote was a resounding 174 to 8—empowering the city to borrow the $30,000 by issuing five per cent debentures maturing in March 1930. The B.C. Sugar Refining Company[7] was incorporated on 27 March, shortly after Rogers arrived back in Vancouver.

By this time the city had agreed to pay $15,000 for the site and had begun tendering contracts to clear it and prepare it for construction. Work proceeded quickly, and by the fall Rogers had the five-storey brick-clad refinery up. In November the company, mindful of the great fire in

Vancouver in June 1886, had the refinery connected to the city's fire alarm system. Raw sugar was ordered from the Orient and, in less than a year from making his proposal to the city, Rogers was producing sugar.

"The first melt was put through on January 16, 1891," Mary Isabella Rogers wrote in *B.C. Sugar*. "It was a tremendous challenge for the managing director; not one of the men employed had ever seen a sugar refinery, much less had any experience at working in one. Rogers had to start with the melt house gang, show them how to do their job, then follow up through blow ups, filters, black house centrifugals, etc., instructing each department, until the finished product, the refined granulated sugar, poured out." With a staff of only twenty, he worked two days and nights without sleep to accomplish this. Bella Rogers, however, assigned too much credit to her husband, who in fact had brought with him from Havemeyers a skilled engineer named Walter Wayte. He helped design the refinery and was its engineer until one morning in March 1894 when Rogers, coming to work with a nasty temper induced by a hangover, scolded Wayte because the barrels of refined sugar were not properly dry. Wayte found himself fired after retorting: "Mr. Rogers, if you were as dry as those barrels, you would have no complaint."[8]

Two weeks after the first melt, Rogers invited the mayor and five of his aldermen to inspect the refinery. They were impressed to find, as they reported to council, that "no expense has been spared to place the works in a thoroughly effective condition . . . We congratulate the city on possessing such a useful industry, and hope that the increase of population and consequent demands may soon require an increased plant to meet the demand."[9] Satisfied that Rogers had met all the conditions he had agreed to a year earlier, they returned the $10,000 bond.

But one detail was overlooked: the deed to the land on which the now functioning refinery sat was still held by the Vancouver Improvement Company in Victoria. At the time, this company, which had been incorporated in 1886, was the second-largest landholder in Vancouver after the CPR. Its shareholders included a number of British Columbia's business leaders, including the ubiquitous Mayor Oppenheimer and his brother Charles. In February 1891 Rogers asked the city for the deed. "As you can understand," he wrote to city clerk Thomas McGuigan, "delay or difficulty in a matter of such grave importance to us as this places this company in a somewhat awkward position."[10]

Rogers would have known the reason for the delay since his president, Alderman Browning, also chaired the city's finance committee. The city had made a commitment to buy the site before it had borrowed the money to finance the deal. The financial arrangements took considerable time. Because the city was slow in paying for the property, the Improvement Company began demanding 8 per cent interest from the date of the initial sale agreement. By January 1891 it was threatening to void the sale, which would indeed have put Rogers in an difficult position. The city, however, heeding its own legal advice that interest need not be paid, was stalling the Improvement Company.

Rogers finally lost his patience in April, testily advising the city that "it is with great regret, therefore, that we see nothing before us now, if this delay is continued, but an appeal to the law courts."[11] The threat worked. In May council sent a $15,525 cheque to the Improvement Company, and Rogers finally received clear title to the land on which his refinery had been built the previous year.

2

Mistakes Are Unavoidable

B. T. ROGERS SURVIVES MISCALCULATION AND MISFORTUNE.

The refinery's first years were precarious. Trouble appeared on 12 December 1890, a month before the first sugar was made, when the Vancouver *News-Advertiser* carried a news item from Ottawa that jolted B. T. Rogers. "The Dominion Government, in negotiating with the British West Indies for closer trade relations, offered to give sugar grown there a rebate duty of $8.50 per short ton." Rogers sent the clipping and a brief letter to William Van Horne: "If there is any truth in the enclosed report from Ottawa," Rogers wrote, "it is a matter of serious consequence to our company here."[1] The report was accurate: the Dominion cabinet authorized this concession to the West Indies within a week. It reduced the cost of raw sugar to the Montreal refiners, who bought from the West Indies, and improved their ability to compete more vigorously for sales on the Prairies. Rogers had ordered his raw sugar from the Philippines and Java, which would not qualify for a duty rebate. The Montreal refiners suddenly had an unforeseen advantage which could confine Rogers to markets west of the Rockies when he had designed a refinery large enough to supply the entire Canadian West.

Rogers quickly conceived a remedy and marshalled support. He suggested that Ottawa should extend the same concession to the Sandwich Islands, as Hawaii was then known. Rogers, counting on the powerful

Van Horne to lobby his friends in the Dominion Cabinet, explained: "We have concluded that it is an excellent opportunity now, to urge the government to adopt a similar policy, in order to promote trade with the islands of the Pacific." The refinery could buy about one thousand tons of raw sugar a month from Hawaii—a cargo which, he reminded Van Horne, would benefit the proposed steamship service between Australia and Vancouver. Rogers also asked all members of Parliament from British Columbia and the rest of Western Canada to support reduced duties for raw sugar from Hawaii. The idea failed because Hawaii became an American possession whereas the West Indies was part of the British Empire and an important export market for Eastern Canada.

Also threatening the refinery was a seemingly modest change in American sugar tariffs proposed late in 1890 to become effective 1 April 1891. The Canadian refiners had been operating behind a tariff which discouraged American competitors. Refined sugar coming into Canada from the United States faced a duty of 1.5 cents a pound and a further ad valorem duty, set at 35 per cent of the market value of the refined sugar in the United States. This priced American sugar comfortably above Canadian refined sugar. Until 1890 the American government had levied an import duty on raw sugar. The change passed by Congress that year eliminated the duty, thereby lowering the refiners' costs. Canadian refiners, on the other hand, paid an import duty of 1.8 cents a pound on raw sugar, except for that purchased from the West Indies by eastern refiners. Rogers found himself being squeezed from two directions: the Montreal refiners had been rendered more competitive in the midwest while the San Francisco refineries would now be able to sell surplus production in British Columbia. "This part of Canadian soil may be looked upon as a convenient dumping ground for the various refineries in the Pacific states to the south," Rogers warned in a lengthy letter drafted in November 1890 to George Kirkpatrick, a Dominion cabinet minister, a Canadian Pacific director and a shareholder of BC Sugar.[2]

Rogers explained that "this refinery of ours occupies a peculiar position here and it is quite possible that the change may affect our profits very considerably. As you are aware, the principal inducement that led to the establishment of a sugar refinery at this point was the knowledge that we should get the advantage of the saving effected in freight charges; or to put it in other words, that in selling our sugars, we should get the one cent per pound which at present goes to the Railway Company for bringing Montreal sugars hither." That penny was a critical margin. Rogers asked the Canadian government to restore protection by increasing its tariff on refined sugar by seven-tenths of a cent.

The following spring several consignments of sugar from Claus Spreckels's Western Sugar Refinery Company in San Francisco were sold to Victoria merchants.[3] Rogers's refinery was forced to shut down for several weeks, covering its embarrassment by saying it was closed for repairs. Rogers retaliated, taking advantage of reduced American duties on imported refined sugar to offer Vancouver sugar in Seattle and Tacoma. This set off a sugar price war in the Pacific Northwest. "They came in to rob us of our market and played havoc with us for the time being," he told the *Daily World*, "and now we have a chance to pay them back in their own coin." He then succeeded in striking an arrangement under which he withdrew from Spreckels's trading area and the San Francisco refiner withdrew from British Columbia. The *Victoria Daily Colonist* commented sarcastically that the Vancouver refinery had fallen "into line . . . at the tail end of a gigantic sugar trust." Then Ottawa, in its June 1891 budget, dropped the Canadian duty on raw sugar. That put Rogers on an even footing with his Montreal competitors and restored the effectiveness of the Canadian protection against refined American sugar.

The refinery lost $13,105 in its first business year, which ended 31 March 1891.[4] Rogers blamed the loss on battling low-priced American sugar and on refining poor quality Manila raw sugar, the best he could get when the refinery started. The refinery's initial capacity, he concluded, also was too small for efficient operation. With the American problem resolved and higher-quality Java raws on order, he convinced his directors to authorize a $10,000 expansion at the refinery, increasing capacity from one hundred barrels a day to three hundred barrels and thereby reducing the refining cost from 1.33 cents a pound to .44 cents a pound. The extra sugar would be sold in markets as far as Winnipeg. "With small meltings, even when selling in British Columbia at high prices, we make little or nothing," Rogers explained in a memorandum to a directors' meeting in July. "With large meltings and selling in Winnipeg and the North West at low prices and in competition with Montreal, we make good profits."[5]

Having decided to capture the entire Manitoba market, Rogers had ordered a substantial quantity of raw sugar. Four ships carrying 5971 tons of raw sugar arrived at the BC Sugar dock during 1891. Three arrived in 1892 with 6370 tons and a fourth, the *Morayshire,* was due early in 1893 with another 2037 tons. Rogers's aggressive move into the Winnipeg market triggered a price war with the Montreal refiners. One angry Montreal refiner went straight to Van Horne, one of the largest individual shareholders of BC Sugar, warning that if Rogers did not leave the Winnipeg market, Montreal sugar would be dumped onto the British Columbia market. Van Horne passed on this threat and Rogers retreated, even though the Vancouver refinery had a large surplus of raw sugar.[6] After May 1892 the refinery shipped no sugar east of Medicine Hat.

The Manitoba foray attracted unwanted attention of another sort. In a private letter in September 1892, Rogers confided to Ernst Gerbracht—his New York mentor and now a shareholder—that George Drummond, president of Montreal's Redpath refinery, was trying to buy control of BC Sugar. "What does this mean?" Rogers wondered. "I don't believe D. is the man to buy up anyone else unless they had a [competing] sugar that was going to interfere with his plans."

He had continued to sell in Manitoba as long as he had—Rogers explained to another shareholder—because of pressure from his bank. The aggressive Rogers had financed substantial raw sugar purchases with slightly more than $400,000 in loans at a hefty 7 per cent interest rate.[7] "Unfortunately we had heavy advances from one bank on the stock of raw sugar, and although I was aware of the danger of continuing in Manitoba, I was practically forced to do so, the bank having informed me they *needed* the money & that it was absolutely imperative our sales should not be reduced."[8] In desperation Rogers sold 1700 tons of BC Sugar's now-surplus raw sugar to the Spreckels refinery. He lost $8,619 on the sale but raised cash to reduce the bank debt. "The Manitoba policy was a mistake and misfortune, I admit," he confessed to Gerbracht. "But mistakes are unavoidable, we have sold our surplus stock to Spreckels . . . and got on a solid foundation."[9]

As if the commercial problems were not enough, a smallpox epidemic swept through British Columbia's Indian bands in the spring of 1892. Rogers lamented to Gerbracht: "The smallpox has considerably interfered with our sales here this summer, but it is now about over and I hope for a brisk business—the Indians however are very much afraid of the disease & *may* not come down from the north for supplies as usual, if they do not, it will make considerable difference, as they are our most voracious consumers."

However, sales recovered so quickly that summer that the refinery was able to pay its first dividend in November. Rogers wrote Van Horne: "I have yourself and my New York friends to thank . . . in holding on when things looked a little blue."[10] And he exulted to Gerbracht: "I hope you are satisfied with the dividend declared. . . . Compared with the position we were in last June (owing the bank $420,000) I think we have done exceedingly well—we owe the bank only $38,000 with outstanding bills due about $5,000 & have sufficient raw sugar on hand to last us until the end of March."[11]

Indeed, sales had revived so well that Rogers kept the refinery melting sugar to mid-December, before setting off to New York for Christmas with his bride of six months. The refinery resumed making sugar as soon as he returned in late January. "The reports from all over the country are excellent," he wrote Gerbracht on 3 February 1893. "More farms have been taken up in the N.W. [Northwest] by actual settlers than ever before—and the mining districts of B.C. are filling up *very* rapidly—the lowest estimates for the Kootenay country alone this year is 20,000."

Before long, Rogers regretted having been forced to sell some of his stock to satisfy the bank. The *Morayshire* left Java 21 October 1892 with 2100 tons of raws on what should have been a sea journey of 110 days. The ship never arrived and was presumed lost at sea. Incredibly, the *Blair Athole*, which left Java 2 March 1893 with 2326 tons of raw sugar, also was lost at sea. "I have never heard before of two A1 steel ships being lost in succession," Rogers wrote to a friend in New York. The refinery now was short of raw sugar. Rogers turned again to San Francisco, buying at current market prices which averaged 30 per cent higher than they had been when the Java contracts had been made. Rogers had bought the Java raws so cheaply that, had the vessels arrived, he believed the refinery's profit on the cargoes would have been 100 per cent. It was small consolation that prudent insurance against loss of cargo enabled the refinery to show a modest profit in 1893.

Rogers's wife in her historical memoir of the company wrote: ". . . the loss of two successive cargoes was a great blow for the company, and the tragedy of it hung about the office for months, as mail kept arriving from their homes in Scotland for members of the crews, among whom were some boy apprentices. Nothing was ever heard of either ship, but some years later a sextant, thought to belong to the *Blair Athole,* was found on Warren Hastings Island, in the mid-Pacific Ocean."

3

This Chinese Sugar Question

HOW B. T. ROGERS MET THE THREAT OF IMPORTED SUGAR.

The most dangerous business rival B. T. Rogers faced was Robert Paterson Rithet. When the youthful Rogers arrived in Vancouver in 1889 with his sugar refinery proposal, Rithet, forty-five and a powerful merchant in Victoria and San Francisco, was planning a refinery in Victoria and did what he could to bring the new Vancouver venture to its knees.

Rithet, a farmer's son from Dumfriesshire in Scotland, began his business career with a shipping agent in Liverpool before striking out in 1862 for Victoria.[1] After an unsuccessful fling in the Cariboo gold rush, he joined Gilbert H. Sproat, whose sawmills near Alberni sold lumber both to Victoria, then booming, and to San Francisco.[2] Rithet supervised Sproat's Victoria sales outlet and in 1869 was placed in charge of Sproat's San Francisco branch. The following year, back in Victoria, he established his own agency, Welch, Rithet & Company, in partnership with San Francisco merchant Andrew Welch. Rithet soon was juggling an active business career with political and social prominence. He was Victoria's mayor in 1885 and was elected to the legislature in 1889. Near the city's Beacon Hill, he built a grand estate called Hollybank whose extensive grounds included tennis and croquet courts, stables and a rose garden. Historians Howay and Scholefield characterized him as being "hard-headed as is typical of his race."

When Welch died in 1888, the firm became Rithet & Company and included Welch's San Francisco business. Victoria and San Francisco were then the two most important commercial cities on the west coast of North America, and Victoria business was slow to grasp that its place in the sun had begun to end when Canadian Pacific chose Vancouver as the terminus of the transcontinental railway.

Talk of a sugar refinery on Canada's Pacific coast had been in the air for some time. In San Francisco, refiner Claus Spreckels had established the Western Sugar Refinery Company to process raw cane sugar from Hawaii. Rithet's firm, representing a number of Hawaiian cane mills, was one of Spreckels's suppliers. Rithet had built a commercial dock in Victoria and was considering a new refinery next to those wharves when B. T. Rogers arrived in Vancouver. One of Rithet's business partners was James Angus, Rogers's future father-in-law, who unsuccessfully tried to convince the young American to build his refinery in Victoria. On 20 April 1890—just as preparation of the BC Sugar site in Vancouver was starting—one Victoria newspaper carried this item: "It is reported upon excellent authority that the next three or four weeks at the latest will see the foundation for the long-looked-forward-to sugar refinery laid on Mr. R. P. Rithet's property, at the outer wharf . . . by the end of the year it is probable that the refinery will be in operation." But the progress Rogers made stopped that rumoured Victoria refinery before it started.

Rithet exemplified the rivalry between Victoria and Vancouver. "Victoria people hate Vancouver & all its works," BC Sugar director Forrest Angus—a Victoria resident himself—once observed in a letter to William Van Horne. Several Victoria merchants, including Rithet, turned to Hong Kong for refined sugar. "In the effort to gain the market, the sugar was offered at prices below that prevailing in British Columbia," Bella Rogers recounted in her memoir of the BC Sugar Company.[3] In the directors' minutes for September 1891, B. T. Rogers recorded that Chinese sugars were landed in Victoria at 5 cents a pound while his refinery was wholesaling its granulated sugar for 5.5 cents. Rogers petitioned Ottawa to raise the tariffs against the Chinese sugars "but I regret to say the minister's reply was most unfavorable," he confessed to his directors.[4]

Rogers wrote confidentially to his wholesale merchants around British Columbia, offering a discount of one-quarter cent a pound to those who promised to handle only his sugar. Oppenheimer Brothers agreed immediately; two other jobbers did not reply to the letter and several, including Hudson's Bay Company and Rithet, refused to go along. Rogers then found he had to increase the discount to Oppenheimer to three-eighths of a cent to compete with the Chinese sugars. He warned his directors that the refinery could suffer a $40,000 annual loss if he was forced to make more deep discount contracts. Director Forrest Angus was asked to seek exclusive contracts with the Victoria merchants. The refinery did have some leverage. The Chinese sugars were imported only in granulated form and in large bags; merchants who required fancy grades of sugar or smaller packages had to buy them from Rogers. Angus threatened that Rogers might deny them the fancy grades and packages if they continued buying Chinese sugar. While all Victoria merchants resented this, only Rithet refused to come to what the BC Sugar's minutes termed "a satisfactory understanding."

"He delights in annoying us," Rogers complained about Rithet in an 1893 letter to Forrest Angus. Rogers's strategy now was to make "much lighter and finer sugars" than Rithet was selling. "I think this better than cutting prices which is just what he wants to see. I think he is going to have a hard time disposing of his soft sugar—the sample we got *stinks.*"[5]

Rogers's ability to compete was harmed when the Canadian government reduced its tariff against imported refined sugars from 80 cents a hundred pounds to 60 cents. This occurred early in April 1894, as Rogers was distracted by the death in California of his younger brother, Theodore. Forrest Angus, who had succeeded Browning as president of BC Sugar, fired identical telegrams to the refinery's two most powerful shareholders, his brother R. B. Angus of the Bank of Montreal and Van Horne: "Reduction refined sugar tariff affects local refinery interests seriously. For last three months we have been selling at less than Montreal prices yet Chinese sugars been coming in freely. Importations last month alone amounted to eight hundred thousand pounds or more than entire consumption of province." As a minimum Angus wanted Van Horne to press for a restoration of the former tariff. At the same time he asked Thomas Earle, a British Columbia Member of Parliament, and the first Victoria merchant to buy sugar from Rogers, to press for a tariff specifically aimed at giving extra protection to BC Sugar against imports. He reported this also in a wire to Van Horne, adding: "Chinese attempting close refinery."

Van Horne swung into action. The day after getting Angus's first wire, he raised the matter with George Foster, the finance minister in Ottawa. The minister's reply was not encouraging. "I am looking into the matter but the difficulty is to make any exceptional legislation for the Pacific coast while freer sugar is required by the country generally." Rogers, now back from his brother's funeral, wired Van Horne on 18 April: "I leave for Ottawa Friday to present our case in person to the government." His intervention was no more successful.

Throughout late spring and early summer of 1894, the lobbying continued in Ottawa for protection against the imported refined sugar. "I wish we could get this Chinese sugar question settled," Rogers wrote to Van Horne. "It is getting worse if anything & the outlook at present is pretty blue—I have been asking for an additional duty of 30 cents per 100 pounds of refined sugar from Chinese ports . . . the government seems to find difficulty in doing anything."[6] Van Horne again failed to extract any concessions from Ottawa. Exasperated, Rogers wrote him on 12 July 1895: "If the new Tariff is now entirely beyond hope of amendment, I suppose the matter might as well be dropped."[7]

Rogers blamed price competition from Chinese sugar for the refinery showing a $7,897 net loss in the six months to the end of September 1894. "There will be no margin of profit unless we can make some favorable arrangement with Mr. Rithet, who is our most active opponent," Rogers told Montreal shareholder A. R. G. Heward (Canadian Pacific's secretary) in mid-November. "I understand Mr. Rithet is now on very friendly terms with the C.P.R.—might not a hint from one of them help to mend matters? All other grocers are favorable to an arrangement for maintaining prices but no combination can stand . . . with Rithet out of it."[8] In July 1895 Rogers confronted Rithet directly in Victoria where Rithet proposed that he and Rogers divide the B.C. sugar business equally, setting the prices at a level at which both could profit. "This proposition I of course rejected," Rogers reported to his shareholders.

Rogers told his directors that the business year to 31 March 1895 was "the worst on record": the refinery had operated only two-thirds of the year; sales were down 16 per cent and the net loss was $29,582. Chinese sugar was only part of the reason. In mid-1894, after Rogers bought his raw sugar cargoes, world sugar prices declined 40 per cent. Rogers was forced to write down the value of his raw sugar inventory by $103,000. In addition, reductions in rail freight rates from eastern Canada once again enabled the eastern refiners to grab three-quarters of the sales on the Prairies.[9] Forrest Angus wrote plaintively to Van Horne in March 1895: "I am not so sanguine as Mr. Rogers is about the future of the Refinery."[10]

The company's ill fortune was also a personal reverse for Rogers who had been buying BC Sugar shares whenever some came available, if necessary borrowing from the bank—and once even from his mother—to finance the transactions. He had purchased $30,000 worth in 1894. But in May 1895 he offered Charles Senff, one of his original New York backers, fifty shares at the $100 par value. "Owing to the past year having been such a bad one for our business, and no dividend coming, I find I cannot hang on to all the stock I bought last year besides interest charges [and] my mother and sisters to look after."[11] He was offering Senff a bargain: in 1893, when earnings were better, the shares had sold privately as high as $200 each.

In order to help the refinery develop its alternative hinterland markets, Forrest Angus pressed the railway for lower freight rates. "If we can open up a trade in the interior, so as to do the most of it which looks natural from distance from Refinery we may prosper again. I hope you will be able to help us; or be able to put Mr. Rogers in the way of helping himself." The railway agreed, charging Rogers 67 cents a hundred pounds for sugar shipments to the Kootenay region of eastern British Columbia, 10 cents less than the rate from Victoria.

How much Rogers counted on Canadian Pacific is shown by his reaction late in 1894 when he learned that Van Horne and R. B. Angus had left for a six-week vacation in France while the refinery was seeking lower freight rates to the Prairies. Rogers lamented to Forrest Angus: "I depended most on Van Horne for getting low rates to the N.W." Early in 1895, with the previous year's loss casting a pall over BC Sugar's future, Angus renewed the appeal to Van Horne, now back from his vacation. "Mr. Rogers leaves for Montreal in a day or two, at my request, to lay the facts fully before you," Angus wrote. "In the meantime I may say that we are not doing one fourth the business there [Manitoba and the Prairies] we ought to." Rogers negotiated significant rebates, lowering the 1895 shipping costs and returning the refinery to profitability. "I am pleased to inform you," he wrote Van Horne in January 1896, "the result of the lower freight rates you granted us last summer to North West points has been fully as satisfactory as I had hoped it would be."[12]

♦

After BC Sugar's annual meeting in September 1895, Rogers sailed to the Orient for the first time. He intended to explore sales prospects for refined sugar in Japan. He also wanted to negotiate directly with Butterfield & Swire to end the dumping of Chinese sugar in British Columbia, although he doubted the Hong Kong company would agree. (Nor did it: but Rogers learned that the company had been losing money on its B.C. shipments for eighteen months. The volume of Chinese sugars abated early in 1896 only because Butterfield & Swire tired of losing money in competition with the resolute Rogers.) Finally, he wanted to contract raw sugar from Australia now that there was reliable steamship service to Vancouver.

Rogers asked Canadian Pacific vice-president Thomas Shaughnessy for free passage to the Far East on that firm's *Empress of China* steamship: "As I should like to take Mrs. Rogers along with me & have no money I will be extremely obliged if you will give us transportation." The request—and he did get free tickets—was not unusual for Rogers. During the refinery's early years, he often asked the railway for free transportation either for himself or for his staff. In February 1893 he applied for a rail pass for refinery employee William Baxter; the best the CPR offered was half fare but with no sleeping car reduction. Rogers was perhaps at his most audacious in December 1903, when he asked for an entire railcar to be put at his disposal for a trip to California. That time Shaughnessy said no. "Under the railway agreements the rule requiring payment of eighteen first class fares is absolute excepting in the case of Railway officers," Shaughnessy wrote quite firmly.

Rogers, who travelled with great enthusiasm, arranged that he and his wife use the trip as a grand tour of the Orient, with stops in Japan, Saigon, Singapore and Java before arriving in Australia on 1 December, six weeks after leaving Vancouver. The Sydney *Daily Telegraph* reported that Rogers "was looking for 4000 tons of sugar and cannot find it anywhere. . . . He is now returning to Canada, a commercially grieved and disappointed man." However, he succeeded in establishing a valuable relationship with the Colonial Sugar Refining Company and, on the return journey to Vancouver after Christmas, stopped in Fiji to look at some of Colonial's sugar plantations there. The need for a supply source with reliable steamship service to Vancouver was underlined in early 1896 when the oft-becalmed sailing vessel *Cambusdoon* took 182 days to travel from Java to Vancouver, double the usual passage time. The refinery had to suspend melting for several weeks when it exhausted its store of raw sugar. It was the last straw for Rogers, who stopped chartering sailing vessels for sugar cargoes. "Happily," he told his directors in November 1896, "we have seen the last of sailing vessels from Java."[13] The raws would come either from Java in small steamers or from Peru, a new source, in schooners.

Rogers believed he had found a Japanese market for refined sugar[14]—providing that Canadian Pacific co-operated. "I understand," he wrote Shaughnessy, "flour is now being taken as far as Hong-Kong at $2 per ton. If you could grant us an equally low rate or lower rate to Yokohama, I believe we could successfully compete with the Hong-Kong refiners. . . . Should you see your way to giving us a rate low enough to permit our shipping to Yokohama, I feel sure it would go far towards helping us to drive China sugar from this market, and, as many of the C.P.R. shareholders are also shareholders in this company, I trust you will take this into consideration in fixing the rate." Rogers did not appreciate that this so-called "fighting rate" was an unprofitable one with which Canadian Pacific was buying business for its newly introduced shipping service. The target rate was $6. The line offered to charge Rogers $3 a ton for sugar.

But Canadian Pacific's freight services also were available to his competitors. In the summer of 1897, C.P.'s *Empress of India* unloaded 800 bags of Chinese sugar in British Columbia. "If this is going to be repeated," Rogers protested in an angry wire to Shaughnessy, [we] "will ship no more sugar to Japan by your line." Shaughnessy replied that if Canadian Pacific had refused that remunerative cargo—the line had been able to charge $7 a ton—competing steamship lines would have carried it to Vancouver in any event.

Rogers fired back: "You are entirely wrong in the view you have taken in this matter." Rogers had been able to confine Rithet's Chinese sugars to Vancouver Island since 1894. The *Empress of India*'s cargo, the first Chinese sugar to be unloaded in Vancouver harbour in three years, was commercially disruptive out of proportion to its small size. "The quantity is less than 40 tons or equal to some $280 freight to your steamers," Rogers contended. "The sugar has already been offered and some sold both here and in the Kootenay, and by breaking our prices the loss to us will probably be $2,500. Assuming you adhere to your determination to carry this sugar, the most you will get will not exceed 500 tons per year. This will hardly help your profits to any great extent, but will do me incalculable harm." He had dealt with the hard-headed Canadian Pacific long enough, however, to realize that his protests would be more effective if wedded to a carrot. "On the other hand," he continued, "I had hoped to gradually increase shipments from here to Japan and to eventually do 4000 to 5000 tons per year. There is little or no profit to us in these shipments and unless I can make a fair profit in the British Columbia market, I shall discontinue shipping to Japan."

In the end, the Japanese market could not be penetrated permanently by a refinery in Vancouver. Rogers again turned to his hinterland, this time looking for ways to encourage fruit-processing and jam-making in British Columbia, since such industries would become large sugar users. "A successfully operated factory of this description in B.C. would considerably increase the consumption of our sugars," he wrote Van Horne early in 1897.[15]

The Chinese battle continued throughout most of the decade before Rogers finally won. The boom caused by the 1898 Klondike gold rush and the rapid settlement of the Prairies created markets for all the sugar Rogers could sell, and then some. The company sold $1 million of sugar in the business year to 31 March 1899, having doubled sales in just two years. The refinery emerged from a very difficult decade as a firmly established Vancouver business—and one well-seasoned to handle the competition which emerged when other Vancouver merchants began importing sugar both from Hong Kong and from Europe. In 1902, for example, some Vancouver wholesalers imported beet sugar from Europe, briefly setting off a price war. The Vancouver *Province* reported: "Some retailers are sticking to the local sugar and selling it at five cents a pound, while others handling both qualities are selling 21 pounds for a dollar. It is predicted that the price will take another tumble at an early date."[16]

The *Victoria Daily Times*, on 18 April 1901, had speculated that Rithet was about to build the long-rumoured sugar refinery. In fact, Rithet already had his own refinery—in San Francisco. Spreckels in 1897 had cancelled a sugar supply contract with Rithet's firm when Rithet began selling raw cane sugar to a newly organized rival, the California Beet Sugar and Refining Company. As the name suggests, the refinery intended to process sugar beets grown in the San Francisco Bay area but was unable to enlist enough growers. Rithet, looking for a new outlet for the Hawaiian sugar he represented, had the new company re-organized, as the California and Hawaiian Sugar Refining Company (now California and Hawaiian Sugar Company) with himself as president and with Hawaiian plantation owners as shareholders. Rithet remained president until he died at his Hollybanks estate in Victoria in April 1919. (He outlived his Vancouver rival by one year.)

Other proposals for new refineries in British Columbia appeared regularly. In 1902 when Spreckels was considering a Montreal refinery—it was never built—he was quoted in the press as saying: "The first works will be in Montreal and when everything is in good running order, a second one will be erected on the Pacific coast." When the Vancouver press speculated that BC Sugar would be absorbed by Spreckels, Rogers retorted that there was no need for a second Vancouver refinery. In 1907 investors formed the Prince Rupert Sugar Company to spend $1 million on a refinery at Prince Rupert, the western terminus for the Grand Trunk Pacific Railway Company of Montreal. This venture collapsed with the failure of the Grand Trunk.

In September 1909 wholesaler Robert Kelly, a founder of Kelly Douglas & Company, formed a syndicate to establish the Vancouver Sugar Refining Company. In 1910 a $300,000 beet factory called Fraser Valley Sugar Works Limited was proposed for Mission. In 1917 a company called The B.C. Sugar Inc., capitalized at $1,250,000, was formed to build a beet factory in the Fraser Valley. None of these companies proceeded. But that they were even proposed indicates how successful the refinery had become after Rogers survived Rithet's challenge.

4

The Tropics Drive Men Crazy

THE FIJI PLANTATION, THE COMPANY'S FIRST FOREIGN VENTURE.

The Colonial Sugar Refining Company of Australia was already fifty years old in 1905, with a history of profits and dividends, when B. T. Rogers adopted one of its strategies for success. Colonial controlled its sources of raw sugar in Queensland and in Fiji, where it had established a plantation and a large sugar cane mill in 1882, twenty years after cane first was planted in Fiji. With Colonial's plantation at Nausori, sugar cane became that nation's major crop and sugar became its leading export.

BC Sugar began ordering Fiji raw sugar, when it could get it, after the Canadian government in 1898 adopted a preferential tariff on goods imported from Britain and her possessions, of which Fiji was one. At first, BC Sugar had been buying its raw sugar either from Java or from Peru, neither of which source was reliable. After 1902, when the refinery bought a large shipment and several smaller ones of Fiji raws, Fiji became BC Sugar's major sugar supplier (and remained so into the 1970s when it was displaced by Australia). Rogers seized the chance when he learned that the British-owned Fiji Sugar Company, headquartered in Bristol, was selling the mill it had built in 1884 on Fiji's south coast near the mouth of the Navua River. "My main object in going into sugar growing," he explained later to London sugar broker Caesar Czarnikow, "was to eliminate to a certain extent anyhow, the horrible speculative element which it seems must always be an inseparable feature of the sugar refining business." This was BC Sugar's first international investment; the company had to amend its articles of incorporation to confirm its legal power to invest outside Canada.

Late in 1904 Rogers commissioned from A. M. Brodziak & Company, a Fiji land dealer, a report on the Navua mill and on the potential to expand the plantation. Brodziak advised that there was more than enough acreage "to keep an up to date 500 ton mill going."[1] However, Rogers remained unaware of Navua's major drawback: the south coast of Viti Levu, Fiji's main island, received much more rain than the north coast where Colonial's three mills were located. The drier growing areas produced cane with a higher sugar content.

Brodziak did tell Rogers that the Fiji Sugar Company treated its growers meanly. While Colonial gave its independent growers contracts with assured prices for their cane, Fiji Sugar bought its cane at open-market prices for as little as possible. Fiji Sugar controlled only 200 acres of its own cane and was at the mercy of growers, who had threatened to strike in 1904. Brodziak warned that the Navua growers remained alienated and were marginal. "Although they live on the proverbial smell of an oily rag, a very few shillings a week being in many instances sufficient for them to subsist on," Brodziak cautioned, "they have failed to make cane growing a success." Rogers was advised to pay "a fair price with the view to securing a higher cultivation and improvement in standards."

Rogers pushed ahead. Had he been less determined, he would have been discouraged by recalling the sugar plantation experience of his father, Samuel Blythe Rogers. Just after the American Civil War, the elder Rogers had persuaded his brother-in-law, Henry S. Sanford, to invest with him in a Louisiana plantation. "I can't see how any money can be lost," he had reassured Sanford. In January 1869 they purchased a plantation about fifty miles north of New Orleans. Samuel Rogers, who had been a successful refinery manager, came to regret his words. He had labour problems; he battled flooding which destroyed a quarter of the crop; the crushing mill burned down; and raw sugar prices dropped to uneconomic levels. In 1876, as a family history puts it, Sanford "eased out" Samuel Rogers.

B. T. Rogers, after a ten-day inspection tour in Fiji in February 1905, returned to Vancouver and bargained by letter and cable with Fiji Sugar's British owners. The British asked 80,000 pounds sterling—about $390,000 Canadian at the exchange rate of the time—and Rogers countered with 60,000 pounds. On 7 June 1905, they split the difference at 70,000 pounds.

Rogers now formed the Vancouver–Fiji Sugar Company, which sold 3500 common shares at $100 each to BC Sugar and 2500 preferred shares, also at $100 each and paying seven per cent, to individuals all of whom also were BC Sugar shareholders.[2] (The company redeemed the preferreds at a premium in 1908.) This total subscription of $600,000 enabled Rogers to buy and rebuild the Fiji plantation.[3]

Rogers sailed back to Fiji in July, accompanied this time by his wife, Bella, and by J. W. Fordham Johnson, the BC Sugar executive who was to manage the new mill temporarily—for Rogers had found the existing management there "execrable." The plantation, accessible only by boat from the Fiji capital of Suva, about thirty-five miles farther east along the coast, needed a great deal of improvement. It had lost $6,400 in the year ended 31 March 1903 and only made $19,222 on sales of $270,591 in the following year. "I feel sometimes a little dazed when I contemplate what I have undertaken," Rogers confessed to Toronto financier and shareholder Wilmot Matthews.[4] Bella Rogers, seeing the mill and the plantation for the first time on 23 July 1905, confided to her diary: "A small quantity of the machinery looked in good condition, but the majority of the property is shockingly out of repair & makeshift." It was not only the mill that was run down. A few days later she visited the hospital. "The whole place needs rebuilding & in a new plan there is urgent need for a dispensary office & operating room, separate from the main buildings, an isolation ward, a nursery, better kitchen & a mortuary. Promised to send them a stove." Her husband made all of her recommended improvements, including a new hospital and the mortuary since illness and death among the plantation workers proved a serious problem. B. T. and Bella spent a month there until the mill began to process that season's cane crop. When they sailed back to Vancouver on 15 August, the cargo hold of the same vessel carried 1000 tons (in 200-pound sacks) of raw sugar, the production of the first three weeks' crushing at the Navua mill.

In the first seven months after Rogers bought Vancouver–Fiji Sugar, more than $270,000 was spent there. While that included the cost of buying sugar cane and the salaries and wages of staff, there were major capital investments. From Mirrlees Watson Company, leading sugar cane refinery equipment builders in Glasgow, Rogers ordered a crushing mill capable of processing 750 tons of cane daily—half again as large as Brodziak had recommended in his report. By the end of 1906, the capacity of the mill had been raised to produce 15,000 tons of raw sugar a season, and Rogers was pressing his local management to contract more acreage. He spent $15,500 in Australia to buy an old cargo-carrying vessel called the *Woosung* which became a floating warehouse. Three new barges costing $8,000 were built to freight sugar from the mill's new wharf to Suva. Tenders were called in September 1905 for a steel bridge across the Navua River which, when completed the following year, provided access to the mill for cane planted on acreage there.

Isolation and disease made it difficult to keep reliable managers at Tamunua, the plantation's community. Rogers often shared his concerns with Matthews, who sympathized in a letter in 1913: "Your experience about finding the proper kind of men to manage large interests seems to be the trouble the world over. Men who can be put into responsible positions 6000 miles away command good prices." Fordham Johnson and William Allen, the Vancouver refinery superintendent who had gone to Tamanua to supervise the mill reconstruction, both became gravely ill from tropical diseases. Johnson, who endured nearly two years there, almost died from intestinal infections and was never able to live in the tropics again.

A Scot named S. R. Cochran, whom Rogers hired as manager during Johnson's illness in the spring of 1906, committed suicide after being dismissed in April 1907. His incredulous widow in Glasgow wrote Rogers to ask why he was fired. "He told me you were a good, straight man, so I ask you plainly to tell me what cause of dis-satisfaction he gave you." Ella Cochran got a straight answer: her husband had become addicted to drugs he was taking for symptoms of malaria and insomnia. The dependency had so incapacited him that he could no longer handle the job and Rogers, in severance, had offered him three months' salary and passage home. Cochran's addiction had worsened: "There seems to be no doubt that Mr. Cochran was out of his mind when he met his death," Rogers wrote.[5] "I must thank you for replying frankly to my letter," she wrote a second time. "I am glad to know the truth about my husband—hard as it is, it is easier to hear than the uncertainty."[6]

The Fiji company finally got a reliable long-term resident manager in 1912 when Edward Duncan, an Australian who had worked for Colonial, was hired on a five-year contract at a starting salary of $8,700 a year, rising to $9,700 by the third year. It was a handsome salary for the time and was supplemented with accommodation and paid transportation for home leave. Rogers was not entirely happy with Duncan. "In fact, the plantation has caused me the greatest worry and anxiety," he confessed in a letter to Matthews on 8 April 1914. "It seems about impossible to get a manager there who understands the word economy—I sometimes think the tropics drive men crazy." When Duncan's contract ended, he was succeeded by his carefully nurtured assistant, Reginald Hales Farrar.

Vancouver–Fiji was modestly profitable (with one loss) for several years under BC Sugar management until a downturn in world sugar prices in 1911 pushed it into the red. Discouraged, Rogers asked Colonial Sugar in August to buy the Fiji plantation. "As you are possibly aware," he wrote to Colonial general manager Edward W. Knox, "I have had a great deal of trouble with the management of Tamunua Estate, in the Fiji Islands, ever since I took over the property. I have about reached the conclusion that not only is the Estate too far away to make the management of it from here practical, but I have also not the organization to do it with proper economy." If Colonial bought the plantation, he promised that BC Sugar would buy raw sugar from it. Knox declined. He thought it preferrable that several foreign companies should run plantations in Fiji, supporting each other in dealing with the colonial government and with the planters.

The losses continued for four years, through to the twelve months ending 28 February 1914, when the $47,000 deficit was the highest yet. The previous October Rogers had had the Vancouver–Fiji Sugar Company convene a special shareholders' meeting in Vancouver "for the purpose of considering, and if deemed advisable, authorizing a sale of the assets of the Company, and for the purpose of authorizing the President thereof, Mr. B. T. Rogers, to enter into any negotiations . . . to sell the same. . . ." The asking price was 300,000 pounds. No sale was concluded before World War I began. Once the European conflict started, sugar prices jumped; the Fiji company suddenly was impressively profitable and no longer for sale.

A continuing problem facing Rogers was securing a work force for the plantation. The native Fijians shunned the miserably unpleasant tasks of cultivating and cutting cane, and the government of Fiji, to sustain the industry, was forced to recruit in India. After the abolition of slavery in the previous century, the British colonies of Natal and Mauritius in Africa, British Guiana and Trinidad had all turned to India for field labour. The Fiji plantation owners reimbursed their government about one hundred dollars for each labourer the government "introduced" to the colony, as recruitment was termed. These indentured workers—referred to as "coolies"—were provided transportation to Fiji and rudimentary housing and employment on their arrival in exchange for agreeing to stay at least five years. When the Vancouver–Fiji Sugar Company took over the Navua plantation, the assets included $30,141.21 shown on the books as the investment in "coolie introduction." Rogers took over a coolie population of 387 men, 152 women and 90 children, some of whom were old enough to work. Within four years, the expanding plantation's coolie population numbered 1059. It peaked at 1533 in 1916, the year in which India put an end to the recruitment of indentured labour triggering a serious labour shortage for the plantation.

Trying to cope, the company paid $1,700 for a crawler tractor in 1918 and bought a second one in 1919. It also tried to buy cane from many of the former indentured workers who had established themselves on plots in the neighbourhood of the Tamunua mill, often on farms of no more than two or three acres in size. These farmers received advances from the company to plant or cultivate their plots but did not always grow enough cane to cover these advances. In 1919–20 the company wrote off as bad debts $5,678 of advances. Productivity soon declined both on the company's estates and from surrounding growers.

Short of labour by the 1918 crop, Vancouver–Fiji had given up half the plantation acreage it had cultivated just two years earlier. Costs of production began to rise, and manager Farrar accompanied the 1918–19 financial statement with a handwritten, private letter of explanation to Vancouver. "With the depletion of labour forces & cutters it has not been possible to keep the factory supplied with sufficient cane to ensure constant employment," he wrote. "This has had the effect of increasing coolie wages per ton. . . ."[7] The problems were compounded when the global influenza epidemic swept through Fiji. The cost of running the hospital that year was nearly $4,000. (Some of the treatment must have been more soothing than therapeutic, for that year's accounts include $136 for "whisky for patients.")

By 1920 the mill crushed only half as much cane as in 1916. The cost of producing raw sugar, given indentured labour and effective plantation management, had been as low as £7.13 a ton in 1906 and no higher than £14.11 in 1918. But with the end of indentured labour—contracts which had not expired were cancelled by the government in January 1920, and many Indian labourers returned to India—the production cost jumped to £20 (nearly $100 Canadian) and more a ton. In 1921 Fordham Johnson was refused when he applied to the Fiji government to recruit five hundred Japanese labourers. A subsequent feeler to bring in Chinese workers also was rebuffed. The labour shortage coincided with a collapse of sugar prices, sealing the plantation's fate.

Because the supply of sugar was reduced by the war that began in 1914, the price of sugar soared. As a result, Vancouver–Fiji Sugar recovered from its 1913–14 loss to enjoy seven consecutive years of profits. Its most spectacular year was 1919–20, when the profit was $454,333. Blythe Rogers, now BC Sugar's president, wrote E. B. Osler in Toronto in February 1920: "Fiji is 'over the top' having at last become a creditor of this Company. . . ."[8] Flush with funds, Vancouver–Fiji undertook major capital programs ranging from overhauling all machinery to renovating plantation housing. Farrar, after detailing $5,000 worth of expenditures on housing, explained in the 1920–21 accounts "that the buildings have been given a very thorough overhaul which was very necessary." The deputy manager's house, for instance, had been badly damaged by an infestation of white ants. But sugar prices were collapsing, and Vancouver–Fiji recorded a loss of $84,752 in the 1921–22 year. The plantation's economics deteriorated further because its own acreage declined by 58 per cent between 1916 and 1924 while the independent planters not only failed to make up the difference but also produced less.

Late in 1921 Fordham Johnson asked C. Czarnikow Limited, the London sugar brokers, to canvass the trade for a buyer. The London company replied that no one was interested. Johnson was philosophic: "I am not surprised from your letter of the 19th December that there is no chance of interesting anyone in our Fiji Sugar Estate, but I wished to leave no stone unturned in my efforts to dispose of the property as a 'going concern' instead of just closing down and realizing what we can on our assets in Fiji. I am sorry to say I am faced with the latter proposition now."[9] One last time, he offered the plantation to Colonial, which still was not interested.

The decision to close the operation was communicated in January 1922 to the 700 independent growers of the Navua district who fought it all season. Finally in September, in a plaintive petition, they begged the company to reconsider. Resident manager Farrar forwarded the petition to Vancouver. The reply was brought back in November by Ernest Rogers, the second-oldest son of B. T. Rogers. Then twenty-five and a recently discharged second lieutenant in the Royal Air Force, Ernest came to Fiji to handle personally the closure of the company. His answer was firm: "The Company's decision to cease operations is definite and final."

Assets were sold wherever a buyer could be found. The Fiji government bought the hospital for $9,700, with the exception of a wing which was purchased by the Methodist Mission and converted into a school. The Colonial Sugar Company—which remained in Fiji until 1973—bought horses and mill stores. Tanks and some other equipment from the mill were dismantled and shipped to Vancouver. Machinery, floating stock, housing and furniture were auctioned, and the land was sold to a local property company. BC Sugar's records indicate that the company realized only about $90,000. Johnson acknowledged to one of his shareholders that this was not very much. "However, I have been able to eliminate what I always considered a very doubtful asset. . . ."[10]

5

I Will Not Recognize Any Union

THE TOUGH GENERALSHIP OF B. T. ROGERS.

The 1917 strike began timidly that April when a refinery worker remembered now only by the nickname Irish Johnny, initiated a petition for higher wages and shorter hours. Signed by nearly all the refinery's 206 men and 36 women, it was left in a storeroom where the timekeeper found it and took it to management. It triggered a seventy-eight-day confrontation so bitter that B. T. Rogers compared the harassment of the non-strikers and replacement workers to "indignities as bad as that practised by the Huns in Belgium."

The strike, the company's first, occurred against a backdrop of much other industrial unrest. Work stoppages in Vancouver that spring involved the B.C. Electric Company street car drivers, the longshoremen in the port and shipyard workers. Since the turn of the century, both union membership and labour strife had been increasing across North America.[1] Among these were several strikes close to home for B. T. Rogers: coal miners on Vancouver Island struck in 1903 (and were fired) and staged another series of violent strikes between 1912 and 1914. Employers invariably took a hard line. In 1908, when Canadian Pacific's 8000 shop mechanics struck, the railway broke the strike by having the strikers arrested and replacing them with British and American immigrants.[2]

Labour relations in the United States between 1900 and 1915 were even more violent, culminating in a bloody seven-month coal miners' strike in Colorado during which there were fatal gunbattles between strikers and troops. Business in North America began to fear revolution. There had already been a socialist revolution in Mexico, and Russia was in the midst of another. In the United States and western Canada, the radical Industrial Workers of the World spread alarm. "The IWW had always preached revolution, anti-militarism, and anti-patriotism," Melvyn Dubofsky wrote in *We Shall Be All,* a history of the IWW. The union opposed American intervention in the world war. "Instead of going abroad to slay capitalist-created dragons, Wobblies"—as the union members were dubbed—"were advised to remain at home in order to fight their bosses in the only worthwhile war: the class war."[3] Headquartered in Chicago, the Wobblies led major strikes in Washington state and began organizing in British Columbia after the 1914 war began. IWW rallying bulletins from the Vancouver Labour Temple were collected by the employers of British Columbia, B. T. Rogers included, who feared unions, especially the IWW.

Refinery employees were not Wobbly revolutionaries. During the first week of the strike, the Vancouver *Daily World* editorialized: "Almost all of them are what in labour circles are designated 'white,' that is to say, they belonged to that race which, by whatever channels these representatives reached Vancouver and the sugar refinery, has its ancestral home in the British Isle. They are a grave, sturdy lot, the older men grave and self-contained, the boys delighted to escape a day or two from the daily round and common task, the girls chattering among themselves after their kind and plainly excited by the enterprise on which they had embarked, that of joining a real labour union and opposing the will of him who had reigned so many years as undisputed master of the sugar works."

Discontent began building before Christmas 1916, when popular plant superintendent William Allen died and was replaced by a martinet, William Aitchison. "We believe the trouble would never have been, had Mr. Allan [*sic*] the late superintendent been in charge," one striking employee told B. T. Rogers in an anonymous letter on 6 May, when the strike was in its third week. "We believe the rank & file of your employees have no serious grievances with you or Mr. Rogers, Junior"—a reference to Blythe Rogers—"but the rank & file we are certain are tired, sick & disgusted with Mr. Acheson [*sic*]. No matter when or how the employees return to work there will be serious friction as long as this man is in charge. We could name about 20 instances of Mr. Acheson's craziness, meanness, & insulting ways, in dealing with men of long service who have far more intelligence than he, himself. . . . We think he is incapable of handling men."[4]

However capricious Aitchison may have been, the circumstances were difficult. Because wartime shipping disruptions delayed the arrival of raw sugar cargoes, the refinery was closed for eleven weeks after Christmas. When it resumed production, it operated at half the normal capacity. The workers were deprived of predictable pay envelopes at a time when living costs were inflating alarmingly. The *World* observed tartly: "It was quite apparent that the men were of a steady, thrifty sort. A man must be steady to hold up his end for a nominal ten-hour day, which frequently stretches to twelve or fourteen hours—at least so it was asserted—and he must be thrifty to keep his family on a wage of 32½ cents an hour, when the works have a way of closing down for weeks at a stretch."

The employees petitioned for a basic wage for men of 40 cents an hour, with time and a half for overtime and Sunday work, and for a guarantee of a maximum ten-hour day and a minimum five-day week. The petitioners also sought a 20 per cent wage increase for mechanics, watchmen and women. Women, whose duties included bagging refined sugar and sewing shut the bags, earned 20 cents an hour but were served, without charge, a daily hot lunch.

The company pinned its reply in the employee dressing room at 4:30 P.M. on Thursday 19 April, just before the end of the day shift. "After due consideration," it read, "it has been decided to grant an advance of 10% to all men working by the hour. . . . This, taken with the advance put into effect about this time last year, will equal 20%, which is the maximum it is possible to go." No increase was offered to women and no guarantees were offered on hours of work.

On Saturday morning, when Rogers sailed to the Gulf Islands on his yacht *Aquilo,* a crewman told him that serious labour trouble was brewing at the refinery. Rogers sent a radiogram to Robert Adamson, the refinery manager: "Tell Aitchison I learn the melting house gang intends to quit Sunday morning unless given time and a half. Are led by a man known as

Irish Johnny." There being no immediate reply, he sent a similar message to Aitchison at six o'clock that evening, suggesting that "if you can identify this man you may avoid trouble by letting him out immediately." Aitchison wired back: "Things are going all right so far No sign of any strike Will discharge Irish Johnny in the morning." Adamson, however, cautioned that it might not be advisable to fire the man "if there is no sign of trouble in the morning because such action might cause other men to quit." Rogers wired back: "My opinion is to fire the man."[5]

On Sunday morning Aitchison not only dismissed Irish Johnny but also, after a sharp exchange of words, one of the refinery foremen. About 160 of the workers walked out and marched to the Vancouver Labour Temple where they listened to speeches from the president and secretary of the Vancouver Trades and Labour Council and then decided to form a union. It was a fateful decision, given the widespread employer fear that unions were the precursor of revolution. The strident columns of the *British Columbia Federationist,* the Council's newspaper, fostered this notion by viewing the strike as class warfare. "There are employers and employers," it began a front-page 23 April essay on the strike. "All are bad."

While his employees were being aroused by speeches at the Labour Temple, Rogers, after spending the night on board the *Aquilo,* sailed back to Vancouver and issued a statement to the newspapers: "The men went out on strike because the superintendent saw fit to let out one of the labourers. The men want him re-instated. I don't know what reason the superintendent had for discharging him, but I will stand behind the superintendent until the crack of doom."[6] The *Federationist* fell on that statement with intemperate relish. "It sounds," the labour newspaper thundered, "something like the late Czar of Russia when, at the outbreak of the war, he declared he would 'go to Berlin if it costs me my last moujik.' " (A moujik was a Russian peasant.)

The day after the strike began, Rogers retained the Thiel detective agency which provided not just refinery security but daily intelligence reports on the strikers.[7] Thiel operatives, as they styled themselves, infiltrated the sugar workers' union and other unions, providing inside accounts of union meetings. It was routine at that time for employers to engage detective agencies, so much so that the Trades and Labour Congress of Canada at its 1913 convention passed a resolution demanding an end to the use of detectives in labour disputes.

Thiel Detective Service Company of Canada was owned by a U.S. firm started in 1873 which by 1917 had grown to twenty branches in North America, including Mexico City. The Canadian arm was headquartered in Montreal with branches in Toronto, Winnipeg, Edmonton and Vancouver. Its only competitor in Vancouver, the Vancouver Detective Agency run by former city police detective John O'Grady, several times volunteered alarming information about possible employee sabotage in an unsuccessful effort to be retained by Rogers.

The infiltrating Thiel detectives learned that the strikers were peaceable, refraining initially from applying the epithet "scab" to non-strikers. The workers also were sanguine. A Thiel double agent identified as C.E.D. "found the strikers whom he talked to in a confident mood generally. They believe it will be only a matter of time before the company is compelled to give in and grant their demands as the stock of sugar on hand has run low and the company will not be able to get enough help to keep up the production necessary to supply the trade." Several strikers told a Thiel detective that "Mr. Rogers was the hardest man on the Pacific Coast to do anything with but that this time he would be taught a lesson." That reference was to a stillborn effort several years earlier to form a union.

The newspaper reporters swarmed around the refinery. "It's like measles," B. T. Rogers is quoted as telling the *World*. "These labour troubles always break out in the spring." He took the reporter into the dining room where women employees were having what Rogers described as a "plentiful hot lunch free of charge." The *World* described "a large, airy room dotted about with small tables, each with places for four and of appointments unexceptional. Visible evidence of the meal that was presently being served consisted of soup, roast pork, several vegetables, pudding and the usual accessories. . . . And everything was good after its kind."

The atmosphere changed after the employees formed a union and sought a meeting with Rogers. "There will be no conference between myself and any union," he told the *Province*. "I will receive a deputation of the men as individuals anytime, but I will not recognize any union or union official." At mid-week, the union began to picket the refinery. The president of the Vancouver Trades and Labour Council, James H. McVety, raised the rhetoric a notch by observing that while the refinery did not employ Asians, it did employ whites in Asian conditions.

By the end of the first week, the Sugar Workers Union had applied for a charter, had received a $100 donation from the streetcar drivers' union and, unknown to them, had enrolled a Thiel detective. Detective H., the new union member, soon reported that at a Labour Temple meeting, which attracted 120 men and 7 women from the refinery, the editor of the *Federationist* advised the strikers to go back to work until they had their union properly organized and recognized by the company (advice he was to repeat later in the strike as well). "This seemed to somewhat discourage the strikers and a good many of them were undecided as to what to do," H. reported. For public consumption, that same editor was shrieking wrath against Rogers. "Not only does everyone around here hate him, including the members of his own tribe of industrial despots and profit chasers," the paper declared on its front page on 27 April, "but this sugar lord knows that they all hate him, and apparently does all he can to put the immortal cinch upon that hate so that none of it can ever get away from him."[8]

Perhaps because it rained very hard on Sunday, 29 April, the first week of the strike ended quietly. But on Monday morning one detective overheard a threatening exchange between a striker and a worker entering the plant. At a Labour Temple meeting at noon that day, the longshoremen's union, one of the toughest and most seasoned in the city, told the refinery workers that their picket line was too mild-mannered to dissuade new arrivals from taking refinery jobs.

The first serious incidents occurred Tuesday afternoon, 1 May, when the shift was leaving the plant after 5:30 P.M. "During the afternoon," according to a detailed account in the Vancouver *Daily World*, "a crowd of considerably over 100 strikers and sympathizers were gathered at the gates. They howled and catcalled at those inside, inviting them to come out." When a merchant attempted to deliver a load of blankets for strikebreakers sleeping in the refinery, the strikers burned the blankets. A milk wagon driven by a boy was turned back by the strikers before it could deliver milk to the refinery's dining room. The refinery workers waited until after six o'clock when a squad of police arrived to protect them. Those who did leave now ran a gauntlet of jeering pickets and, when they were out of sight in side streets, found themselves pursued by strikers. "Somebody threw a stone at one man," the *World* reported, "and it struck him on the forehead, inflicting a cut. This man when overtaken was fisticuffed." Several others also were roughed up.

Another newspaper reported that William Purchas, one of the BC Sugar employees, was tricked into leaving the refinery by a telephoned message that his wife was dying at home. Outside the plant, he was beaten badly enough to be hospitalized. The sugar workers' union denied that this event ever took place, a denial which outraged B. T. Rogers. He told the press: "If my word after 27 years residence here is not as good as theirs on a matter of veracity, then things have indeed reached a pretty pass."

After the 1 May incidents, Rogers—despite the contingent of detectives he had retained—complained angrily to Vancouver Mayor Malcolm McBeath about inadequate police protection. Rogers had a point: because of wartime demands on manpower, the entire city depended on a mere eighty-person police force, down from the prewar force of three hundred. On 2 May Rogers wired the British Columbia Attorney General, M. A. Macdonald, that "a strike organized by a partial number of our employees has paralyzed our business. Flagrant intimidation of our loyal employees has forced them to quit work to preserve their lives. . . . I appeal to you to take whatever steps you may consider necessary to provide proper protection." The attorney general passed the buck back to the Vancouver mayor as the proper authority to provide protection, adding that he was informed it was orderly at the refinery. Rogers shot back: "Replying police have no control. Things quiet because men intimidated." And he sent Macdonald detective reports of the confrontation.

By the end of the second week, the sugar workers union had scored a victory with the help of the longshoremen who refused to unload an arriving cargo. The ship, *Yubari Maru,* with 5000 tons of raw sugar, was diverted to Seattle and the sugar had to be delivered to the refinery by rail and truck. This delay in receiving the sugar left the refinery's stocks dangerously low. Rogers tried to reassure customers through a statement in the *Province* that "he had plenty of sugar on hand for ordinary requirements and that wholesalers would get all they needed if they sent their own trucks for it."

With sugar supplies on the way, the refinery planned to resume melting with whatever workers could be recruited and housed on the plant premises, well protected by Thiel detectives. "All quiet about the plant," Blythe Rogers jotted in his diary of the strike. "Busy bringing in men and supplies by taxi. Reports of dissension amongst the strikers grow every day"—a reference to the comprehensive inside reports from the detectives.[9]

On Thursday, 10 May, with the strike nearly three weeks old, the men on the picket line noted smoke from the steam boilers. "They all thought this another bluff on the part of the company," one Thiel detective reported to the company. However, another detective that day reported a different attitude, a "growing despondency. . . . The fact that smoke was seen coming from the stacks and many guards at work did not serve to cheer them up any." The company now offered to raise the hourly wages for men to 38 cents, in line with a recent civic wage settlement, and to 22 cents for the women. The strikers, as the Thiel detectives informed their client, thought the money quite acceptable. On 11 May a delegation of two strikers met with B. T. Rogers to discuss the offer. Blythe Rogers took notes of what was a very short and tough meeting.

"In the first place," B. T. Rogers told the men, "I want it definitely understood. Are you here as representatives of the union or as a deputation of the men. If you come from the union, stop right here, because I will not recognize any union." He was asked whether he would take the strikers back as a body. The answer was no: the refinery expected to be melting only limited quantities of sugar and would take back employees only as required.

One of the delegation, William McIntosh, persistently returned to the question of a union. (A few days later detective C.E.D.'s report described McIntosh as someone who would be "a trouble maker even if taken back to work under normal conditions.") McIntosh asked: "The men would like to know if they can have a union of their own. Would you discriminate against any man for that?"

Rogers bristled. "I will have nothing whatever to do with any union or union man, and I will not have a union man at work in the refinery. I will discharge whoever I want to and employ whoever I want to, without reference to any union. I will not have the few more years I have left to run this refinery spoilt by any union. The men have the right to work or quit work as they see fit, and I insist on my right to employ or discharge who *I* see fit. . . . Meanwhile, the men's jobs are rapidly being filled, and

I warn you that unless the men return soon they will not be taken on. We are melting enough to supply the market. You men know that I have not lied to you during the 27 years I have been here. I am not going to begin now, and you may take my word for it that no man will be discharged who is working here today to make way for a striker to resume work." After that withering blast, the chastened delegation withdrew, McIntosh privately concluding from the reception they had received that he would never be rehired, whatever the outcome of the strike.[10]

The refinery prepared to resume melting raw sugar, securely protected by so many detectives that one union leader told the press the refinery "swarms with armed men." The detective reports had given Rogers reason for concern when they warned repeatedly that the tough longshoremen urged the sugar workers to hold out for union recognition and to resort to violence if necessary. "As Operative has previously stated," read one Thiel report for 12 May, "if it were not for the Longshoremen's Union, the men would have gone back to work. . . ."

On that day, according to Blythe's diary, the refinery, staffed by seventy-six, including fourteen Thiel detectives and the crew of the yacht *Aquilo,* melted 200,000 pounds of raw sugar. On 13 May it melted 250,000 pounds, serenaded by jeering from the picketers. The taunts led the company to erect high fences screening the refinery property. Several Thiel detectives who had infiltrated the picket line now began urging a return to work, aware that many strikers had exhausted their personal resources.

During this the fourth week of the strike, the refinery melted sugar every day but Saturday, 19 May, with an ever-increasing number of employees in the plant. By 20 May Blythe Rogers recorded 103 men at work, including two "from Moose Jaw." New employees were being spirited into the refinery in the Black Maria, a taxi whose window blinds hid the passengers. Detective H. warned: "There seems to be a growing feeling against the automobile used for bringing in men and operative suggests that extra precautions be taken to prevent mischief being done this car." Subsequently, the strikers smashed several of its windows with stones, and S. H. Bellamy, the union's secretary, was fined $25 plus costs for damaging the vehicle.

A Japanese freighter, the *Tsurugisan Maru,* was due shortly with a cargo of raw sugar. The company, warned by a detective that strikers considered storming the refinery, ringed it with barbed wire fences and a number of guards: in his diary, Blythe Rogers proudly sketched what he called the defences. But the ship was diverted to Seattle after the longshoremen again refused to unload it. Some of the sugar then was transferred to Vancouver by small coastal freighters and unloaded by strikebreakers, while the rest came by rail and truck. The sugar workers failed to dissuade the railway workers from handling the cars of sugar, and the amply supplied refinery melted 325,000 pounds on Sunday, 2 June.

Blythe Rogers noted in his diary on 8 June that the "pickets are reported to be getting very desperate." Detectives said that the union was almost broke and relied on the charity of other unions for the money to pay picketers $2 a day and to pay other costs—including the fines imposed for several picket line incidents. The sugar workers' union raised $1,100 in donations during the strike, the most generous donor being the 650-member longshoremen's union. The strike had deprived longshoremen of the jobs which the two sugar ships would have created; and a third ship was expected shortly.

By now many of the strikers had drifted to other jobs. Some had taken jobs in the city's busy shipyards, only to get caught up in a brief strike in one of those yards. Thiel detectives, in two separate reports, said that the strikers were weary of labour disruptions. They "appear to be sickening of labour unions, as this is the first experience most of them had with strikes." The refinery by late June was operating so smoothly that the company dispensed with the Black Maria and considered no longer housing workers overnight in the refinery.

But militancy was not quite dead. After one striker slipped into the plant on a one-day spying assignment, the strikers decided to rough up strikebreakers caught away from the refinery. In one incident, a stone thrown at Blythe Rogers just missed him. The refinery quickly beefed up security again, resumed using the Black Maria and settled down to win the strike once and for all.

The leadership of the longshoremen finally decided enough was enough. On 20 July a committee of strikers and longshoremen summoned J. D. McNiven, the federal Fair Wages Officer in Vancouver, and asked him to see B. T. Rogers, "without intimating it was at their request." McNiven, who had tried several times before to mediate the dispute, called on Rogers that afternoon and discovered, as he later wrote to the deputy minister of labour in Ottawa, that Rogers remained adamant against dealing with a union but that "he was more disposed to be conciliatory. He agreed to re-instate as many of his former employees as there were vacancies . . . without discrimination, except as to those who had been convicted of violations of law and order."

McNiven advised the strikers to accept this offer. In his report to Ottawa, he said: "I intimated that in my opinion the strike was lost to them, and that the wise course would be to call it off and allow as many as possible to return to their usual occupation, particularly as their demands on the wages question has been practically conceded. All but the number comprising the picket had found other employment." On Sunday 22 July the sugar workers voted to end the strike and seek their jobs back.

Those that were rehired received the additional 20 per cent that had been sought in April, had working hours regularized to ten hours a day and began receiving inexpensive noonday meals for all in the company dining room. "They seem well pleased with the other conditions and especially with the mid day meal and the low price they have to pay for it," reported a Thiel detective who worked inside the refinery during the first three weeks after the strike ended.

There was tension between the former strikers and those refinery workers who had refused to strike. For the most part, the two groups avoided each other. But in the melt house, a former striker named Alex McKinnon made it a point to refer to non-strikers as "scabs." This was reported to the company by a Thiel detective (in his final report of 16 August) who wrote: "It is evident to the Operative that this man McKinnon is creating dissension and promoting ill feeling and if it is possible to replace him, Operative believes it would be a good thing in the interests of harmony." McKinnon was fired at noon that day.

To help restore harmony, the company that summer sponsored the first of the day-long employee picnics which became immensely popular during the next two decades. Time healed many wounds: even McKinnon was soon rehired, and when he finally left the refinery on 30 November 1944, he had accumulated forty-eight years of service with BC Sugar. The company's employees, in the final analysis, were not Wobbly class warriors after all, as even Thiel's detectives recognized. "Operative states," one detective reported from inside the plant, "that those men who have gone back to work seem to be a very good class of workmen, being steady, sober and reliable and unless some agitator works his way in among them he does not look for any trouble for some time to come."

6

I Have Nothing To Hide

THE COMPANY EMERGES UNSCATHED FROM A PUBLIC INQUIRY.

On 2 February 1917 William F. O'Connor, the Cost of Living Commissioner in Ottawa, responsible for preventing profiteering and price-fixing in foodstuffs in Canada during the war, accused BC Sugar of engaging in a criminal conspiracy to fix sugar prices. This was the first of several inquiries or prosecutions targeting the company, brought on by its position as the major—and since 1956, the only—sugar refiner in Western Canada.

Well before 1914, sugar had become a staple in the industrial world. Global production of sugar, a mere one million short tons in 1844, doubled within two decades and then doubled again to 4.2 million tons in 1882. Production had risen to 11.2 million tons by 1900 and had been above 18 million tons for three years when world war began in 1914.[1] Depressed by excess production, Cuban raw sugar in New York was selling for as little as 1.5 cents a pound by 1913. It strengthened the following spring but still was only 2.9 cents a pound in April 1914.[2]

The outbreak of war in Europe destroyed the established sugar trade. Britain, a major importer, was cut off from its largest suppliers, Germany and the Austrian-Hungarian Empire, and faced reduced supplies as the the beet farms of Belgium, France and Holland were ravaged by trench warfare. The full extent of the supply dislocation was described by B. T.

Rogers in a 1916 letter to the Vancouver newspapers when the refinery was being criticized for having raised prices. He wrote: "Immediately the war broke out and our blockade of the enemies' ports became effective, these 8,250,000 tons of beet sugars [in Europe] were inaccessible. Now suddenly withdraw that enormous quantity of sugar from the markets of the world and one thing is bound to happen—the price will go up."

Within days of the declaration of war, Seattle and Tacoma buyers sought sugar in Vancouver. Rogers refused to sell: he also forbad his wholesalers to resell to the Americans and, by telegram, he asked the Canadian government to stop sugar exports. "Prices in Seattle today are three cents higher than here," he wrote in August 1914 to Huntly R. Drummond, president of Canada Sugar Refining Company in Montreal. "I fear our stocks will be depleted and there will be nothing left for our own people unless something is done quickly." He threatened to match the higher Seattle prices if the exports were not stopped. "I had to conserve the supply of sugar for the people of B.C.," he explained later. "I could have sold my whole stock of sugar to the United States at the time for a million and a half dollars more than I sold it for in Canada."[3] Indeed, there was a widely held suspicion in Vancouver that, as soon as war broke out, the refinery held back sugar to speculate on future price increases. By 12 August, less than two weeks after war began, BC Sugar addressed the rumour in a large advertisement in the *Daily News-Advertiser.* "If your grocer tells you he cannot get sugar, it is not true," the refinery said. "What we have done is to eliminate speculative orders only, which action is entirely in the public interest." Nevertheless, consumer hoarding dried up sugar supplies and forced BC Sugar to withdraw from the Manitoba market.

Sir George Foster, the minister of trade and commerce, summoned refiners to meet in Ottawa on 18 August 1914. Rogers was unable to get there but wired his views to Drummond. The other refiners agreed that export sales be prohibited to prevent speculation in refined sugar. All refiners were alarmed when it seemed that Foster would go further and control prices. Rogers wired his reaction to Drummond: "Am anxious to keep prices reasonable as long as possible but must myself be the judge of when higher prices required."[4] He decided to increase prices in September, as he explained to shareholder W. D. Matthews: "Until just now I considered it good policy to keep prices of Refined Sugar as low as possible. I think now, however, in order to compel the consumer to economise, prices will have to go gradually up until they reach a point which will conform to the prices ruling in other parts of the world. You are doubtless aware that sugar in Canada has since the war been selling at a lower price than in any other country in the world."[5]

The war injected considerable volatility into raw sugar markets. They surged upwards in August only to retreat in mid-September: during a six-day period ending 23 September, the raw sugar price in New York fell from 5.25 cents a pound to 4 cents. "This business is a most extraordinary and dangerous one to operate in," Canada Sugar's Drummond wrote to Foster, justifying a reluctance by the refiners to reduce their prices immediately. "Sugar that we have all bought already at high prices could not now be sold without loss."[6] But early in November, when BC Sugar began reducing refined sugar prices, Foster prodded Drummond and the other eastern refiners to do the same. The eastern refiners grumbled that BC Sugar was in a different situation, not having participated in an expensive purchase of British West Indies sugar in August. Yet the eastern refiners soon began rolling back prices when a new lower-cost shipment of raw sugar arrived in Montreal.

Commodity prices, after remaining reasonably steady in 1914 and 1915, began to surge upwards in 1916. Ottawa responded with a pair of orders-in-council in November of that year setting up its Commission on the Cost of Living with independent power to investigate and with authority to delegate these powers to local municipalities. For example, Vancouver city council examined trading in seven basic commodities: meat, butter, fish, poultry, vegetables, potatoes—and sugar. Ottawa soon took the sugar investigation back after O'Connor concluded that price fixing had become general in Canada and that action had to be initiated against one corporation to deter others. The orders-in-council prohibited arrangements to "prevent or lessen competition" and gave O'Connor substantial investigative authority.

BC Sugar's secretary, J. W. Fordham Johnson, completed one of O'Connor's probing questionnaires on 26 January 1917.[7] The accompanying sixteen pages of schedules detailed the company's affairs, showing that its profit margin on the sale of sugar was "a trifle over two per cent." The schedules also included typical sales contracts between BC Sugar and its forty-six wholesalers across western Canada. "We have a tacit understanding with Jobbers that our sugars should be sold at prices quoted in our price lists," Johnson wrote in his reply, a sworn statement. "But, without being able to submit proof, we are confident that in many cases special discounts are given. The arrangement therefore cannot be said to be adhered to." The understanding was a little stronger than just tacit. Among the documents that Johnson attached to his statement was a letter from the W. H. Malkin Company of Vancouver. Malkin sales manager Herbert W. Taylor had agreed that: "In consideration of your offer to us of a discount of six per cent from all purchases made during the month of November last, we certify that from the commencement of the aforesaid month to the present time we have not sold, nor have we permitted any of our travellers, or salesmen, or agents to sell . . . at a lower price than the current price of the Refinery as made known from day to day. . . . We further certify that during the same period, we have bought and sold and dealt in sugar of your company's manufacture solely." Letters of agreement with other jobbers were similar, except that some got discounts of 5.5 per cent and others 7 per cent. Johnson concluded his deposition by recommending the government forbid such discounts. "While our competitors in the East follow the practice of giving discounts on a fixed sale price, we must adhere to the same policy or be threatened with a loss of business."

O'Connor responded sternly on 2 February. "I have to point out that the return discloses a method of operation which is clearly criminal." It was unnecessary for Ottawa to forbid the discounts. "It has been, for a long time, a criminal offence to be a party to any combination in restraint of competition."

The company tried to forestall prosecution. "We assure you that we are entirely innocent of intention to do anything illegal," Johnson wrote O'Connor on 9 February. He also enclosed a circular letter which BC Sugar proposed sending to its jobbers, if advised to do so by the government. This letter stated that because the Cost of Living Commissioner believed the business practice illegal, all discounting would end and the new price list would reduce prices to the extent of the discounts. O'Connor was not moved. He wired the company immediately that because price maintenance schemes were becoming general and because all involved "plead ignorance of the law, publicity [is] the remedy." He asked the attorneys general of British Columbia and Alberta for leave to prosecute.

Rogers now found himself on the front pages. "I have nothing to hide or be ashamed of," he told the *Daily News-Advertiser.* Privately, he was outraged, however. In April he wrote to Matthews: "I dare say that you have heard of them indicting me for 'criminal conspiracy' both in Alberta and in B.C. They certainly made it public enough and I can assure you it was most unpleasant for me—After what I did for the country when the war broke out, I think their action perfectly contemptible."[8] The reference was to making the yacht *Aquilo* available as an auxiliary naval vessel. He might also had added that the company, in 1915, had subscribed to $490,000 worth of Anglo-French war bonds and later also subscribed to Canadian war bonds.

When the conspiracy charge become public, Rogers maintained that his business practices were those which had existed in the sugar refining industry for fifty years. "I only fell in with the custom in vogue when I came and if the government says it is wrong I am perfectly willing to make what change is desired." Rogers admitted to the *Daily News-Advertiser* that the wholesalers had agreed to maintain the retail selling price set by the refinery. "That is correct," he told the newspaper. "But if we did not have that, prices would be all cut up. . . . If the jobbers are left to themselves they would all be cutting each other's prices and there would be no stability in the trade at all and the whole system of distribution would be upset. It would be pandemonium." His lawyer had advised him that the price maintenance policy was legal. He added: "Legal or not legal, if the government asks us to abandon the discount system, we will do so, reducing list prices accordingly, and leaving the wholesaler to set his own price."

There was more to it, of course, than protecting the jobbers from themselves. The wartime tightening of sugar supplies provided Rogers, finally, with the leverage to deal with those vexatious Chinese sugars: he asked his jobbers to handle the refinery's sugar exclusively. "It would be absurd," Rogers told the *Daily News-Advertiser,* "for a man buying Chinese sugar to come to me and ask me to help him maintain the margin on my sugar. . . . He could buy the Chinese sugar but I would not give him any discount on my sugar."[9]

Alberta quickly granted leave for O'Connor's prosecution, but British Columbia Attorney General M. A. Macdonald first wanted to know whether Ottawa would pay the costs of the action. After an exchange of wires over a three-week period, O'Connor had to remind the tight-fisted Macdonald that "responsibility for and expense of administration of criminal law are constitutionally matters of provincial concern." Macdonald finally wired O'Connor permission to prosecute on 6 March 1917, adding: ". . . the matter of costs standing in abeyance."

But, after all that, the prosecution was abandoned. The report of his investigation, published in May 1917, showed that O'Connor had discovered "an entire absence of any evidence of overcharging." His initial righteousness also had been humbled by what he had learned: "Throughout Canada there are many combinations and arrangements similar to those made by the British Columbia Company with its vendees. Many of these . . . were made in entire ignorance of their illegality. It seems to me unfair to proceed on a prosecution of this refinery unless all other refineries, and as well the hundreds, doubtless, of other manufacturers who have for many years been doing business on a fixed price basis are also prosecuted. It has amended its practices. Many of the others have not."[10]

Sir George Foster accepted O'Connor's conclusions. "It is to be remarked that the actions of the refiners"—including BC Sugar—"has given consumers in Canada sugar at very much cheaper prices than in either Great Britain or the United States," Foster said in a statement in September 1917. The refinery's selling price for sugar in Vancouver had risen from 5.1 cents a pound in mid-August 1914 to 8.5 cents a pound in December 1916, an increase of 66 per cent, driven by the rising cost of raw sugar, the higher world shipping costs and the wartime doubling of the duty the Canadian government charged on raw sugar imports. Consumers in Vancouver still were far better off than those in Britain, where sugar prices in the same period had risen 156 per cent. O'Connor's inquiry also showed that Canadian refiners were far from making unconscionable profits. Three of the six eastern refineries were barely able to service their bond debts, two others had neglible earnings and one was losing money. BC Sugar was more successful, but there was no evidence of price gouging and nothing from which to fashion a test case. The government concluded that the contract BC Sugar had sought from the wholesalers was questionable and the refinery had, as B. T. Rogers said it would, stopped insisting that its wholesalers maintain selling prices.

The irony is that wholesalers throughout the next two decades regularly importuned the company to set resale prices and to discipline merchants who were cutting prices. In 1925 BC Sugar had Vancouver lawyer E. P. Davis provide the company with an opinion explaining why price maintenance was illegal, copies of which were sent to wholesalers who wanted prices fixed. After he became president of the company, Ernest Rogers wrote a Winnipeg wholesaler who requested price-fixing: "We regret that, in view of our experience in 1917, and the carefully considered advice given us by our lawyers, it is not possible to do as you suggest."[11]

7

Everything Was the Finest

THE REFINERY'S SUCCESS AFFORDS B. T. ROGERS A BARONIAL LIFESTYLE

In 1890 factory managers could be hired for $100 a month and workers for a lot less. The directors of BC Sugar, however, rewarded their managing director well from the beginning. B. T. Rogers's initial three-year contract provided an annual salary of $5,000, rising in subsequent renewals to $24,000 in 1912.[1] He also received profit bonuses, the first one being $6,038 in 1897. As the refinery prospered, the bonuses sometimes exceeded the salary. In addition, as a shareholder Rogers also benefitted from the generous dividend policy on which he insisted: once, in 1896, he marshalled the proxies to remove from the board two "stupid directors" who had opposed an accounting manoeuvre that allowed a dividend to be declared. B. T. could afford his taste for a fine lifestyle from the beginning.

Soon after arriving in Vancouver, he bought property on the south side of Georgia street, near Nicola, where the gentle northward-facing slope commanded a view of Coal Harbour and the North Shore from the veranda of the expansive, wood-frame, architecturally designed house he had built in 1890. The house, named simply The Bungalow, was completed about the same time that the refinery melted its first sugar. In addition to such practical comforts as indoor plumbing, the house had a conservatory where Rogers indulged a passion for botany. After he married and the first children were born, he installed a dark room to process his family and travel photographs.[2]

The very first bonus was paid in 1892 when the directors awarded him $20,000 "for services rendered and disbursements incurred in promoting the company." The original employment contract stipulated that he receive treasury shares. Because there was doubt about the legality of this stipulation, the directors instead gave him the cash required to buy 200 shares in the company.[3] Through the rest of his life, he seldom missed an opportunity to buy BC Sugar shares. In 1905, for example, he offered $110 a share for Lord Strathcona's 600 shares (Strathcona's original 150 had been split 4 for 1). Rogers explained: "I am naturally anxious to increase my holdings [in BC Sugar], especially as I hope to see my sons succeed me in it." Strathcona declined to sell.

Enviably affluent after receiving the promotion bonus, Rogers wed Mary Isabella Angus of Victoria in June 1892. A gregarious man, Rogers led his reserved and dignified wife, whom he called Bella, into a life where business and pleasure definitely mixed. Bella's diaries recount trips to New York, to the Orient and to California (where Rogers's widowed mother Clara lived until 1894 when she came to reside with her son and his family in Vancouver). As well, there were travels into the interior of British Columbia after Rogers became interested in mining: along with some of the Toronto financiers who had invested in BC Sugar, Rogers was a shareholder in and president of the Horsefly Hydraulic Mining Company, a gold property in the Kootenays which operated with little success for three seasons then closed in 1899.

Rogers loved machinery, preferably fast and powerful. His first automobile, an electric car which he imported from Philadelphia in 1904, steered him into what is believed to have been Vancouver's first traffic accident between a car and a pedestrian. A youth named William Roedde (later a prominent Vancouver printer) was playing at the sandy curb on Barclay Street near Nicola when the passing Rogers accidentally veered or skidded over the boy's leg. Rogers took the frightened but uninjured boy into the car and drove him to the Roedde home, by which time the youth had forgotten his fright in the exhilaration of his first car ride.

In March 1905, just before buying the first of several Pierce Arrows, Rogers was summonsed for, as the *Vancouver Daily Province* reported it, "having driven his toot-toot wagon on a bicycle path on Powell Street." Never one to submit easily to authority, Rogers had his lawyer Osborne Plunkett argue the case. The lawyer contended that no city by-law designated any part of Powell as a cycle path, but the magistrate noted that the path was clearly marked for cyclists. The police indignantly entered evidence that the pneumatic tires of Rogers's vehicle had left wheel marks on either side of the path, "breaking off the edges as it moved along."[4] Plunkett, a family friend who also acted for the sugar company, paid a $5 fine on his client's behalf.

While there are receipts in his private papers indicating that Rogers in 1907 bought a Franklin Runabout,[5] his preference settled on Pierce Arrow, then the builder of some of America's most luxurious cars. He bought the first one in 1905 during a holiday in California. In 1911 he paid $8,000 for a 48-hp Pierce Arrow limousine, less a $2,000 trade-in allowance. The limousine had two bodies: an enclosed one for winter and a canvas-topped touring one for summer. "Twice a year workers would be sent up from the sugar refinery to help the chauffeur make the change," said Forrest Rogers, who once, as a five-year-old with a small hand, was asked to fish a lost nut from the coachwork. "I was very proud of myself, naturally," he said of this feat.

In 1898 Rogers paid $4,000 for three lots on Davie Street at Nicola on which to erect what would be Vancouver's most elegant mansion of that day. By this time he and Bella had three children: Blythe born in 1893, Mary born in 1894 and Ernest born in 1897. They were still living in The Bungalow when Elspeth was born in 1900. Three more children were born after they moved to the mansion in mid-1901: Philip in 1908, Margaret in 1910 and Forrest in 1912.

The $25,000 mansion, called Gabriola after the island from which the exterior stone was quarried, was designed by Samuel MacLure, then the leading young British Columbia architect. MacLure, the first white child in British Columbia whose birth was recorded at New Westminster (on 11 April 1860), had already designed coal magnate Sir James Dunsmuir's baronial home in Victoria, regarded by contemporary historians F. W. Howay and E. O. S. Scholefield as "the finest home in Canada."[6]

Gabriola was to be even more elegant. "Everything was the finest," recalled Kathleen Bell-Irving, a frequent guest of the Rogers's eldest daughters. The two-and-one-half storey home, which survives as a heritage building (and is currently used as a restaurant), had stained glass windows, wood panelling imported from Britain, eighteen fireplaces and the first concrete-lined basement of any home in the city. Among its furnishings was a $1,200 Steinway grand piano. After the Rogers family moved in, a coach house and stable, also designed by MacLure, was erected next door. This building, which was demolished in 1978, was itself large enough to accommodate six horses, several cars and carriages and, in a two-bedroom second-floor apartment, a groom to look after the horses. Rogers, who also liked to gamble at the card table, on occasion would race his horse-owning neighbours, with money bet on the outcome.

The staff at Gabriola included a butler and a nurse to look after the children. "He [B. T.] was very fond of his children," Mrs. Bell-Irving said. A doting father, he relished bringing home small gifts. When Margaret, the youngest daughter, was six, he returned from a weekend cruise to Victoria with a Pomeranian puppy for her which he had obtained from his friend, Robert P. Butchart.

The children usually dined separately, with Rogers and his wife dressing for dinner later. "We were just allowed in the dining room for a few minutes," Margaret recalled. Rogers, a bon vivant, entertained grandly at the mansion. "There was always the best of wine and plenty of it," Mrs. Bell-Irving remembered. "I think he probably drank too much for his health." Rogers's private papers contain receipts for quantity orders, either for the house or for his yacht. One example: a 1918 order through Henry Wootten & Son, mail-order liquor merchants in Vancouver, for five cases of port, five cases of scotch and one case of Heering's cherry brandy. Turkish cigarettes were imported directly from Benson & Hedges in London while the cigars were Cuban, ordered in quantity from suppliers in Vancouver.

The impression that emerges from Bella Rogers's diaries—journals she kept for most of her long adult life—is that she was the leavening influence in the boisterous Rogers household. While both she and her husband enjoyed music, she was a talented amateur, having learned the violin in her youth in Manchester. She joined a ladies' orchestra that gave concerts in Vancouver during the 1890s. Two decades later she became one of the founding patrons of the Vancouver Symphony Orchestra, a sponsorship that involved her writing personal cheques to cover the deficit at the end of each season. Indeed, she pursued a number of philanthropies during her life, beginning in 1901 when she joined the women's committee raising money for the new Vancouver General Hospital. (B. T. Rogers, not notably interested in philanthropies, was persuaded to support his wife in this one.) After her husband's death, she emerged in her own right as a person of stature and influence in Vancouver. Her extensive community involvement, besides the symphony, included active membership on the art gallery's board. As well, she was an eminent hostess. Her house guests typically were leading musicians—including eccentric pianist Glenn Gould, who wore an overcoat and gloves during lunch. The regal and vice-regal guests included the King and Queen of Siam, who dined with her in 1931 during a Vancouver stopover. A capable manager of her own business affairs, she was a director of BC Sugar for 47 years until retiring in 1960 in favour of Peter Cherniavsky, her grandson.

B. T. Rogers was an enthusiastic yachtsman. In 1899 he ordered a $6,700, fifty-foot, steam-powered yacht from A. S. Gordon & Company in Hong Kong. "I would like the boat named the Po Ping or Mo Ping, which ever means foreign devil," he instructed the builders. The *Mouping,* as she was called, was registered in his wife's name because Rogers had not yet become a British subject and, as an American, was not permitted to register the yacht in his name.[7] Joining the Royal Vancouver Yacht Club, he became its Commodore for six years from 1912 to 1918, longer than any other member in that position. "During the war years when Club activities were at a low ebb, Commodore Rogers acted as Host at a series of memorable dinners he gave for Club members and those returning from overseas," report the Club's Annals. In 1914 Rogers commissioned the building of a racing sloop, the *Turenga*, but she turned out to be a disappointment since she never won a major race.

After selling the *Mouping* to another member of the Royal Vancouver Yacht Club, Rogers in 1912 bought what became the grandest private yacht sailing from Vancouver at that time, the 160-foot *Aquilo.* Built in Boston in 1901, for William Eno of the fruit salts company, she was sailed by a professional crew of nineteen from the U.S. Atlantic coast around Cape Horn for delivery to new owners in Seattle in 1910. Rogers bought her cheaply two years later after a collapse of real estate values diminished the owners' fortunes.

When World War I began in August 1914, British Columbia premier Sir Richard McBride bought two submarines as the province's contribution to the Canadian navy. Rogers promptly hoisted the navy's white ensign on the *Aquilo* and made her available for several weeks as a submarine supply boat. Blythe Rogers, B. T.'s mechanically adept eldest son, installed radios in the submarines as well as the yacht. The *Aquilo* patrolled off Vancouver Island that summer when it was feared that a German warship in the Pacific, the *Leipzig,* would attack the British Columbia coast. Rogers, who spent many of his weekends at sea, sailed on one of her naval patrols.[8]

Bella Rogers often called her husband by his yacht club title, "the Commodore"—a reflection of the decorum with which the *Aquilo* was run. On board, he wore a peaked cap, white trousers and a double-breasted navy blazer with two rings on the sleeves, a uniform not out of place on the bridge of a Cunard liner. (He even had his portrait painted in this uniform.) The first mate always fired a ceremonial cannon and lowered the flag at sundown. Even on the yacht, Rogers and his guests dressed for dinner. "Everything was very proper, well-done and very shipshape," recalled Mrs. Bell-Irving, a frequent weekend guest when Rogers took his older children sailing. After her husband's death, Bella Rogers, who suffered from seasickness, sold the *Aquilo* in 1919 for $55,000. The yacht later had a varied career, which included passenger cruising to Alaska, until she burned and sank in September 1966 off Fort Bragg, California.

As the refinery flourished, B. T. Rogers conceived a grand country estate. Vancouver's west end had already begun its drift towards rooming houses and apartments, and the Rogers's social peers were beginning to build in the Shaughnessy Heights district. In 1912 Rogers paid Canadian Pacific $40,400 for ten acres of land well beyond the southern end of the Granville street car line. The property fronted on Granville and Shannon Road (now 57th Avenue), named for the neighbourhood's dairy farmer, William Shannon. Rogers commissioned what was to be the most luxurious residence west of Toronto.

Shannon, as the estate was called, brought Rogers together with contractor Charles Bentall, the British-born engineer who had become assistant general manager of Dominion Construction Company shortly after it was founded in 1911. The work that this firm was to do for BC

Sugar during the next decades contributed largely to Dominion Construction's surviving the Depression and thriving.[9]

Rogers hired Seattle architects Somervell and Putnam to design a forty-room Georgian-style house of reinforced concrete and brick. The eighteen-foot wall around the estate enclosed a gatehouse and stables as well as a magnificent garden filled with fruit and other trees. A pipe organ was ordered from the Aeolian Company of New York. During one business trip to New York, Rogers also began planning the interior decoration with L. Alavoine & Company, a Paris firm with a New York gallery. It is a measure of Rogers's wealth that he was able to launch such a vast project even though a business recession had begun in 1913.

Architect Somervell was elated when he was retained in September 1913. He assured Rogers: "At this stage, with the general stagnation of business in British Columbia and here, we would be in a position to give your house our entire attention, and I would thus be able to retain on my force for this purpose men whom I must shortly let go unless business picks up." The architect did not work as expeditiously as promised. Rogers prodded him with this letter on 23 March 1915: "There is a rumour around the Vancouver Club that you have finished the tentative plans for my house on Shannon Road. If so, would you be kind enough to let me have two copies." A perfectionist, Rogers insisted on enough design changes that the project took longer than intended which led to an unpleasant dispute later over the architect's fee.

After an expenditure of $125,000, the stable, the garage and the exterior shell of the mansion were complete by June 1918 when Rogers's sudden death occurred. Mrs. Bell-Irving recalls returning with the Rogers family from "a very happy cruise" on the *Aquilo* Sunday evening 17 June. Later that night B. T. Rogers suffered a fatal cerebral hemorrage. His widow asked Dominion to stop work until she was able to sell Gabriola—a difficult task in the depressed postwar real estate market. "It was his dream" Mrs. Bell-Irving believed. "Shannon meant a great deal to him. He enjoyed building it. I remember Mrs. Rogers saying, after he died, that 'Ben would have enjoyed entertaining at Shannon.' " The widow had his ashes placed in the ornamental gardens.[10]

It was not until 1925 that Bella Rogers devised a way to sell Gabriola and complete Shannon, living there for more than a decade until selling it in 1936 for $105,600 to mining promoter Austin Taylor. (Shannon survives today as an elegant 160-unit rental estate.) According to Shirley Bentall: "Mrs. Rogers, who was still unable to sell Gabriola for what she considered to be a reasonable price, came to an agreement with Charles [Bentall] regarding the Davie Street property. Mrs. Rogers was an intelligent businesswoman, high-principled and exceedingly fair. . . . She agreed to turn over the Davie Street house and property to a company that would be organized to retain it and develop an apartment building in connection with it. Mrs. Rogers accepted $75,000 worth of shares in the new company, while the Dominion Construction Company contributed its building of the adjoining structure for shares."[11] Gabriola and the attached buildings were called the Angus Apartments (Bella Rogers's maiden name) and the units quickly rented to brokers and other affluent tennants, including Charles Bentall, who raised his family and lived there until his death in 1974. His work for the Rogers family—his firm also built Blythe Rogers's mansion in 1920—resulted in Dominion Construction's receiving major commercial contracts at the refinery and in Alberta after the company entered the beet sugar business.

Rogers's success with the refinery had earned him the respect of powerful business figures, both in Vancouver and elsewhere. Typical was his relationship with Wilmot D. Matthews, an influential Toronto businessman with whom he frequently exchanged views and advice. In June 1910, as an example, Matthews asked about rumours that Montreal businessmen associated with Commercial Trust Company were trying to establish a sugar refinery in Vancouver. Rogers was not concerned: "The Trust Company you mention is composed of men of 'straw' and totally unable to financially carry out such an enterprise. Our papers are constantly full of rumours of all kinds of schemes, but I find most of them emanate from street talk. The real estate element here are using desperate efforts to boost land in Vancouver higher than it is already, and, to my mind it is now beyond the bounds of reason. If I knew of anything else to invest in, I should like to sell some of my property at the present prices, provided I could get *cash,* but these boomers are never ready to pay more than a small amount of cash."[12] The property included the Glencoe Lodge, a classy residential hotel at Burrard and Georgia which Rogers owned and later sold to the manager, who had trouble servicing the mortgage.

An April 1914 letter to Rogers from Matthews further confirms their relationship: "On our trip west last fall, you were about the only man living west of Winnipeg who would admit that we were in for dull times and I thought then that you were not only prudent, but courageous in expressing your opinion and told me that you intended to reduce the output of your refinery in order to meet the anticipated demand."

When war broke out, Matthews wrote: "I hope everything is shaping up all right with you and that you have—with your usual foresight—laid in a good stock of sugar that is going to see you through, and which no doubt will be profitable to the Company." Rogers indeed had done that, as he wrote Sir Edmund Osler in April 1915: "At the outbreak of the war, prices being low, I was carrying—as I have made a practice of doing at low prices—a heavy stock of raws . . . so that the financial result of our year's work is going to be highly satisfactory."[13]

When Harry Abbott died in 1916, his founders' shares in BC Sugar were placed on the market. Rogers wanted them for his eldest son, Blythe, who was joining the company. He was surprised when Matthews and Osler, unaware that Rogers was in the market, outbid him for the shares. Testily, he suggested that they should co-operate next time. There was a consolation. "I am glad the shares are in the hands of friends of mine," Rogers wrote Matthews. "This reminds me that I am creditably informed that the 1200 shares in our Company belonging to the estate of the late Lord Strathcona, may be on the market shortly. I have endeavoured quietly to get the executors to fix a price for me, but so far without success. Perhaps you can suggest a way of approaching the executors." Strathcona's heirs retained the shares, perhaps because they rewarded their owners so well, having again been split since last Rogers tried to buy them. On the refinery's twenty-fifth anniversary, in April 1916, Rogers boasted to Osler that the $3,099,575 which had been paid in total dividends during that time were equal to "1,239 ¾% on the original capital" or an average of 50 per cent a year.[14]

In the same letter in which he asked Matthews's help to get the Strathcona shares, Rogers disclosed that he had invested $60,000 in a sugar refinery being built at Savannah, Georgia. He knew and trusted the backers; and he believed the refinery's proximity to Cuba gave it access to ready sugar supplies. "It has occurred to me since that the scope of the enterprise might possibly be broadened and the profits doubly assured by 'hitching it up' with the Van Horne interests in Cuba."[15] He asked Matthews whether he and Osler were close to the Van Horne interests. Matthews and Osler immediately agreed to join Rogers in investing in the refinery. Rogers had agreed to take 750 preferred shares in the Georgia company at $80 each, receiving 375 common shares as a bonus. He paid $10,000 down and the balance on 15 May, using his dividend from BC Sugar. He now offered one-third of these to Matthews at cost if Matthews would sell, at his cost, sixty of Abbott's BC Sugar shares to his eldest son, Blythe. This particular transaction never took place because Matthews had purchased Abbott's shares for his own son. When Rogers died, Matthews sent a quick handwritten note to Blythe, saying: "I valued and appreciated his opinions not only about his own business but about matters generally. We will miss him greatly."[16]

A Vancouver newspaper, the *Saturday Chinook*, published a sour but revealing obituary of BC Sugar's founder.

> Mr. Rogers was honest in his way. If he didn't like a man or a proposition he usually said so out loud and plain. He spoke his mind in other words. . . . Some say that the deceased failed as a citizen. Not having all the facts before us we cannot pass upon this. Surely he did not take interest in politics. Probably he was too busy at his place. They say he knew every detail of every machine in his mighty factory and had invented many machines there and had improved many that others had invented. He worked with his hands as well as with his head and must have been kept busy. He was not a church worker. He belonged to none of the artistic clubs. He did not go in for city beautiful other than that he always kept his property in splendid shape, keeping a small army constantly at work with cleaning up and painting. He had a mania for keeping things tidy and in order.
>
> They say he wasn't generous with his money. Surely the press has not carried announcements of Rogers' gifts here and there. . . . We have learned, however, of a case where someone caused a ten thousand dollar instrument to be placed in a certain hospital for the use and benefit of mankind. When Rogers was asked if he had placed it there, he said he refused to give money to public bodies because they usually squander and waste any money placed in their hands.[17]

There was no doubt he was wealthy: the value of his estate at the time of his death was $1,125,000. But in a time when income tax was just being introduced, it was still modest compared with the great fortunes of the time.

He would have preferred as an epitaph a note he had written proudly that February to Matthews. "It will interest you to know that since I started in business here . . . with a paid up capital of $250,000, The Co has earned $10,566,909 of which $5,289,375 has been paid out in dividends to shareholders. Is it not true that there are few manufacturing enterprises in Canada which can equal that record? Certainly there are none in British Columbia."[19]

8

Quite Without Foundation

THE STRESS OF A SECOND PUBLIC INQUIRY HASTENS BLYTHE ROGERS'S DEATH.

During the autumn of 1919, $300,000 worth of British Columbia fruit went unsold when neither the processors nor the home canners were able to get enough sugar. BC Sugar was accused of manipulating supplies to increase the price and of diverting sugar to markets elsewhere. Early in 1920 the provincial legislature struck a committee of inquiry which targetted the company. Blythe Rogers, who was now the president, wrote to reassure shareholder Sir Edmund Osler in Toronto: "Of course both charges are quite without foundation and very easily disproved, so that except for some unpleasant publicity we have nothing to fear at their hands."[1]

In fact, BC Sugar was in for a rough ride. Frank Giolma, a soldier-member for Victoria who introduced the resolution for the inquiry on 20 February, said—according to the report in the Vancouver *World*—"that he did not pose as a sugar expert, but public feeling was bitter about this matter, and they should know whether it was due to world shortage or to a restraint in trade." Fellow politician George Bell was more openly suspicious: "Sugar conditions in British Columbia have not been in a healthy state for twenty-five years, except for the sugar refinery."[2] R. H. Pooley, another of the five members of the select committee, complained that his house had been without sugar for five days. He suggested that the refinery was paying more attention to its customers in Alberta and Saskatchewan than to those in its home market. Committee member Mrs. Ralph Smith, reported the *Vancouver Daily Province,* "expressed the opinion that large shipments of sugar were going to the United States."

By 1917 wartime demand for shipping made it impossible for BC Sugar to charter all the vessels necessary to maintain the refinery's supply of raw sugar. B. T. Rogers had 25,000 tons of Fiji raw sugar available but was able to get vessel space only for shipments of 1800 tons to 2500 tons each, sometimes in unsatisfactory ships.[3] In April 1918 the company began reducing shipments to its jobbers. During the next three years, the refinery had its customers on allotment much of the time, either because of shipping difficulties or raw sugar shortages.

The worldwide sugar shortage was the consequence of the collapse in the European beet sugar industry. While production had reached 8.8 million tons before the war, the beet harvest of 1919 was only 2.3 million tonnes. In Russia, civil war in the Ukraine, where 80 per cent of its beet sugar was produced, had left the farms and the sugar factories—in the words of a contemporary observer—"in complete ruins."[4] In Germany, sugar production plunged after the repatriation of prisoners of war deprived beet farms of labour. In France, where there had been about 200 beet processing factories before the war, only 61 had escaped destruction or pillage at the hands of the Germans, and most of these were idle because there were no beets. Dutch authority Dr. H. C. Prinsen Geerligs, European columnist for the trade journal *Louisiana Planter and Sugar Manufacturer,* wrote plaintively in February 1919: "The scarcity of sugar prevails in every continental country, the crops having been small, the initial stocks almost nothing and the craving for sugar and sugared food is intense, because other food is only to be had in small quantities and is not sufficient to feed the population properly." The craving was demonstrated in the summer of 1920 by a riot in a waiting room at Ellis Island, the New York harbour clearing point for European migrants to the United States. To sweeten coffee and tea, the immigrants were given sugar instead of the usual molasses. "As these unfortunates had not seen sugar for the past five years there was a great rush for the bowls, some of which the men tried to pocket," recounted the *Louisiana Planter.* "The delving into the sugar bowls caused a scramble, then a scuffle, then a fight and a number of aliens had to be removed to hospitals."[5]

Aggravating the sugar shortage was Prohibition in the United States and Canada. Denied alcoholic beverages, consumers turned to sugar-intensive alternatives, including candy, soft drinks and sweetened coffee. Victoria candymaker James W. Rogers (not related to the refinery Rogers) told the legislative inquiry in March 1920: "Since prohibition much more candy has been consumed than before."[6]

Americans and Canadians had the benefit of more ample supplies of domestic beet and cane sugar as well as cane sugar from the Caribbean. In September 1919 the wholesale price of refined sugar in New York was still 9 cents a pound, compared with 13.46 cents in Britain and 17.5 cents in France. The United States Sugar Equalization Board, which had been set up to stabilize sugar prices, paid an average of 4.6 cents a pound for Cuba's 1918 sugar crop and contracted the 1919 crop for 5.5 cents a pound. Ignoring signals that sugar prices were about to soar, they offered a modest 6.5 cents a pound for the 1920 crop.

The *Louisiana Planter,* to which BC Sugar subscribed, warned in a front-page editorial on 3 January 1920: "The various governments of the world that have any credit they can possibly utilize will now be interested in buying sugar in Cuba in competition with the United States. . . ." The Cubans, who had seen the Americans resell at a profit a portion of that 1919 crop to Britain, started holding back sugar at the beginning of 1920. A Cuban banker quoted by the trade paper in July recounted what happened: "When the world shortage of sugar occurred buyers were sent to Cuba from all European countries, even from Asia; the demand for this commodity started a rise in price which by leaps and bounds sent sugar to 10, 11, 12 and up to 18 cents a pound, there being cases lately when sugar has sold as high as 20 cents per pound."[7] In fact, the wholesale price of refined sugar soared in New York from 9 cents at the start of 1920 to peak at 23.5 cents a pound in May. For Cuba it seemed a bonanza. "The sugar crop of 1919–1920 was sold at $1,022,000,000 and brought the island more money than had all the crops from 1900 to 1914," Cuban historian Luis A. Aguilar has written.[8] In sugar history, this period is always referred to as The Dance of the Millions.

Both the American and Canadian governments tried to restrain sugar prices and prevent hoarding and profiteering. The Canadian government's sugar price controls in mid-1919 required wholesalers to sell sugar at prices that would yield retailers a profit of 1.5 cents a pound; the maximum retail sales price appears to have been 15 cents. This untenable order was rescinded seven months later, in February 1920, rising raw sugar prices having made it unrealistic.[9] The American government also empowered itself to dictate retail sugar prices and to prosecute those who overcharged. Some of the most aggressive enforcement occurred in Wisconsin where, in October 1919, the U.S. District Attorney warned: "The Government has set a price and I am here to see that dealers do not charge any more. If dealers want to keep out of jail I would advise them to be satisfied with the 11 cents [a pound] allowed them." Early in the new year, he constituted a federal grand jury to investigate profiteering. Dozens of investigations, prosecutions and arrests occurred across the United States in 1920 as the authorities rooted out presumed or actual profiteering in sugar. This only stopped after the U.S. Supreme Court in March 1921 ruled that the price control legislation was unconstitutional.

When the British Columbia legislature began its investigation, Blythe Rogers, like his father before him, was confident that the company had nothing to hide. No sugar had been exported to the United States because the Canadian Trade Commission in Ottawa refused export licences to refiners despite demand from potential American buyers. Rogers, who was in poor health, wired Premier John Oliver, inviting the committee to visit the refinery where he would place the records at their disposal. The committee insisted on public hearings in Victoria.

♦

Blythe Dupuy Rogers was born on 22 May 1893, eight days before the death of B. T.'s oldest and closest brother, after whom he was named. B. T.'s sudden death plunged Blythe into the presidency of BC Sugar when he was only twenty-five and in frail health. His education for business had begun in 1907 when he was sent to St. Alban's, a private boys' school in Brockville, Ontario, which prepared him for subsequent technical studies at the Royal Military College in Kingston. His surviving letters home portray a sensitive, sheltered youth forced to mature in a hurry. The school had the boys awake at 6:45 A.M. and in chapel at 7 A.M. The remainder of the day and the entire week were tightly programmed. Sunday afternoon, he complained in a 7 September letter, even included two hours devoted to "*compulsory walk* in a *given direction* (always the same)."[10]

"You said that I would have to keep clean at school," he wrote his mother. "How can I, when I get a *cold* water bath once a week, and always have to wash in *cold* water. Not a drop of hot water for four months. Just think of it."[10] There was the inevitable bullying by the other boys and the homesickness which, he admitted, reduced him to tears from time to time. "I broke some more of my front tooth and some of the gold in it playing football, and for the first time in my life I enjoyed going to the dentist because I could not go to football. I am perfectly sick of this place. . . ." That plaintive letter seems to have led his mother to write directly to St. Alban's headmaster, for on 28 September, Blythe wrote her: "But, for goodness sakes, DONT WRITE ANY BABY'S LETTERS TO MR. ORCHARD, about cycling or anything like or unlike it, or you will establish a laughing stock in the school in the form of me. . . ." He was, he wrote, beginning to like the school. Next spring, after he had been invited onto the editorial board of the school newspaper, he actually lauded the school in verse:

> St Albans is just, & by no means the worst,
> Of all *the* schools, I ween:
> Its gains are many, Its losses, if any,
> Are few & far between.

He survived St. Alban's and went on to the Royal Military College. His interest in technology also is evident from his letters home from St. Alban's. In one to his father—Blythe addressed him as Dear Dada—he asked: "Will you please ask mother if she will send some weekly or monthly paper (Except the Scientific American, because Mr. Orchard lends me that). . . ." In the same letter, he asked knowledgeably about the conversion from coal to oil his father had ordered for the yacht, *Mouping.* "Will you get a higher speed off her if she burns oil? Will you have a tank for her oil on the wharf, or draw on the Refinery oil for it?"

Blythe joined the army soon after the war began in 1914. His father expressed concern about this to W. D. Matthews in Toronto. Matthews, replying to Rogers reassured him: "I can readily appreciate your feeling of anxiety about your oldest son going to the front. The sentiment that causes him to feel it is a duty to go is, of course, very patriotic and much to be commended. . . . Is your son already at Salisbury, or is he going with the 2nd regiment?"[11] In fact, he had become a lieutenant in the Sixth Field Company Engineers, a unit of the army which particularly suited his technical bent. But during final training in Ottawa with the engineers in April 1915, Blythe Rogers was injured in a fall from a horse and, while in hospital, contracted influenza.

"He was invalided home with a badly damaged heart," his mother recounted in her dispassionate memoir of BC Sugar. "After a long convalescence he returned to the Refinery, where he had previously worked for awhile in the drafting department, was made a director and elected Vice President . . . in October 1915." The young man's progress pleased his father who wrote Matthews in 1916: "My eldest son has joined the staff of the Refinery here, and I am glad to say, is taking a very keen interest in his work. I have given him some shares in the Company, and he is anxious to become possessed of some more, but I want him to borrow the money himself to pay for them, because I consider a matter of this kind an important part of his business training." But in a 1975 interview Forrest Rogers said that Blythe "knew he was doomed to die at a very, very early age."

◆

When the legislature began its inquiry, there was a presumption that the refinery had manipulated sugar supplies. One rumour had sugar from the refinery on sale in Honolulu at 8 cents a pound. Improbable as that was—Hawaii was a major sugar producing state—Premier John Oliver had the British consul there check it out. The committee had just begun its hearings when, one day early in March, Victoria pharmacist W. S. Terry, who ran several stores with restaurants and soda fountains, had a ton of freezing salt delivered to the sidewalk outside his Pandora Street store. By coincidence Terry testified at the inquiry that day and remarked on the curiosity the white mound had stirred among passersby. "That's interesting," broke in committee member Smith. "I received a telephone message this morning saying that a ton of sugar was on Terry's sidewalk."

Blythe Rogers went to Victoria for a three-hour session before the committee on the afternoon of Monday, 15 March 1920. His health had deteriorated and his mother wrote later that "he had risen from a sick bed to attend the inquiry sessions. . . ."[12] He began his testimony by reviewing how the war had disrupted Europe's capacity to supply sugar and how, with the war ended, the British had joined the Americans in bidding for the Cuban crop. "Then [in June 1919] France surprised the world by removing all restrictions on sugar," he said. "French buyers entered every market and bid up prices. At the same time came the news of the drought in India which reduced that crop by one million tons."[13] A longshoremen's strike in mid-June, which lasted a month, prevented the delivery of several raw sugar cargoes and forced the refinery to withdraw from raw sugar markets. Once the strike ended, BC Sugar tried to buy more raws, only to find that the French had bid up the prices and were buying "everything they could get."

The refinery now joined the scramble for sugar, locating small quantities in Peru—where a hurricane damaged the ship while it was loading—and in San Francisco. The Canadian government refused the refinery a licence to import American sugar and, to Rogers's intense irritation, neglected to include the Vancouver refinery in a pool of eastern refiners buying from Cuba at 5.5 cents a pound. "Except when they want taxes, the Ottawa Government thinks that Canada consists of Ontario and Quebec," Rogers complained. "Normally when governments don't interfere with the distribution of sugar our competitors have to buy it at the same prices we do."[14]

BC Sugar eventually contracted for Cuban raw sugar somewhat above the pool price only to discover that the Cubans wanted even more money when prices began to soar early in 1920. "The Cuban grower has put every possible stumbling block in our way to provoke us to cancel our contracts because he can sell this sugar elsewhere at much better prices," Rogers told the committee. "All our shipments have been delayed. Our December shipment did not leave until January 13 and our January shipment not until March 7. Our February shipment is just starting to load. We have just got to lie down and take these things as they come or we don't get any sugar." In fact, the vendor of an 11,000-ton cargo of raw sugar from Southeast Asia had just broken his contract with BC Sugar and sold the cargo elsewhere.

He assured the committee that, even with all these problems, the refinery had contracted for about 65,000 tons of raw sugar, about 20 per cent more than in 1919, and enough to meet consumer needs—at a price. Later, he told the newspapers that he "could not conceive" that the selling price of refined sugar at the refinery would be higher than 20 cents a pound.

The testimony of Rogers and of the thirty-two other witnesses called before the committee convinced the legislators that, indeed, there was a global shortage of sugar, attributable chiefly to the war. Their report also suggested that "a large measure of recent hardship" had been caused by the postwar controls of the Canadian government, which restrained domestic prices but allowed exports to Britain and the United States where prices were higher. Between January and November 1919, nearly 114,000 tons of refined sugar was exported by the eastern refiners, a significant quantity given that Canadian consumption was about 400,000 tons. BC Sugar's response to the shortage and to serving its markets was judged above criticism. Its refinery, the committee's report noted, was the only one of the Canadian refiners positioned to serve that quarter of the population in the West. "There is no evidence that this refinery abuses its monopoly," the committee stated.[15]

On the contrary, the committee learned that for a period in 1919 "British Columbia sugar, though limited in quantity, was the cheapest sugar on the American continent and consistently sold at approximately two cents per pound less than sugar in Eastern Canada or throughout the United States." Blythe Rogers was vindicated. As he wrote one of his shareholders: "I am glad to say that we have been able to turn the tables on them [the legislature's committee] and make them feel that they have made utter fools of themselves."[16] He was not to savour his victory too long: on 6 May 1920, a month after the legislature's committee reported, he was dead at the age of twenty-seven.

The committee, while clearing the company of fault, worried that 1919's shortage would worsen in 1920 and recommended that the province buy 1000 to 2000 tons of refined sugar to assure consumers with adequate supplies for fruit processing that autumn. Premier Oliver wired two eastern refiners but failed to get any sugar.

The committee's recommendation illustrated the sugar panic that gripped Canadian governments in the spring of 1920. The national government prohibited exports of refined sugar, conserving stocks for domestic use. The refiners all complained that they were unable to get bank financing to store high-cost sugar inventories and asked the government to finance this store. The Canadian government then decided to pass the problem on to the consumer: in advertisements across Canada, it urged consumers to buy their sugar needs well in advance of the fall canning season. This counsel to hoard sugar was meant to generate cash with which the refineries could go back to an escalating world market and buy more raw sugar. Conventional wisdom was, as the select committee put it, that the demand for sugar would be strong and prices "will be high and increasing." They could not have been more wrong.

As it turned out, BC Sugar was fortunate not to have been included in the eastern buying pool. The Canadian government's inept intervention into the sugar business left the eastern refiners with ruinous losses. The bubble of speculation broke in Cuba in June 1920 when the American refiners refused to continue bidding up raw sugar prices. Suddenly the speculators in Cuba found themselves holding vast tonnages of unwanted (at the price) sugar, all of which they had financed with short-term bank loans. When the bankers began asking for their money back, sugar was dumped onto the market, and the price collapsed even more rapidly than it had soared. By December Cuban sugar could be had again for 5.5 cents a pound. Shareholder Osler had already written the company in October, asking about the impact of falling prices. "I have only one cargo which is fairly high priced, but that was not bought anywhere near the top of the market," replied J. W. Fordham Johnson, who had succeeded Blythe Rogers as president. He believed the "large" profit the company had made since April would be "a fine reserve to meet declining prices."[17]

The eastern Canadian refiners, at the urging of government, had contracted heavily that summer for sugar. When the market turned, they had on hand or were committed for 80 million pounds of beet sugar and 280 million pounds of raw cane sugar, purchased at an average price of 19 cents a pound—some $63 million of unrefined inventory. They now faced massive losses on that inventory. The retail price in the United States was below that and still falling, with the result that Canadian wholesalers and retailers were about to import American refined sugar. A delegation of eastern refiners—again BC Sugar was not included—met with officials of Prime Minister Arthur Meighen's government. The refiners believed they were owed a favour: the government, by prohibiting Canadian sugar exports to the United States between June 1918 and June 1919, had prevented the refiners from realizing a windfall profit estimated as high as $10 million. Now, stuck with expensive sugar, they faced a potential $10 million loss.

The solution seemed simple. The Board of Commerce of Canada, a government agency, issued an order 13 October 1920, ordering all wholesalers and commercial users to buy from Canadian refiners. The order fixed the maximum retail price of granulated sugar at 21 cents a pound until the end of the year. This was triple the raw sugar price in New York at the time.

Outrage exploded across Canada—from hostile newspaper editorials to a stern resolution from Vancouver City Council—and the Meighen cabinet rescinded the order almost immediately. The *Vancouver Sun* editorialized on its front page: "Never before have the Canadian people witnessed such a brazen attempt at highway robbery . . . The people of British Columbia will pay 21 cents a pound for sugar while people in Seattle are getting it for thirteen. . . . The Canadian consumer is simply being robbed for the benefit of the sugar barons." When the year ended, the eastern refiners all reported major losses. "These losses," said W. A. Hobbins, the angry president of Atlantic Sugar Refineries, "are a direct result of a breach of faith on the part of the government. . . ."[18]

But BC Sugar, not having been included in the Cuban pool, emerged from 1920 in reasonable shape. Johnson had been forced to write down sugar inventories by $450,000 which gave the company a loss of $321,047 for the fifteen months ended 31 March 1921 (then the firm's fiscal year). He wrote shareholder Osler that he considered the result "satisfactory, in view of the extraordinary conditions which prevailed during the last six or seven months."[19] The company's reputation also had survived. When Vancouver mayor R. H. Gale fired an angry telegram to Ottawa in October 1920 protesting the sugar price order, he distinguished between the eastern refiners and BC Sugar. The *Vancouver Province* paraphrased his view: "During the war or the times when sugar was short, the B.C. Refinery did its level best, thought His Worship, to cater to public wants and he believed did not take advantage of situations which opened the way for unfair treatment of consumers had they so desired."[20]

9

Forty-Seven Years Of Experience

THE REGENCY OF FORDHAM JOHNSON, THE FRUGAL BANKER.

John William Fordham Johnson, the banker who was BC Sugar's president during the 1920s, was the only chief executive in the company's first century not a member of the Rogers family. While the company did have non-family presidents during its first decade—J. M. Browning and Forrest Angus—these men only represented senior shareholders while founder B. T. Rogers called the shots as general manager. Johnson was the company's chief financial officer when the deaths of Rogers, in 1918, and his eldest son, Blythe, in 1920 thrust him into the top job.

It is likely that he was expected to remain there until B. T.'s second-oldest son, Ernest, had been groomed. But he settled into the job so forcefully that, by the time his regency ended, a lingering coolness had settled between Johnson and the Rogers family. It began during Blythe's brief presidency. Forrest Rogers, youngest of B. T.'s four sons, believed Blythe disliked Johnson. As well, others of the Rogers family took the view that Johnson did not give the ailing Blythe all the assistance he required. Johnson was such an austere penny-pincher that others in the company dubbed him "Can't Afford 'Em Johnson." Forrest Rogers, in a 1975 interview, said: "The company was not in good financial condition when Johnson took it over and he ran it, as I understand it, like the receiver of a company might have done. He didn't spend a nickel on the refinery and there was no modernization done in this period."[1] When Philip Rogers learned that a Johnson grandson had taken a job at the refinery during the 1950s, he snapped to the youth's astonished mother that the refinery did not need any more Johnsons. "There are enough Rogers to take over." (The grandson, William Wood, was unaware of this exchange and left of his own volition to join the army and later to become an economist at the University of British Columbia.[2])

Johnson was born in England on 28 November 1866 and, at twenty-two, came to North America to work in the Portland branch of the first Bank of British Columbia (which was taken over in 1900 by the Canadian Bank of Commerce). In 1898 the bank transferred him to Vancouver. A year later he joined the bank's client, BC Sugar, to handle its accounting and banking affairs, freeing B. T. Rogers to deal with the other problems of business.

The volatile Rogers and the phlegmatic Johnson were contrasting personalities. "He was certainly not what you would call quick-tempered," Johnson's daughter, Beatrice (Wood), said of her father. "I would say he was very even-tempered."[3] A sister-in-law who was Johnson's tour guide to London during an 1897 vacation, later wrote: "Everyone was delighted with his charm and gaiety and everyone wanted to see more of him."[4] Johnson's leisure tastes ran to bridge, golf and tennis while Rogers preferred boats and botany. Johnson seldom participated in the poker games, fishing trips and horse races that his employer relished. However, the families—notably the wives—became friends: the Johnson home was not far from Gabriola, and the children grew close. Johnson was the godfather for B. T. Rogers's third son, Philip. Beatrice, a close friend of Mary, B. T.'s eldest daughter, was a frequent guest at Gabriola and sometimes accompanied the Rogers family on weekend cruises on the *Aquilo*.

When Rogers bought the Fiji sugar plantation in 1905, he needed a reliable manager and turned to Johnson, naming him president of the Vancouver–Fiji Sugar Company. Johnson sailed for Fiji on 21 June 1905 and arranged for his American-born wife Helen to follow in September with their children: Beatrice, who was only five and Helen, a baby who had not yet begun to speak. After living six months in hot, humid Suva, they moved into a newly completed, rambling manager's house at Tamunua.

Helen Johnson's diary revealed that her husband, whom she called

Billy, had exposed himself and his family to discomfort and risk. "Mosquito and flies a perfect pest," Mrs. Johnson complained. "*Awful.*"[5] Beatrice soon was confined to bed with what the plantation doctor diagnosed as "poisoning from mosquito bites." Johnson's own health held until after B. T. Rogers had visited the plantation in the third week in March 1906. But by the end of March Johnson was forced to bed with what the doctor called a "slight congestion of the liver." Beatrice, who later became a nurse, said: "The trouble was in those days they didn't know a great deal about public health and he [Johnson] used to ride over the plantation to oversee the cutting of the cane and so on and drink from polluted streams. He got amoebic dysentery and it settled on his liver."[6]

Johnson was gravely ill. On 21 April he was taken on a stretcher to hospital in Suva where surgeons advised his wife to "prepare for the worst" when they operated to deal with an abscess of the liver. He came through surgery but made a very slow recovery. In June Rogers hired Scotsman S. R. Cochran to run the plantation and oversee the rebuilding of the Tamanua mill while Johnson was recuperating. On 16 June Johnson left hospital but stayed in Suva so that the surgeons could monitor his recovery. He had, his wife wrote, "dressed for the first time since March 30." It had been a close call. His wife confided to her diary that she "did not think he would recover." That also was the opinion of doctors in Australia when Johnson suffered a setback while in Sydney in July for further treatment. He spent a month in a private hospital, nourished by milk and arrowroot biscuits, before completing his convalescence in rented accommodation. On 8 August, his wife wrote in her diary: "He had his first whiskey & soda for dinner which did him good."

He was able to return to Tamunua on 3 October, in time to preside over the opening of the new crushing mill. The governor of Fiji had been invited, the mill was decked out with flags and bunting, and cake and champagne were on hand. (The governor was detained by what he called "affairs of state" but sent his wife to represent him.) Now recovered, but tiring easily, Johnson settled into the routine of getting the mill running well. The Navua bridge was completed in late November and the mill's crushing facilities, after an erratic start, began working well. It rained heavily almost every day in November and December: when the sun came out on 30 December 1906, Mrs. Johnson described it as "the first ray in a month, the 2nd in six weeks." She confided to her diary that it was the end of "the most trying and troublesome year we have ever spent."

Johnson moved back to Vancouver in mid-1907. He retained the presidency of the Vancouver–Fiji Sugar Company and periodically returned on inspection trips. "But my father was not allowed to live in the tropics," Beatrice said, "because he never really completely recovered." A recurrence of illness forced Johnson to resign as BC Sugar's secretary in July 1919. The directors agreed to retain him as an advisor if his health allowed, and in March 1920, his health improved, Johnson was rehired as vice-president.[7]

When Blythe died, Johnson's twenty-two years experience in the company made him the obvious choice to run it. He is believed to have demanded and been given a ten-year contract. It seems reasonable that capable Ernest Rogers would have been chafing to take over by the end of the Johnson regency although he was certainly too well-mannered to engage in a power struggle.

The refinery when Johnson took over was beginning to show its age. Wilfred Kenyon, who went to work in the laboratory in 1921, recalled in a 1975 interview: "It was a rather dark and gloomy place."[8] Early in 1922 Johnson asked a New York consulting engineer, R. S. Kent, to design a new pan house and a new packing house, with construction to begin in the fall of 1923. But in October 1922, after the company had been unsuccessful in recovering much capital from the closure of the Fiji mill, Kent was wired that BC Sugar had decided "to postpone indefinitely any extensive alterations." It was another five years before this expansion was brought forward—and then again delayed by the cautious Johnson who authorized only modest changes. In 1923 $51,000 was spent to add three floors to the the refinery's three-storey No. 1 warehouse and a sixth floor to the No. 2 warehouse. Several years later the refinery's filter house was remodelled and new controls were installed when chief chemist Robert Boyd convinced Johnson that sloppy process controls were costing the company money.

Several times during Johnson's term, sugar from foreign suppliers disrupted BC Sugar's marketplace. Refined sugar from Central America reached Vancouver priced so cheaply that Johnson charged it was being dumped (sold for less in Canada than it sold at home). Johnson's persistent complaints led to an investigation by Canadian authorities in the fall of 1926 which established that sugar from El Salvador and Guatemala indeed was being dumped. An appropriate anti-dumping duty was levied in 1927.[9] When a cargo from the Dominican Republic was landed in Vancouver late in 1928, Johnson again succeeded in getting a protective duty.

He was not always successful. The Dominion government in 1926 had allowed a duty remission on sugar imports used to make loganberry wine, a measure aimed specifically to help Growers Wine Company of Victoria. In June 1927 Growers imported 2500 bags of white sugar from Central America. The tariff remission, Johnson complained angrily to federal finance minister J. A. Robb, made it "absolutely impossible for my Company to compete against such importations of foreign sugar." Robb responded that a comparable duty drawback on sugar for other wine production had been in place since 1910, and no one had complained. The answer overlooked the fact that wine production, well established in Ontario, only began in British Columbia after World War I.

Despite occasional breaches in the tariff wall, BC Sugar recovered from its 1921 loss to prosper during Johnson's decade. "He did get the company back on a good financial footing, no doubt about that," Forrest Rogers admitted later.[10] The company paid generous annual dividends averaging 10 per cent of profits to its shareholders (and Johnson became a large shareholder). Surpluses generated by the business were placed either in blue-chip securities or in the money market until, by the end of the decade, BC Sugar owned a remarkable portfolio. In 1930 this included 14,400 shares of Canadian Pacific Railway Company; 1,000 preferred shares of Steel Company of Canada; $100,000 in Bell Telephone 5 per cent first mortgage bonds; $5.3 million in Dominion of Canada 5.5 per cent bonds; $265,000 in B.C. Telephone Company 7 per cent preferred shares; $50,000 worth of Montreal Island Power Company bonds; and shares in several U.S. telephone utilities. Johnson also invested cash in the New York money market where the company had had a commercial account with National City Bank since 1917 and where the 6 per cent return was double that earned in the company's Bank of Montreal savings account.[11]

With a secrecy typical of that era, none of this nor any other significant financial information was disclosed to shareholders. B. T. Rogers had presided at an annual shareholders' meeting early in the company's history which passed a resolution prohibiting such disclosure and this policy remained until the company was listed on stock exchanges in 1962. There seemed a cogent reason for non-disclosure. Johnson, replying to a prospective New York investor in May 1929, explained: "This company produces a necessary food product under a certain amount of protection. The payment of large dividends per annum on a percentage basis might, if known, be used against the industry by the free trade advocates in this country, and, unfortunately, there are many in Canada." The letter was marked, of course, Private and Confidential.[12] In the spring of 1929, when the company split its shares five for one, several shareholders wrote for annual financial statements. Johnson firmly rebuffed one Toronto shareholder: "Mrs. Mason must realize that this company produces a necessary article of food, and is dependent on the protective policy of Canada. Any broadcasting of its affairs might have an injurious effect on this condition and so, with the approval of the shareholders, it was decided wiser not to issue any statements."[13]

Johnson's cautious husbanding of cash also was done with an eye to threats from renewed beet sugar production. In December 1924 the Utah–Idaho Sugar Company announced a $1 million beet factory at Bellingham in Washington state. This spurred interest in beet growing in the Fraser Valley. E. D. Barrow, British Columbia's minister of agriculture, suggested that Canadian beet farmers could deliver their crop to Bellingham—even though they had to overcome a duty of 85 cents a ton—until a beet sugar factory could be set up at Sumas. Johnson discouraged the idea. "Personally, I doubt if it could be made a success," he told the *Vancouver Sun*. "Some experimenting was carried on in the Ladner District with beet growing a few years ago and it was found that there was not enough sunshine to develop the saccharine content of the beet sufficiently."[14] After the Bellingham factory opened in 1927, about forty farmers signed beet contracts and sold their beets across the border until the 1933 harvest, after which the U.S. government banned sugar beet imports.

Johnson was more apprehensive when Utah–Idaho opened a sugar beet factory at Raymond, Alberta, in 1925. That February, Johnson wrote one shareholder that he hoped to maintain the company's dividend if the new factory could be prevented from eroding BC Sugar's sales on the Prairies. "I expect I shall have to give them a fight this fall and thus discourage them from starting new factories."[15]

Utah–Idaho's activity in Bellingham motivated a proposal in 1926 for a beet factory at New Westminster. That autumn Fraser Valley farmers incorporated the B.C. Beet Growers Association and asked John Oliver's government in Victoria to provide an annual $50,000 subsidy for five years to support the proposed factory. Johnson swung into action immediately to stop Oliver from granting a subsidy. In a three-page memorandum to the premier, Johnson wrote: "Our Company is a very heavy tax payer in the Province, both to the Provincial and the Municipal governments, and I cannot too strongly oppose the diversion of tax payers' money to subsidize a rival industry, the success of which is open to doubt." Oliver was aware—Johnson may have brought this to his attention during a personal meeting in Victoria—that the Ontario government had sunk $375,000 into beet factory subsidies during the previous five years with mixed results. In December 1926, when the Dominion Sugar Company advertised its failed Kitchener plant, Johnson pointedly sent the premier a newspaper clipping of the advertisement. Oliver refused the subsidy.

The New Westminster venture got new life in 1927 when a proposal supposedly backed by British capital surfaced. Again, a subsidy was sought and refused. It is not known whether Johnson lobbied against this potential rival, but he certainly checked out the backers through Czarnikow's in London. The sugar brokers reported that G. T. Fleming, one of the British investors, was less than substantial. "They say that he is not wealthy, quite the contrary; he teaches music."[16]

When the stock market crashed in 1929, heralding the onset of the Depression, Johnson quickly conserved cash. One of his first moves was to cut the hourly wage in the refinery from 47.5 cents to 43.5 cents.[17] His steady but tight-fisted administration left the company in solid financial shape—if not in the best mechanical shape—to confront both the challenge and opportunity of the Depression. The value of the company's shares, reflected in rare private transactions, had risen from about $100 in 1923 to $165 in 1928. The company's nest egg of cash and quality securities (such as Dominion of Canada Victory Loan bonds and B.C. Telephone preferred shares) was not badly hurt by the 1929 crash, leaving Ernest Rogers with the resources to enter the Alberta sugar beet industry and thus preserve BC Sugar's dominant position in sugar in Western Canada.

Johnson retired in May 1930, six months before his sixty-fifth birthday, and rewarded himself by taking a trip around the world with his wife Alice. (His first wife, Helen, died in 1915.) Johnson had risen to wealth and social prominence, with business interests beyond the refinery. He was chairman of a land development company and a member of the Royal Trust advisory board. In addition to owning a large home in Vancouver, the Johnsons also kept a country estate near Qualicum Beach on Vancouver Island where, according to one newspaper, "on several occasions royalty was entertained." The royalty, whom they also entertained in Vancouver, included the playboy Edward VIII (later Duke of Windsor) who had enjoyed the company of Johnson's socialite younger daughter, Helen.[18]

Johnson's standing with the royal family may have accounted for his appointment in July 1931 as British Columbia's lieutenant-governor. Until he resigned four years later because of failing health, he was as steady and conventional in this job as he had been at the refinery. Public speeches were used as the occasion to spoon out nostrums of encouragement and optimism in the depths of the Depression. "I have had forty-seven years of experience in business," Johnson declared when he became lieutenant-governor. "Speaking with that experience in mind, I feel safe in predicting that within a short while we shall see a gradual but safe resumption of better times, accompanied by a marked improvement in the distressing and difficult problem of unemployment. . . . I have passed through a crisis, 1893–94, just as serious as the present one. My experience has taught me that once a spirit of confidence in the future takes hold of people, the return of prosperity cannot be delayed."[19]

10

Lucky From the Start

THE COMPANY ENTERS THE SUGAR BEET INDUSTRY IN ALBERTA.

Land agent C. A. Magrath underestimated Will and Raymond Knight when they arrived in Lethbridge in 1901 to buy ranchland. Magrath was the agent for a British syndicate, the Canada Northwest Irrigation Company (later acquired by Canadian Pacific) which owned and proposed to irrigate vast stretches of arid prairie land south of the town. The Knight boys had been sent from Salt Lake City by their father, Jesse Knight, a wealthy miner and Mormon elder, to buy resettlement tracts for persecuted Mormons. Magrath formed the impression that they would buy about 1200 acres. He was surprised when Jesse Knight bought 30,000 acres.

The earliest Mormon immigrants had established the town of Cardston, southwest of Lethbridge, in 1877, and land agents like Magrath recognized that these were ideal settlers. In Utah, the Mormons had pioneered both irrigation and the cultivation of sugar beets, a cash crop important to their prosperity. Magrath in 1900 distributed about fifty pounds of beet seed among the Alberta Mormons to show that beet growing was viable. Jesse Knight, who contracted for another 226,000 acres from Magrath, now decided to build Alberta's first sugar factory to attract Mormon beet farmers to settle on his land.

Site preparation began in the spring of 1902. The Canadian government agreed to waive taxes on the factory for twelve years in exchange for a commitment to produce sugar for at least that long. About 3000 acres of virgin land were cultivated and prepared for irrigation, with the new settlers using the sod for their first housing. The Knight Sugar Company's $500,000 beet factory, designed by the Dyer Company of Cleveland, was completed in 1903 at a new town called Raymond, after the oldest of the Knight boys. (Raymond Knight also was an enthusiastic cowboy, and the stampede he organized to entertain the new settlers in the summer of 1902 is believed to have been Canada's first.)

B. T. Rogers visited Raymond in September 1903 to inquire whether the new factory could become a domestic source of sugar for BC Sugar. Unfortunately for Rogers, Ephraim P. Ellison, the factory's general manager, was in Utah. Rogers wired Ellison, asking him to return home by way of Vancouver. "I have proposal to make I am sure will be of advantage to your company."[1]

Ellison accepted neither the invitation nor Rogers's proposal that BC Sugar market some of Raymond's sugar. In a letter to Rogers on 23 October, Ellison said: "It is impossible for us to turn out raw sugar, at least so far this season, as our machinery is so constructed that the product will be turned out in a finished condition. We regret very much that we have been unable so far to arrange with you the handling of our small product and while the amount we will have this season is small we would like to have you keep us posted by wire at our expense as to values. We hope by another season to be able to enter into some kind of agreement whereby we shall each be mutually benefitted."

Ellison and Rogers soon became competitors. In late 1905 Ellison asked the Tariff Commission in Ottawa to give beet sugar tariff protection against cane sugar, insulating his business from BC Sugar's aggressive pricing. The Vancouver *News-Advertiser* reported: "The Knight Sugar Company claims to have established a clear case that the sugar refinery in Vancouver is endeavouring to put them out of business through an arrangement with other Canadian refiners. They claim that these have an agreement by which territory is divided among them and Alberta comes within the district alloted to Vancouver. Now this refinery, says the Knight Company, are slaughtering prices in the interior to kill their business, selling sugar in Lethbridge for less than in Vancouver."[2] Further proof that Rogers was up to no good, in Ellison's eyes, was his purchase of the cane plantation in Fiji. The *Raymond Chronicle* quoted Ellison's contention that this "brought Canadian beet growers into competition with coolie labour." Ottawa, however, refused additional tariff protection for beet sugar.

Rogers kept a close eye on Knight Sugar and knew that the company was in continual difficulty. In 1912 meat packer Swift & Company took an option to buy the factory but let it lapse. In a letter to Sir Edmund Osler, Rogers speculated on the reason for this: "The great difficulty in the way of successfully operating a Beet Factory in Alberta is the lack of labour, and this is a condition which I believe will continue for many years. Beet sugar cultivation is, as I daresay you know, very 'intense cultivation,' and requires a great amount of cheap labour. In fact the labour must be very very cheap. In Europe the thinning of beets, which must all be done by hand, is carried out by children, and women also work in the beet fields. People come to Canada particularly to escape this very thing, and I do not think they could be induced to do this kind of work after they reach this country."[3] That was precisely how the Mormons felt. Magrath wrote: "The settlers found it more profitable to grow grain during the War, hence the factory was closed and the machinery taken out and sold in Idaho."[4]

Postwar expansion of irrigation in the Lethbridge area, coinciding with a decline in grain prices, rekindled interest in sugar beets. The boards of trade of the towns of Raymond and Magrath, most of whose members were Mormons, mounted a successful campaign to attract the Utah–Idaho Sugar Company of Salt Lake City. Utah–Idaho, then one of the largest North American beet sugar companies and one controlled by the Mormon Church, was being forced by plant diseases to close two factories in Washington's Yakima Valley. One was moved to Montana and the other became Canadian Sugar Factories Ltd. when it was moved to Raymond in 1925 and rebuilt beside the reservoir and rail lines which had served the Knight factory. BC Sugar president Fordham Johnson quickly countered Utah–Idaho's inroads into the market. In November, as the new rival began producing its first sugar, Johnson ordered a significant reduction of BC Sugar's prices on the Prairies.

This time the Alberta farmers supported the factory: 582 growers produced more than 41,000 tons of beets from which 7.5 million pounds of sugar was made. But most of the growers were novices. During its first four years the Raymond factory, which had a capacity to process 100,000 tons of beets, operated only at one-third capacity because the growers were losing crops to frost, insects and poor cultivation.[5] Consequently, the factory lost money every year but one between 1925 and 1930 and only made $9,000 in the one profitable year of 1929.[6] Yet a major farm crop had been established. By 1928 farmers in newly irrigated land north of Lethbridge had begun to plant beets. The factory received 58,000 tons of beets in the 1929 campaign—as the beet harvesting and processing is called—and about 100,000 tons in each of the 1930 and 1931 campaigns. The main reason that the growers finally embraced beet farming was the dramatic decline in wheat prices with the start of the Great Depression.

By 1930 the Raymond factory had contracted 15,074 acres of sugar beets and was preparing to process the largest crop to that date when a severe October frost snapped across southern Alberta and the northern United States. Harvested beets spoiled in factory piles before they could be sliced, causing a major loss for Utah–Idaho at Raymond and at several American factories. In addition, as the Depression worsened, the price of sugar in 1931 fell to the lowest level in Utah–Idaho's forty-year history, handing the company a major loss on the value of its inventory. Utah–Idaho was forced to report a $446,591 loss for 1931, tripling its accumulated deficit and placing the company in great difficulty. In desperation, the company sent the manager of its Bellingham factory to Vancouver late in 1930 to solicit an offer for the Raymond factory from BC Sugar's new president, Ernest Rogers. The $2.3 million which Rogers agreed to pay in April 1931 for the factory and its inventory enabled Utah–Idaho to resume servicing its bonds and its trade debts.[7]

It was a considerable commercial gamble. Rogers, who had become president a year earlier at age thirty-three, bought the Raymond factory at a time when nearly all the major beet sugar companies in the Western United States were enduring losses. Some Alberta beet growers, in fact, believed that BC Sugar had bought the factory merely to close it. Just three months before BC Sugar bought Raymond, the growers again asked Ottawa for higher tariffs against imported cane sugar. The request failed, but only after Rogers protested to the finance minister: "If, as has been suggested, the tariff is increased sufficiently to allow the beet sugar industry to supply the entire requirements of the three prairie provinces, our industry would be wiped out entirely, for the British Columbia coast market is not large enough to justify the operation of a refinery."[8]

When grower suspicions persisted into 1932, Rogers was summoned to Ottawa to explain the Raymond purchase to the agricultural committee of the House of Commons. "In considering this offer, we could see reasons both for and against accepting it," he wrote in his formal brief. With depressed sugar prices and the Raymond factory's dismal record of losses, "there was little incentive to invest money in the beet industry," Rogers acknowledged. "On the other hand we felt sure that the price of sugar must sooner or later return to normal, and, with an adequate supply of beets practically assured for years to come, we considered the chance for ultimate success quite promising."[9]

Forrest Rogers, Ernest's youngest brother, later said that the purchase of Raymond was one of BC Sugar's "most significant moves" because it secured the market position B. T. Rogers had desired at the very beginning.[10] As Ernest told the Commons committee: "The principal reason however which finally decided us in favour of purchasing the Plant was a desire on our part to familiarize ourselves with the beet sugar industry so that, in the event of any major development, we would be in a position to participate in it, rather than stand aside as straight cane refiners and watch our markets disappearing."[11]

Ernest Rogers, who shared his family's almost genetic love for properly functioning machinery, had acquired a factory where maintenance had been neglected because of Utah–Idaho's financial plight. The consultants hired to evaluate the factory, the Honolulu Iron Works Company, warned Rogers that the neglect was "quite apparent from the lack of cleanliness observed almost everywhere; from the rusty condition of the structural steel in particular; from the leaky condition of the pipes, and from the sloppy condition of the floors, pumps and apparatus throughout the plant."[12] Rogers authorized only urgent minor improvements. He explained to the Commons committee: "As we were not fully conversant with the process of sugar beet manufacture at that time, we decided to delay action on any major changes until we had the benefit of at least one season's operating experience." He soon began touring other beet factories in the United States and Canada, filling little pocket notebooks with details, prices and sketches of machinery. Fortunately for Raymond's new owners, the 1931 campaign was ideal: the weather was

B. T. Rogers (*left*) and his older brother Blythe as private school students.

By 1895 the B.C. Sugar refinery in Vancouver, having survived early miscalculations and determined competition, was ready to supply an expanding market.

A ship unloading raw sugar at BC Sugar dock, about 1900; Rogers's first yacht, the *Mouping*, is on the right.

The company's first president, Vancouver alderman and CPR agent J. M. Browning.

Forrest Angus, the company's second president, represented his family's investments in BC Sugar.

Top: B. T. Rogers's children (*left to right*): Elspeth, Forrest, Ernest, Margaret (*on lower step*), Mary, Philip (*with sailboat*) and Blythe.

Bottom: Cultured, British-born Mary Isabella Angus married B. T. Rogers in 1892.

B. T. Rogers was already a skilled sugar refiner at twenty-five when he started the company in 1890.

Top: The Vancouver-Fiji Sugar Company plantation (residences are shown here) broke the health and spirit of several managers.

Bottom: Fiji plantations depended on indentured labour recruited in India to cultivate and harvest sugar cane.

J. W. Fordham Johnson, company president during the 1920s.

Top: Refinery employees, about 1891; many worked a lifetime at BC Sugar, including members of several families.

Facing page, top: Gabriola was Vancouver's finest home when built in 1901; it survives today as a restaurant. (COURTESY VANCOUVER CITY ARCHIVES)

Facing page, bottom: In its day B. T. Rogers's *Aquilo,* at 160 feet, was the largest private yacht cruising British Columbia waters.

Blythe Rogers, in frail health when he assumed the presidency in 1918, died two years later after surviving a legislative enquiry into sugar supply manipulation.

Ernest Rogers, a former RAF fighter pilot, guided the company through the Depression without laying off a single employee.

Convivial Philip Rogers became president at the beginning of World War II and quickly learned to deal with rationing and sugar shortages.

Forrest Rogers, the only one of B. T. Rogers's four sons to live a normal life span, served as president from 1953 until 1973, and then as chairman until 1977 when he retired.

Shannon, the Rogers's ten-acre estate in Vancouver. (JOHN SCHREINER PHOTOGRAPH)

perfect and the growers delivered a large tonnage of high quality beets. "It seemed that we were lucky from the start," Ernest's brother Philip reflected later.

After the 1931 campaign, $250,000 was spent on the Raymond factory. A reporter from the *Lethbridge Herald* found the factory much improved when he toured it in 1932. "The Raymond plant presents a different air this year. It has taken on stature and it has slicked up. The plant has been added to in every department. . . ." The plant's capacity had been increased to 1400 tons of beets a day, up from 1000 tons. The new owners installed a process called a Steffens House, which enabled the factory to recover additional sugar from the beet molasses, a low-value by-product which was either discarded or fed to animals. "And the leaks have stopped," the newspaper found. "It doesn't take a very big leak working 24 hours a day throughout the 100 days the plant is in operation to run away with a lot of money."

Because BC Sugar knew little about sugar beets, Rogers had asked Utah–Idaho to leave their managers in place at Raymond. Retained at $700 a month in the top job as district manager of Canadian Sugar Factories was T. George Wood. Born in 1887 in Northampton, England, Wood was the son of a plumber who died in 1892. Six years later his widowed mother, a convert to the Church of Jesus Christ of the Latter Day Saints, immigrated to Salt Lake City where Wood completed the eighth grade in school and went to work as a mail boy for Utah–Idaho. Clever and ambitious, he progressed to purchasing agent and, when the Yakima Valley factories were relocated, he was moved to Raymond as manager of both that plant and the one in Montana. Wood, who married the daughter of a former president of the Mormon church, and his Utah-born agricultural superintendent Frank Taylor were prominent Mormon leaders in southern Alberta. They also brought their faith to work: nearly all Canadian Sugar Factory employees were members of the church. "I thought he [Wood] was a really able administrator," said Arledge Hill, who joined Canadian Sugar Factories as an agricultural field man in 1945.[13] "He was always responsible to Vancouver but I think they went along pretty well with the way he operated. He was astute—and he was tighter than bark to a tree."[14]

With the extreme decline in prices received for nearly all other farm crops in the 1930s, BC Sugar found that, as Frank Taylor said later, "everyone was anxious to get on the bandwagon to grow sugar beets." The company was under continual pressure to build more factories. Only one month after acquiring the Raymond factory, the company was approached by the Touchwood Sugar Beet Co-operative Growers of Saskatchewan, based in Lestock, Saskatchewan. Rogers turned them down politely: "During the past year, all the large beet sugar companies operating in the United States sustained heavy losses. . . ." he explained. He gave a similar reply in June 1931 to the Southern Alberta Beet Growers Association. The Boards of Trade in British Columbia's Fraser Valley once again were trying to get a sugar factory established. W. F. Granger, secretary of the Delta board, wrote Ernest Rogers in February 1933: "Two different parties have presented propositions to us but we would wish to deal with a Company of your standing." Rogers replied that the price of sugar was too low to make a factory pay: "The Utah–Idaho Sugar Co., which owns the Bellingham factory, has been losing money for several years."

In August 1931 farmers in the Lethbridge Northern Irrigation District asked Rogers to support their pressure on the provincial government to subsidize a second beet factory. In his pocket notebook, he noted: " I said would be glad to do so but thought pressure on gov't should come from them to which they agreed." But the last thing he wanted to do was build a second factory before BC Sugar was familiar with the beet sugar business. "I pointed out that we could not give any undertaking to build a factory—but they could feel assured we would build if we thought there was a profit in it—but added that inducement would have to be considerable just now as we weren't too sure of the possibilities of making steady profit at Raymond yet."[15]

Worried that the agitation for a second factory just might succeed, Rogers moved behind the scenes to block the American sugar beet companies to which the farmers also had appealed. On 5 April 1932 Rogers privately asked Col. W. A. Hobbins, an executive with the powerful London sugar brokers C. Czarnikow Ltd., to lobby the upcoming Imperial Conference on trade for special duties on beet factory machinery not made in the British Empire. That would stop any of the American sugar companies from relocating closed factories to Alberta. Rogers cautioned Hobbins: "It is obvious that our name should not appear in this, because the change in the tariff referred to above would be in direct opposition to the interests of those who wish to see new factories erected indiscriminately throughout the country."[16]

Meanwhile, the Alberta farmers petitioned Prime Minister R. B. Bennett for the beet factory, and Bennett in turn pressured BC Sugar. Wearily, Rogers reported in a letter in July 1933 to his Montreal director D. Forbes Angus: "Ever since we purchased the Raymond plant, we have been pressed by various Farmers' Delegations, Politicians, Boards of Trade, etc., to build another factory, but so far we have been unable to see any merit in the suggestion." A second plant processing more beets would displace the Vancouver refinery's cane sugar from the Prairies. The Raymond plant had been doubled by BC Sugar and now purchased beets from 714 growers in 1932 compared with 562 in 1930. It was understandable, Rogers admitted, that the success of Canadian Sugar Factories should create a demand for a second factory. He confessed to Angus: "Sooner or later, it may be necessary for us, in self defence, to embark upon such a project. . . ."[17]

The farmers persisted and so did the political pressure on BC Sugar. In January 1934, with Raymond producing half the total sugar consumed in Alberta and Saskatchewan, Ernest Rogers wrote the prime minister: "Because our company supplies the cane sugar as well as the beet sugar consumed in western Canada, we have been criticized severely for the stand we have taken, the suggestion being that we are holding back development of the beet industry on account of our investment in cane sugar refining facilities in Vancouver. This contention is hardly borne out by the facts." He noted that BC Sugar had spent $350,000 on the Raymond factory, doubling its output. "We did this knowing that the gain in output at Raymond would be offset by a corresponding loss at Vancouver, because we have felt all along that, if we did not supply the popular demand for increased beet facilities, someone else would. . . ."

Someone else almost did. In late 1934 the beet growers' association negotiated secretly with the Amalgamated Sugar Company of Ogden, Utah, to build Alberta's second sugar factory. The factory was to be financed by a package which would include a $450,000 guarantee from the government of Alberta. "The beet growers in the interests of both producer and consumer, desired competition in beet refining," the Alberta Co-operative Sugar Beet Growers told its members early in 1935.[18] BC Sugar pre-empted the growers. It agreed to build the factory without a subsidy and got the provincial government's guarantee that Alberta would not subsidize a competitor for ten years. Rogers, having seen Alberta offer concessions to a potential competitor, did not let the province off the hook entirely. The government agreed to provide a free site, a free reservoir, free water and fixed local tax assessment rates for the factory, to be erected at what would be the new town of Picture Butte, north of Lethbridge. The agreement with Alberta was barely concluded when the Manitoba government offered to guarantee bonds for a sugar factory, and asked BC Sugar to build it. However, Rogers decided against investing in Manitoba because he had his hands full in Alberta.

Picture Butte was chosen because, when Utah–Idaho had asked for demonstration plots in 1924, farmers in this district responded with enthusiasm while those in the Taber irrigation district, thirty miles east of Lethbridge, did not. Frank Taylor, who was Utah–Idaho's field man at the time, described that attitude as "cold-shouldered." He wrote: "Sugar beets to them was synonymous with hard work and they were still hoping that irrigation farming could be done on a wheat-farm basis."

The Picture Butte factory, designed by Stearns–Roger of Denver, was completed in 1936 at a cost of $1.5 million. BC Sugar believed it to be one of the most efficient beet factories in the world. It needed to be efficient, for sugar prices had followed other commodity prices down during the Depression. It was a poor time to be entering the market with additional quantities of sugar, especially beet sugar. When Picture Butte opened, Ernest Rogers appealed in the *Lethbridge Herald* for consumers to buy beet sugar. "If the people of Alberta desire to maintain a successful sugar industry," he wrote, "it is essential that they express that desire in action by asking for the local product when placing their orders for sugar."

The Taber farmers who had turned their backs on sugar beets in 1925 had changed their minds and planted extensive acreages by the time the Picture Butte plant opened. Now they began trying to lure Amalgamated to build an Alberta factory. Rogers counselled Wood to "seize the present opportunity to point out in the most emphatic manner possible why we consider the proposal ill-advised and unfair. . . ." Next spring, the growers also demanded contracts for more acres of sugar beets than the company wanted. Rogers, trying to placate the growers, finally agreed to additional acreage but advised Wood to ensure that the growers and the public understood how difficult it was becoming to sell the extra sugar. In the summer of 1937 he suggested that Wood include the growers' association in the marketing of the sugar. He hoped the growers would stop pushing for a third factory if they realized that the market could not absorb more product.

The large 1937 crop forced the company to sell some of its surplus in Manitoba, much to the irritation of Canada & Dominion Sugar Company of Chatham, Ontario. C. H. Houson, the company's president, protested that Manitoba was essentially the market for the eastern refiners. Ernest Rogers responded: "It is true that the territory covered by our Company is very extensive, but unfortunately, it consists very largely of wide open spaces."[19] Rogers explained that Canadian Sugar Factories had produced 65 million pounds of sugar in 1936 and had had a 10 million-pound carryover. "This year from the same acreage we now expect to produce 74,000,000 lbs. so you can see what we are up against."[20] He wanted the eastern refiners to understand that, had BC Sugar not built the Picture Butte factory, the Alberta government would have lured an American competitor, perhaps to build a large factory processing four to five times more sugar beets than BC Sugar contracted initially. Houson suggested that Rogers had let the beet growers bluff him; had he ignored them, no one else would have built a factory. "It is easy for someone who is not familiar with the local situation to make such a statement," Rogers wrote to one of his directors later, "but from all the information I could obtain at the time, and have obtained since, I am quite positive that if we had not undertaken to build, the Amalagamated Sugar Company would have done so. The fact that they built a new factory in California just at the time we were building at Picture Butte, and that they are at present building a new factory in Oregon, at least indicates their interest in expansion."[21]

Late in 1938 Ernest Rogers again gave in to pressure, signing an agreement with the growers to build Alberta's third sugar factory. To seal his good faith, he promised to pay the growers a penalty if construction was delayed more than three years. He explained to Houson: "You will note that we offered either to build a factory at Taber for operation in 1942, or else pay a penalty to each grower unless a factory is established there by other growers in the meantime. . . . This offer was made to win back the growers, or at least a majority of them, to our policy of orderly expansion based on market possibilities, as opposed to over-expansion and ruinous prices." The outbreak of war prevented the company from beginning construction until 1946, and postwar shortages delayed completion of the factory, which cost $5.9 million, to 1950.

Ernest Rogers's willingness to accommodate the Albertans arose partly from his apprehension of the populist William Aberhart, not a lover of big capital, who was elected in 1935 at the head of the radical Social Credit government. At this time the growers were agitating for a share of the additional revenue gained from the operation of the Steffens House, the effectiveness of which certainly contributed to the improvement in Raymond's profitability. The company's position was that it had provided all the investment to install the equipment and was entitled to all the additional revenue. The growers called for a public inquiry into the factory's profits, which had grown rapidly since 1931 and would not be offset until the investment in Picture Butte appeared on the company's books in 1936. Rogers chose to give in to the growers rather than risk an inquiry by a government he mistrusted. "It is obvious that sooner or later there must be a showdown," he wrote Wood in January 1936, "but . . . I think next year would be a much better time to call it."[22]

II

It Is Not Our Intention To Lay Off Anyone

THE COMPANY UNDER ERNEST ROGERS REPRESENTS SECURITY DURING THE DEPRESSION.

The irony of Ernest Rogers's tragic drowning was that it happened to an ardent yachtsman in a family of yachtsmen. About 5:30 P.M. on the warm, breezy afternoon of 25 July 1939, Rogers and his family were sailing off Nelson Island about seven miles from Pender Harbour. They had borrowed the yawl *Andi Lailey*—formerly owned by Ernest but now owned by Forrest Rogers—for what was to be a leisurely ten-day sail in British Columbia coastal waters. On board were Irene Rogers, Ernest's wife, who had the helm; their sixteen-year-old son, John; his friend, Michael McGeer; and two of the Rogers's three daughters, Trish and Mary, the latter a fourteen-year-old nicknamed Lailey, after whom the yacht had been named.

The girls were helping to hoist a sail when a boom, swinging with the wind, knocked Lailey overboard. She was a good swimmer, but her father, galvanized by her cry of fright, dove after her. Both surfaced and began to swim towards the boat, as Irene, an expert sailor, swung it around and dropped the mainsail. "I wish they'd hurry up," Ernest said to his daughter. "This water is cold." With that, he disappeared beneath the surface.[1] The family later concluded that the shock of the cold water may have caused a heart attack. There had been an incident in July 1932 when Ernest suffered a cramp and lost consciousness while swimming in cold water offshore from his Bowen Island property. His mother wrote in her diary at the time: "He was advised to rest for a few days, as his blood pressure is low, which caused the cramp and faint."[2] The cause of death could not be established conclusively because Rogers's body never was found, in spite of an extensive search by three police boats, a number of private yachts and even a plane chartered by the *Vancouver Sun.*

Only forty-one when he died, Ernest Rogers had made a significant mark both on the company and on the community. In contrast to his quick-tempered and fine-living father, he was cool-headed and even a bit shy. Under his direction, the company had begun contributing to local charities. His community roles included joining with four other Vancouver business people in 1933 to take control of floundering, two-year-old St. George's School, reorganizing its finances so that it could become the city's leading private boys' school. "He had character, quiet tastes, and gentlemanly instincts," the *Vancouver Daily Province* said in an obituary. Many others shared that assessment of him. "I found he was really honest in his dealings with us," wrote one Alberta sugar beet grower in a note of condolence to Irene Rogers. Contractor Charles Bentall remarked on Ernest Rogers's "thoughtfulness of others."[3]

His death was a major blow to morale in the company. "Ernest was certainly very much admired by, I think, practically all of the employees," Forrest Rogers recalled.[4] Laboratory technician Wilfred Kenyon agreed: "Mr. Ernest had a much different attitude toward the employees than Mr. Johnson had."[5] Robert Adamson, the company secretary, collapsed with grief and was away from work for many weeks with what Bella Rogers described as "a sort of nervous breakdown." The next oldest of the Rogers brothers, Philip, was pitched into the presidency.

Born on 15 October 1897, Ernest followed his brother Blythe to St. Alban's College in Brockville, Ontario, and was equally unhappy there. Author Michael Kluckner, writing in his privately published biography of Bella Rogers, said that Ernest "endured endless daily chapel services [at St. Alban's] and developed a lifelong distaste for organized religion."[6] He also followed Blythe into Kingston's Royal Military College and, on graduating in 1917, was sent to Britain as a junior army officer. He arrived in early September and, within days, was pursuaded to transfer to the Royal Flying Corps by several Vancouver friends already in the RFC. It did not take much pursuading. He had been keen on flying since early

1914, when the Rogers family all took joyrides on a floatplane while vacationing at San Diego.

British Ministry of Defence records show he joined the RFC on 8 October 1917 and was sent to Egypt for his pilot's training, surviving en route the sinking of his ship by torpedoes. After getting his wings in March 1918, he returned to Britain. He flew with three different squadrons, but the records do not disclose whether he saw combat with any of them. He may not have been posted to the front since there is no indication that he received any decorations. In May 1919 he volunteered to join the British Expeditionary Forces which fought that summer with the White Russians against the Communists. Forrest Rogers said his brother seldom talked about that episode, leaving the family to conclude that he had had some "gruesome experiences." The British force—which included a number of Canadians—began to withdraw in September, with the collapse of the White Russian armies. Ernest Rogers was discharged with the rank of second lieutenant and, in October 1919, returned to Vancouver and a job at the refinery. Because he was only twenty-two and not ready for the presidency when Blythe died in May 1920, the company's directors elevated J. W. Fordham Johnson to the job and made Ernest Rogers vice-president.

His mother, in her memoir of the company, penned a bland portrayal of her son that made him sound dull and narrow: "As vice-president under Mr. Johnson he travelled extensively on business for the company, to Fiji, to Cuba and other cane growing countries; he also visited sugar beet companies in the United States, and the Utah Idaho factory operating in Alberta." He was anything but dull. Trim and good-humoured with smiling grey eyes, he was popular with his siblings. His youngest sister, Margaret, years later described him as "the best of the bunch. . . . He was very funny, in a quiet way."[7] In 1922 he married Irene Cowan, a nurse and childhood friend whose lawyer father owned a large tract of land at Cowan's Point on Bowen Island. Ernest's father-in-law gave the couple property at Cowan's Point where they built a summer home. Ernest later bought a speedboat, the *Saltpeter*, with which he commuted to the refinery during the summers. Like his father, he enjoyed travelling. In 1928 he and Irene made a trip around the world. Having acquired a movie camera, Ernest returned with exotic tourist footage as well as mundane scenes of sugar plantations and irrigation works in India. After the company invested in Alberta, he became a keen hunter, since fortuitously the hunting season and the beet campaign always overlapped.

Fordham Johnson had seldom ventured into the refinery, but Ernest's habit was to materialize quietly at an employee's elbow and watch silently while absorbing the task being done. His growing popularity with employees flowed from his technical grasp and from his involvement with improvements in the refinery. Ernest, who began the tradition of company officers giving brief speeches at the annual Christmas party, noted the changes in his 1927 remarks. "Since our last meeting here, as you all know as well as I do, considerable improvements have been made in the refinery," he said. "It is our endeavour, whenever possible, to include in these improvements better working conditions. . . . Of course, we have quite an old plant, and some of the newest refineries are no doubt ahead of us in some respects."[8]

When Johnson retired in May 1930, he left a company with a $6-million portfolio of stocks, bonds and cash. This enabled the company to weather the Depression without laying off permanent staff and also to expand into the beet sugar business. "On the whole, we're all very lucky to be in the sugar business," Ernest told employees at the 1930 Christmas party—his first as president. "Not many industries today are in a position to celebrate anything." It was true, he added, that the business decline had halted the refinery's modernization program and was reducing its operating rate. "It has become apparent that our present labour force is really more than necessary for the lower rate of melting which must go into effect after the [Christmas] shut down but I want to say this: that as long as we can find any useful work whatsoever to do around the plant, it is not our intention to lay off anyone in our employ during these hard times." In 1933, as the Depression deepened, layoffs were avoided by cutting the refinery's work week from forty-eight to forty hours without any reduction in the wages. At the same time, few new jobs opened in Vancouver. In December 1936, when T. George Wood asked that his son, Lincoln, be hired in the refinery laboratory, Rogers declined: "On checking our laboratory staff, I find that we have not taken on any new men during the last eight years."[9] (Lincoln Wood did receive a job at the Raymond factory, beginning a long career which, by the time he retired, saw him become BC Sugar's purchasing manager based in Vancouver.)

At the 1930 Christmas party, Rogers revealed that the company was inaugurating a medical insurance program. Membership in this Sick Benefit Association was voluntary, Rogers being "quite opposed" to a compulsory scheme. "It is interesting to note," he wrote in 1932, "that only two employees have failed to join the Association, one being a Christian Scientist and the other reporting that he is never ill." The Association provided free medical care by a company doctor and established a fund to offset loss of income during illness. This fund, after starting with a $1,000 company contribution, was built by contributions from both employees and the company. By 1935 the fund was large enough to include surgical expenses and specialists' fees, with hospital coverage added a year later. By today's standard, the program was modest; but for the 1930s it was progressive.

The Christmas parties, held at Templeton High School in East Vancouver, were the venue where Rogers, in mercifully brief speeches, liked to announce new benefit programs. In 1937, for example, when nine men were retiring, he announced that the company would make a lump sum payment ($10 for each year or service) to each retiree. A pension plan was started in 1938 and adequately funded by a company payment of $646,782 in 1939. Seven years later, a question was put to Philip Rogers, then president, whether the company would recover investment profits exceeding the actuarial needs of the pension. Allan Dunlop, who was then the company's chief financial officer, recalled Philip stating emphatically: "The employees have got to benefit. The company puts up its money and it stays."[10]

Ernest's attitude towards charities was more practical than his father's, who was not noted for philanthropy. In 1934, when St. Michael's Hospital in Lethbridge solicited a donation, Rogers instructed T. George Wood, his general manager in Alberta: "I note from your records that you have not been in the habit of incurring expenditure of this kind. I need hardly mention that donations made by corporations cannot be considered as charitable in the true sense of the word, since the money belongs to the shareholders, who are not consulted in the matter. However, the practice is well-established, and, as a means of creating goodwill, I believe it is justified."[11]

That Ernest Rogers was open to new ideas is shown in the company's change from cloth to paper bags for packing sugar. Until the 1930s sugar was routinely packed in cloth, typically 100-pound, cotton-lined jute bags. In 1930 Rogers, during one of his tours of American refineries, "became paper bag conscious," as he put it in a letter to a friend. In March 1931 the Bates Valve Bag Company, a subsidiary of St. Regis Paper Company of New York, convinced Rogers to undertake a trial of wax-lined paper bags for packaging brown sugar, which was prone to harden in cloth. In October the company ordered forty thousand 100-pound paper bags and fifteen thousand 50-pound paper bags. The wax-lined paper bags proved durable in transit, kept brown sugars soft and, unlike cloth, kept very fine icing sugars from leaking. Rogers now began to consider a 25-pound paper bag that St. Regis was developing to replace cotton bags.

St. Regis also sent a machine to sew the bags shut—and discovered what honourable people it was dealing with. When BC Sugar agreed to buy the machine after a six-month trial, the concurrent transactions for bags and the machine had so muddled the St. Regis accounting that they invoiced BC Sugar $165 rather than the correct price, $375. They are "robbing themselves," BC Sugar secretary Robert Adamson noted on the invoice, insisting that BC Sugar be billed correctly.

St. Regis was trying hard to sell paper bags to other sugar companies and ran into unexpected resistance from Canada & Dominion Sugar in Ontario. T. H. Cosford, the director of sales for the St. Regis Bates Valve subsidiary, appealed to Rogers in the spring of 1933 to "supply me with some of the essential facts and arguments that I could use with Canada and Dominion." Rogers replied with a testimonial but also complained that it took longer to sew paper bags, slowing down packing operations. For that reason, BC Sugar continued to pack its granulated white sugar in cloth. When Bates Valve redesigned the bag and perfected the filling machine, BC Sugar still was slow in phasing out cloth sacks because, during the Depression, the sacks "appear to be valued quite highly by the consumers of sugar," as Rogers wrote Cosford on one occasion. The textile sugar bags were not eliminated totally from the Prairie market until the mid-1960s.

Ernest Rogers's decision in 1931 to move into the beet sugar industry was the most strategically important of his business career. The Canadian Sugar Factories' Raymond plant had been no more than a competitive irritant in its troubled first five years, but Rogers recognized that a sugar factory in strong hands could cause his refinery considerable difficulty across the Prairies. The opportunity to buy Raymond neutralized that possibility.

He set out to master the beet sugar industry with a boundless appetite for detail. After making two tours of American beet factories in 1931, he began to pepper T. George Wood with suggestions. He asked his Alberta general manager for a report on agricultural operations, discussing details such as the impact of fertilizers, the optimum time for seeding and for irrigation. Rogers's correspondence—he often wrote to Raymond every day[12]—soon displayed a wide technical grasp and not just of matters relating to refining sugar. In 1936 when the Picture Butte factory and infrastructure were being built and Charles Bentall sent a blueprint of the proposed community swimming pool, Ernest Rogers dug into his notes and his memory to provide comprehensive details on how the town of Brooks had built its pool. Rogers explained to Bentall: "I happen to know of the Brooks layout because I was there two years ago at the time the town of Raymond was interested in the matter of a swimming pool, and I secured complete information from Major Cross of Brooks who had charge of the construction. Subsequently, I wrote to Major Cross for further details and he sent me a white print. . . ." Later, when the pool was actually under construction, Rogers advised Wood that it should be surrounded either by a fence or a windbreak for the comfort of swimmers on windy days. Clearly, his was a hands-on management style. When an October 1933 business trip to Europe coincided with the start of the beet harvest, he instructed Wood to wire him, care of the S.S. *Bremen* in New York harbour, last-minute details on how the campaign was progressing.

His correspondence displayed considerable sensitivity in dealing with Wood, a prickly man jealous of his authority. BC Sugar's chief chemist, Robert Boyd, spent the summer of 1931 at Raymond, doing a detailed and critical review of the factory in preparation for planned renovations. He appears not to have gone out of his way to cultivate Wood, who took Boyd's report as personal criticism and defended himself and his staff in a strong letter to the Vancouver head office. Ernest Rogers undertook to cool him down while at the same time standing behind the critique. "I will take, for example, the statement that the beet receiving station is in an atrocious mechanical condition—if this statement is unfair, to whom is it unfair? I do not hold anyone responsible, for I know perfectly well why portions of the plant were allowed to run down prior to our acquisition of it. . . . As for the statement being an exaggeration, I think that, from an engineer's point of view, it was possibly justified, and if the language was strong, it had at least the desired effect of focussing attention on this point."

Rogers reassured Wood: "I also appreciate the fact that you and Mr. Taylor and others deserve a great deal of credit for establishing the industry under most trying circumstances, and that you have ironed out all the major difficulties in the most important department—that is the agricultural end. We are now trying to bring the plant up to the highest possible state of efficiency, and I would like you to feel that the men to whom we have given this task are working for you and your staff as well as for us, which they will assuredly be doing if the objects in view are attained." In a supplementary letter, Rogers added that Boyd "did not intend to create any ill-feeling and was surprised to learn that he had done so."

Wood and Frank Taylor, the agricultural superintendent, were retained because Rogers had no one in Vancouver skilled at running a sugar beet factory. Because neither man was trained to handle the factory's technical problems, Rogers recruited F. H. Ballou, an engineer from an American beet factory. Abrupt and volatile, Ballou soon came into conflict with the aloof Boyd, setting in train a series of personal and technical disputes which lasted until Ballou retired in 1950. (Boyd died a few months later.) This relationship created needless division between their staffs in Vancouver. Allan Dunlop, who lived with this conflict, believed it could have been ameliorated had Ernest Rogers not been so unfailingly polite with his staff.

12

No War-Time Boom

PHILIP ROGERS COPES WITH SUGAR RATIONING AND OTHER VICISSITUDES OF WAR.

The motor vessel *Donerail,* owned by the United States Maritime Commission but flying the Panamanian flag, left Suva in Fiji for Vancouver on 29 November 1941. Crewed by thirty-three, the 4473-ton vessel carried seven passengers and a cargo of Fijian raw cane sugar. Two days after the 7 December Japanese attack on Pearl Harbor, a Japanese submarine found the *Donerail* 200 miles southeast of Hawaii and pounded her with gunfire until she sank. Sixteen persons died; the captain and twenty-three others sought safety in lifeboats. Only one lifeboat, with eight terrified survivors, made it back to Fiji.

This was BC Sugar's only cargo of sugar lost at sea during World War II. But Japan's sudden sweep across the Pacific prevented enough other sugar cargoes from being shipped that Canada and the United States almost immediately suffered shortages and were forced to adopt sugar rationing. In Canada, when an appeal for voluntary restraint proved ineffective, formal rationing was ordered in June 1942 and remained in place for five years. "Unlike most industries," Philip Rogers wrote in the company's 1948 annual report, "we experienced no war-time boom, and as a matter of fact went through a very difficult period when sugar rationing reached its most severe stage in 1944."

Sugar, along with many other commodities, had come under government control in 1939 within days of the war's start in Europe. The Wartime Prices and Trade Board was established on 3 September of that year to control commodity prices. The Sugar Administration, an agency of the Board, took over the wholesale trade in raw sugar, enforcing price controls and, later, rationing. At the same time, the British Ministry of Food asserted control over all Commonwealth sugar and allocated it among refineries, including those in Canada, throughout the war and for several years thereafter. In Canada, the Sugar Administration bought all raw cane imports and resold them to the refiners as one measure for controlling prices and distribution of this product. At first there was adequate sugar in Canada, there being plentiful stocks outside Europe. Submarines had not yet begun to strangle trade routes. The refinery in Vancouver had been getting almost all its raw sugar from Fiji, with occasional cargoes from Peru, Australia and the Caribbean. On 1 November 1939, in a letter to T. George Wood at the company's Alberta subsidiary, Philip Rogers disclosed: "For the duration of the War we have decided to carry larger than normal stocks of Raw Sugar, in order to protect ourselves against the possible loss of cargo or against any temporary difficulties in securing Raw Sugars."

Philip Rogers had become president of the company only two weeks before war broke out, thrown into the job by Ernest Rogers's drowning. "I'm quite sure to begin with Philip didn't think that he had the necessary qualifications to take over," said Forrest Rogers, who believed that the shock of taking charge contributed to his brother's subsequent alcoholism. "He may have relied on it [drink] for some sort of Dutch courage and of course it got all out of hand."[1] In fact, Philip had worked in the company since 1930 and had become a director in 1938. If he doubted his own qualifications, the probable explanation is that Ernest did not delegate a great deal of responsibility.

Phip, as his family called him, was born 14 February 1908. Perhaps because he suffered a good deal from ear infections and bronchitis as a young child, his mother treated him indulgently. He was sent to Trinity College School in Port Hope, Ontario, and continued on to McGill in 1926. He failed two of his subjects, the consequence of playing harder than studying, and finally left McGill in the middle of his second year. He then enrolled at the University of British Columbia but dropped out after failing the Christmas examinations. After an automobile accident in September 1930, when he required twenty-three stitches for two large head wounds, he settled down to work, to some accounting classes and to marriage in 1933.[2]

He was a man of eclectic interests. One was sailing: he was among the crew on a Canadian yacht at the 1932 Los Angeles Olympics and also somehow managed to carry a javelin in the Olympic parade. At home it was often Philip among all the Rogers children who instigated and organized family entertainments. His youngest sister, Margaret, remembers his starring in a Christmas skit called *Sofie Cooks the Dinner*, put on for his nieces and nephews. The set included a cardboard stove packed with dry ice from the refinery. Philip, as Sophie, put a pet dachshund into the stove and, to the horror of some of the children, pulled out a string of sausages.[3] With this sense of playfulness, he was the most outgoing of B. T. Rogers's four sons. The challenge of running the company during wartime unlocked an entrepreneurship which saw him making several strategic decisions that not only secured the company's business but also enlarged it nationally and internationally.

During the initial year of the war, Canada was not short of sugar. That changed after Pearl Harbor. The Sugar Administration was able to import only 758 million pounds of raw cane sugar in 1942 and 773 million pounds in 1943, down dramatically from one billion pounds in 1940. Several refineries in eastern Canada were forced to suspend operations. BC Sugar's Vancouver refinery, relying on suppliers across the submarine-infested Pacific, received only enough raw sugar in 1941 to sustain a melt of 100 million pounds, down from 140 million pounds in 1940. In the summer of 1942 one-fifth of the raw sugar warehouse was converted to a plate shop, and the company took the subcontract from Burrard Dry Dock Company to make deck houses for Victory ships. The refinery's machine shop also produced crankshafts, engine blocks and bases for diesel engines. Philip Rogers wrote one shareholder: "The above work though fairly remunerative in itself is chiefly useful in helping out our overhead and in keeping our staff intact and usefully employed."

Canadians began hoarding sugar after the Pacific war began. On 24 January 1942 the Wartime Prices and Trade Board declared it illegal for any person to buy more than three-quarters of a pound of sugar a week. The Sugar Administration carved up sugar sales territories in Canada, ordering eastern refined cane sugar withdrawn entirely from Manitoba, and limited BC Sugar's cane product on the Prairies to not more than 20 per cent of its total sugar sales. This meant that Prairies consumers, by and large, would have to rely on beet sugar, like it or not.

The government, trying to pressure consumers to follow rationing voluntarily, suggested that retailers make a list of all purchasers and how much they bought. When the Steinberg grocery stores in Montreal complied, some consumers returned excess sugar in exchange for having their names dropped from the list.[4] In May the ration was reduced to half a pound weekly per person, still on the honour system. But this system proved ineffective, and rationing with coupon books began on 1 July 1942.

The coupons limited individuals to half a pound of sugar a week with an additional allotment for home preserving and with exceptions only for those labourers—such as loggers, miners, workers in isolated construction camps, deepsea fishermen—whose strenuous exertions presumably required them to consume more sugar. H. J. (Jack) Hobbins, Montreal-based technical advisor to the Sugar Administration, explained the rationale in a letter to Reginald Noble, his boss in Ottawa. "For forest workers, one of the reasons for the increased quantity of sugar is to avoid biological requirements of alcohol, which is naturally to be deprecated."[5] One such group of consumers supplied by BC Sugar were the construction workers and soldiers who built the Alaska Highway and the Canol pipeline across the Northwest Territories in 1943.

Rationing regulations limited industrial users of sugar to a percentage—usually 70 per cent—of their 1941 purchases. This was to vary somewhat during the war but always remained less than that of 1941. The loudest complaint came from bakers, particularly smarting from a March 1942 ruling prohibiting them from icing any cakes or sweet buns, except those made for weddings, anniversaries and birthdays. "It has been represented to me," Noble wrote to Hobbins, "that a chocolate cake, if it has not a chocolate covering, is practically unsaleable." One Vancouver baker sought a larger sugar allocation by contending that his was a new business, started a few years earlier, which had lost money for several years and had just turned the corner when rationing came along. His plea, like so many others, had to be denied because there just was not sufficient sugar.

After the Sugar Administration allowed an additional ration for home preserving, Canadian Sugar Factories, in a circular to grocers on 2 July, said that it had packed 250,000 twenty-pound cotton bags of sugar specifically for preserving. "The Sugar Administrator has given his permission for us to publicize, advertise and sell this special 20 lb. package." In conjunction with B.C. Tree Fruits, a grower-owned fruit marketing company in Kelowna, a poster was prepared which outlined how much sugar consumers could buy for preserving. B.C. Tree Fruits even distributed a booklet called *Ration Recipes*. But when the Sugar Adminstration learned of the poster, it ordered that its use be stopped. Hobbins wrote the Kelowna company on September 1942: "Without impugning your good faith we still feel it necessary to prohibit the advertising of sugar for any purpose whatsoever."

At the same time that the Sugar Administration cut back BC Sugar's cane sugar sales on the Prairies, it withdrew most eastern refined cane sugar from Manitoba. Many food processors, especially the soft drink bottlers and candy makers, objected strongly. G. H. Bond, president of Winnipeg chocolate manufacturer Bond & Ronald Ltd., complained angrily to the Sugar Administrator: "We have tried repeatedly to use Beet Sugar and have run into nothing but grief. You are, no doubt, unaware that we have no vacuum cookers, but have open kettles on gas furnaces. The moment we start to boil Beet Sugar, it foams and froths and boils over, and if some person is not on the alert every moment, serious trouble will occur and fires will start. On more than one occasion, it has come so close to burning our place down, that it has reached the stage where we do not wish to bother with this commodity again."[6] But after Bond was told firmly that little cane sugar would be available, the company reluctantly tested beet sugar again, taking particular care while boiling it. "I am very glad to say that it turned out more satisfactorily than we had anticipated." That was often the case.

For the Alberta sugar beet growers, the war provided the opportunity to expand production because the Sugar Administration now was anxious for more domestic sugar production. Reginald Noble, the Administrator, in a letter to Philip Rogers in January 1942, urged: "We trust that no effort will be spared to produce the maximum crop in the present season." In 1939 nearly 22,000 acres of beets were grown in Alberta. This had climbed to 23,800 acres in 1941 while 18,000 new acres of beets came into production in Manitoba. But Noble still worried that the war would induce shortages in a market that had suffered from surplus before the war.

Rogers protested to Noble that rationing "puts me in more of a quandry than before regarding Alberta acreage." On the one hand, rationing was designed to conserve sugar. On the other, additional beet acreage would increase production, the obvious result being such a surplus of sugar in Alberta that it might even have to be shipped as far as Vancouver, forcing BC Sugar to suspend refining entirely. On top of that, the freight costs would be so high that Alberta growers would lose money on this sugar. "The other alternative would be the Ontario market," he wrote Noble. Again, freight costs would make that unprofitable. "The whole question is at present so confusing that it might be better if I go East within the next few days and discuss the matter with you before any acreage is definitely set." He and other sugar refiners met Noble in Montreal early in February 1942 and negotiated a market redistribution that made more sense. Rogers also talked Noble into agreeing that the Sugar Administration would guarantee Canadian Sugar Factories a profitable net return on the sugar made from any new beet acreage above that of 1941. With that assurance, Rogers contracted an extra 4000 acres.

While Alberta growers planted more beets, Manitoba growers responded less enthusiastically and Ontario's beet acreage plunged. The reason was that the wartime labour demand sucked farm workers into better paying urban jobs or into the military. "Our acreage was this year increased the 4,000 acres called for [by the Sugar Administration] and 28,000 acres of beets were planted," Alberta Sugar Beet Growers Association president Philip Baker wrote Noble in June 1942. "If the same effort had been successfully made in Ontario and Manitoba the problem of Canadian sugar supply would be much easier to handle." Alberta sugar was shipped as far as Ontario during the war years, significantly easing the threat of shortage. The extra freight costs reduced the net return for both the growers and the company, but that apparently was the price of patriotism. Philip Baker was turned down when he asked the Sugar Administration for a bonus payment to offset the freight costs.

Philip Rogers once admitted that he found it "most embarrassing" to take the dictatorial stance with his customers the Sugar Administration advised. Soon after he became president, he hired Alan Robertson, a personal friend, as BC Sugar's first sales manager. Robertson was a suave and dapper former stockbroker with an easy charm. He began calling regularly on the company's distributors and major customers, often accompanied either by Philip or Forrest Rogers. The sales trips both improved the company's public relations and sharpened its competitive stance. These trips during wartime were useful opportunities to straighten out problems created by the involved rationing rules.

Because rationing inspired cheating, complaints about adulterated sugar became frequent. Most commonly, cheaters stretched sugar with salt. A Vernon grocer in 1943 returned two 100-pound bags of sugar which the refinery found contained 14.5 per cent salt. On this occasion, as on all others where salt was found in sugar, the refinery declined responsibility since salt was never handled in the plant. Salt was not the only material used by cheaters. Again in 1943, Anweiler's Ltd. of Melville, Saskatchewan, complained that adulterated icing sugar had ruined a cake. The foreign substance this time was bicarbonate of soda. "Although we were obviously not responsible," an internal refinery report said, "we refunded $1.83 to Anweiler's because they made such an issue of it and we did not want trouble at a future competitive point." On another occasion, a Wells, B.C., grocer returned a five-pound bag of sugar which was found contaminated with citric acid, also a white crystalline substance. This grocer lacked Anweiler's leverage and received no refund.

The war enabled BC Sugar to export to the Soviet Union. The United States, under its so-called Lend-Lease program to supply weapons and commodities to its allies, had undertaken to ship the Russians 196,000 long tons (2,240 pounds to a long ton) of refined sugar from both Atlantic and Pacific ports during the twelve months beginning 1 July 1943. By the end of that year the Americans were having difficulty fulfilling commitments from the West Coast because those ports were congested with Pacific-bound war traffic and because the midwestern U.S. beet crop was inadequate. Late in 1943 Jack Hobbins suggested to the Americans that BC Sugar assume some of the contracts. The company agreed enthusiastically "provided we could get fuel and containers and that he [Hobbins] could supply the necessary raw sugar." The supplies were made available.

The first contract, for 3500 long tons (7.8 million pounds), was awarded in January 1944. In total, BC Sugar shipped to Russia 14,112,032 pounds in 1944 and 41,820,000 pounds in 1945.[7] The company also exported sugar cubes to Russia: 448,000 pounds in 1944 and 1.5 million pounds in 1945. This was welcome and profitable business which enabled the refinery to operate at more efficient volumes. However, the red tape required to complete these contracts, involving several agencies of the Canadian, American and Russian governments, was particularly onerous. A wire Robertson sent in April 1945 to his Washington contact trying to get one sugar consignment loaded on a ship bound for the Soviet Union shows typical frustration: "Russian representative Vancouver has been advised by Russians Ottawa that they know nothing about the 8,000 long tons granulated now ready for shipment and that the Russians in Washington have no information on it Stop Would you please have Russians in Washington advised. . . ."

The ultimate bureaucratic footnote was a claim made by the American government in January 1947, seeking $31.48 compensation after alleging that eight cases of sugar cubes were missing from a shipment of 1 June 1945. Robertson, justifiably incensed, replied: "Although we are anxious to be quite fair in this matter, it seems rather extraordinary to us that a year and a half after a shipment is made, received and paid for, a claim for a shortage should be made. . . . This company handled more than 50 million pounds of sugar for the United States government and this is the first time that it has been suggested we made an error in shipment." After further correspondence, Robertson agreed to pay half the claim rather than prolong the argument.[8]

During the first half of 1944, the refinery also was asked to sell sugar to the British navy, whose supply ships, calling at New Westminster, took delivery of 1.8 million pounds during 1944 and an equal amount in 1945.

When the war ended, the Sugar Administration continued to enforce the ration allocations. The British Ministry of Food wanted to avoid a repeat of the catastrophic 1920 price spike. One of the uncertainties involved how much sugar was to be available from producing areas that had been occupied. There were rumours, inaccurate as it turned out, that stocks of sugar were to be found in Java after the Japanese withdrawal. A pessimistic Jack Hobbins visited the refinery in December 1945 to warn that households in 1946 were unlikely to be allowed to buy any greater quantities of sugar than in the previous year. He doubted that there would be much improvement in the supply of raw sugar and if there were, industrial users such as the grousing bakers, limited now to 50 per cent of 1941 purchases, would be the first to get more.

Even with continued rationing, the refinery's sales in the last three months of 1945 were strong. The company's internal distribution report for that quarter credited this strength to the special sugar allotment of five pounds a person which the government had created for service men and women on their discharge. "As a great number . . . chose British Columbia for discharge, this undoubtedly affected B.C. sugar sales."

In November 1945 Robertson and T. George Wood set off on one of their three-week tours to visit their distributors and customers on the Prairies. "No complaints were received during the trip," the distribution report noted. "It is obvious that customer relationship is excellent." The two also concluded that the prejudice against beet sugar, widespread in the 1930s, had diminished significantly during the war when many had no choice but use it. "Manufacturers on the Prairies, with the exception of bottlers, seem to be quite satisfied with beet sugar." (Bottlers objected because they sometimes experienced a harmless but unsightly precipitate in clear drinks when using sugar made from beets.)

Sugar rationing remained in effect in Canada until November 1947. This meant that the Vancouver refinery had worked below capacity almost six consecutive years. But after rationing the demand for sugar exploded so dramatically that the refinery was forced to work long overtime hours in 1948—so much so that the B.C. Department of Labour asked why additional employees were not hired. General superintendent Robert Boyd pointed out that "we had no way of knowing what the demand would be when rationing was removed. . . ."[9] Also, buying habits had changed during the war: at one time, all large stores had purchased sugar in bulk, typically 100-pound bags, and repackaged it for sale. During the war the refinery had begun packaging sugar in small bags, five or ten pounds each, or in small cartons, which retailers found so convenient that they were not prepared to resume repackaging from bulk. Consequently, the refinery's packaging machinery was running twenty-four hours a day and still was unable to keep up to the orders. Larger capacity equipment was ordered in 1948; meanwhile the refinery had to cope as best as it could.

Several unusual events in 1948 made it even harder for the company to meet the demand for sugar. Severe spring flooding of the Fraser River halted rail shipping for several weeks, and refining had to be halted temporarily when the warehouse became jammed with sugar which ordinarily would have been shipped to distribution points. "When railway connections were re-established," Boyd explained in a letter to the government in October 1948, "our stocks were quickly exhausted and we were forced to work long hours to meet the situation." The large 1948 strawberry and raspberry crops in the Fraser Valley and the large wild berry harvest across the Prairies added to the demand for sugar for making jams and other preserves. Because the 1947 beet sugar yield had been low, the Prairies looked to Vancouver for additional cane sugar. "The threat of loss of fruit for lack of sugar to preserve it was serious and we did everything possible to meet the emergency," Boyd wrote.

13

A Cross to Bear

TWO RIVALS AND THEIR LEGACIES.

Frederick H. Ballou, the company's first chief engineer, was a Coloradan whom Ernest Rogers hired in 1931 to handle the reconstruction of the newly acquired Raymond beet sugar factory. Ballou arrived in the fall, when the campaign was already underway, and crossed swords almost immediately with Robert Boyd, BC Sugar's chief chemist and general superintendent. It was the beginning of a divisive feud between the company's two top technical officers which continued until Ballou retired in 1950. Despite their intense personal rivalry, both made significant contributions. Boyd, the developer of Rogers' Golden Syrup, ensured that the refinery's processing methods were brought to the technical forefront of sugar refining. Ballou played a role in the engineering of three sugar beet factories and set in motion the rebuilding of the Vancouver refinery.

Roger's Golden Syrup, one of Canada's most long-lived consumer products, was developed just before World War I. The model was Lyle's Golden Syrup, which British refiner Abram Lyle had begun making in 1882. (It is still being made by Tate & Lyle.) Boyd, a graduate of the Royal Technical College in Scotland, was lecturing in chemistry at the University of Toronto when B. T. Rogers hired him in 1913. There is an unconfirmed belief that Rogers acquired the "secret" of Golden Syrup by recruiting Boyd. William Blankenbach, who was Boyd's assistant and later his successor, insisted that Boyd developed the syrup in Vancouver. "The technology wasn't private knowledge. The way Lyle's produced it of course was probably a very secretive thing. I think you have to give him [Boyd] credit for developing the Golden Syrup process." Boyd visited the Tate & Lyle refinery several times during his long career but never succeeded in gaining access to the details of its syrup process.[1]

The Vancouver refinery had been trying for several years to market the syrupy by-product of refining cane sugar with little success. "I can't 'give away' Cane syrup," B. T. Rogers complained to W. D. Matthews in 1911.[2] The Golden Syrup that Boyd created went through a naturally induced chemical change which prevented it from crystallizing rapidly. Its stability as a syrup was the key to its appeal as a consumer product. Getting it established was not easy, as is shown by a letter written in 1916 by Fordham Johnson to Nicholson & Bain, the company's agents on the Prairies: "We assume that your Salesmen have been pushing the sale of our Syrup. Since Rogers' Golden Syrup was put on the market, it has been sold below the cost of manufacturing, and this undoubtedly has much to do with the demand." Ultimately, the strategy of buying market worked. "Our syrup has largely supplanted Lyle's in Canada," Johnson noted in October 1926.[3]

Selling Golden Syrup against competitive products sharpened the company's consumer marketing. The company had done so little advertising that it came in for criticism from Robert Cromie, the publisher of the *Vancouver Sun.* In a letter in which he referred to a Bee Hive corn syrup advertisement in the *Montreal Gazette,* Cromie told Ernest Rogers: "They [Eastern sugar refiners] consistently use the newspapers there to sell their products in a good big way instead of sitting on a monopoly with a buy or leave it policy." BC Sugar had spent a mere $857 in 1934 and slightly less in 1935 advertising the syrup in the *Sun.* Rogers replied that this was consistent with the quantity being sold in the market. He added: "In the refining industry all over the world there is little scope for advertising, because everyone knows that refined sugar is a standard product, and any claims made that a particular brand is superior are without foundation. For this reason, little advertising is done by refineries on this continent, or elsewhere as far as I know, and consequently I do not think your reference to us as a 'monopoly with a buy it or leave it policy' is in any way justified."

In 1932 BC Sugar retained the Vancouver advertising agency of J. J. Gibbons, whose account executive James Lovick was a rising star. He focussed the company's advertising and promotion on Golden Syrup, particularly its place in children's diets. Lovick's prose from 1933 newspaper advertising in various B.C. dailies proclaimed that: "Children love Rogers' Golden Syrup. The school lunch or 'tween meal sandwich, buttered and spread with Rogers' Syrup, disappears with greater zest than usual. . . . It is absolutely pure, a product of the luscious ripe sugar cane. A natural food that every child and adult requires daily, to replace spent energy." The five advertisements that Lovick designed for the 1934 campaign all featured drawings of children, usually playing very actively. "Rogers' is also the spread for those between meal sandwiches, every active child craves during cold winter days."

In September 1933 the company agreed to participate in a cooking school which the Safeway grocery chain was running in Vancouver. In return for having lecturers plug their products, BC Sugar and other participants paid for the school's newspaper advertising and supplied samples for the students. This concept proved so popular that the Vancouver *Daily Province* developed its so-called Modern Kitchen to demonstrate food products provided by sponsoring processors. In 1939 BC Sugar paid a fee to have its syrup used in cooking classes held across the West by the School of Canadian Cookery, a commercial firm based in Winnipeg. Each person attending the classes also received a two-pound tin of syrup and the popular Golden Syrup cookbook (the first printing was 10,000 copies and there was a larger second printing.) BC Sugar declined to participate in the classes in 1940 after the school decided to demonstrate rival corn syrup as well.

Because Rogers' Golden Syrup was not marketed in eastern Canada before the war, the product was overlooked in 1940 when the Department of Munitions and Supply drew up a list of food products to be purchased for the military from Canadian processors. BC Sugar became aware of this when the department's Regina office sent out tender invitations which mentioned only corn and maple syrups. Alan Robertson, the company's sales manager, asked Ottawa in January 1941 to add cane syrup to the tender. John Eaton, the department's director of purchases, replied curtly: "This matter has been taken up with the Department of National Defence, who advise that they are not prepared at the present time to make any changes to their standard ration list." The military did not reverse its policy until April 1943. The Sugar Administration also had overlooked Golden Syrup when imposing rationing, with the result that syrup sales boomed in the first five months of 1942 and BC Sugar was permitted production quotas based on those strong months. Then, in the face of a jam shortage on the Prairies in 1943, the company was permitted to make 10 million pounds annually, more than twice its 1941 sales.

Wartime metal shortages forced the company to improvise Golden Syrup's packaging. In July 1942 the Metals Controller prohibited the use of two-pound and twenty-pound tins once the refinery's supplies were used up late in the year. Shortly thereafter, the company also was told to stop using five- and ten-pound tins and to switch to three-and-a-half-pound glass jars. The first jars were packed during the last week in March 1943. Glass had not been used before because it was heavier to transport and because excessive breakage was feared. Breakage proved to be minor, but the weight was a problem, and wartime price controls prevented the company from raising prices to recover the additional shipping charges. Philip Rogers complained in July 1943 to the Sugar Administrator: "Syrup in the new package has been on the market since March and . . . every case sold results in a direct loss to our Company." The company also used one-pound wax paper containers for about a year. While these were lighter, they were unpopular with consumers and were discontinued in the fall of 1944 when the refinery was permitted to resume using tins. The tins, ubiquitous as lunch pails at country schools across the West, remained in use until the early 1970s when they were again replaced by glass and later by plastic containers.

The company first began selling Golden Syrup in Ontario late in 1941, at the suggestion of Donald Bain of Winnipeg, a leading distributor of BC Sugar products. Bain's manager in Toronto was a brother-in-law of the buyer for Loblaw's and talked the grocery chain into a trial order of one carload. A corn syrup shortage in 1943 enabled Golden Syrup to consolidate its hold on Prairie consumers and make inroads in Ontario immediately after the war. Golden Syrup's best sales year nationally was

1947, when the company sold 13.3 million pounds, penetrating not only Ontario but also Quebec and the Maritimes. In 1948 the corn syrup producers finally secured adequate supplies of corn and lavished $250,000 on advertising to recapture their share of the syrup market. "Competition is very keen and the corn syrup advertising is good," BC Sugar conceded in an internal sales report at the end of 1948. Gradually, the competitors, aided by the high cost of shipping the syrup from Vancouver, took back the eastern market while Maritimers showed a distinct preference for molasses. BC Sugar briefly probed the United States but withdrew when it became clear that the cost of launching Golden Syrup there would be enormous. By 1952 Golden Syrup production was 5.5 million pounds, back to the volume made a decade earlier.

The company was slow to expand the breadth of the product line on the Golden Syrup base. That it had been considered even before the war is illustrated by some charming correspondence between Forrest Rogers and his nephews in 1938. A trial of a honeylike version was made at Port Cowan, one of the family's summer homes. The children, who liked the product, sent a letter addressed to "Dear Uncle Forrie" and signed themselves the "Rogers Troops." After having sampled the thick syrup on their bread, they urged: "We think you should start up a new branch of the sugar business, making this as imitation honey. We think it would be very profitable." They gave seven arguments for their case, including the following: "Its energy-giving qualities would make skiiers ski better, make children be healthy, make sailors stay awake, and make frowning office executives grin." Forrest responded by challenging the Troops to come up with a trade name. Whether or not they did, the product never was made.

In 1955 Rogers' Light Syrup, a thinner version of Golden Syrup packed in sixteen-ounce bottles, was launched as a pancake syrup. A six-week-long promotion and contest keyed to that fall's Grey Cup football championship flopped because the syrup was not distributed to enough retailers when the contest began. It was relaunched in mid-1957 as Rogers' Pancake Syrup. W. A. Davies, a retired BC Sugar sales manager, recalled that at the time the company decided against making a maple-flavoured version even though the wholesalers were asking for one. Davies explained: "There were so many of our own customers producing maple-flavoured syrups using our sugar that to put out our own maple-flavoured pancake syrup, we would really be competing with our own customers. So we never did."[4] It was not until 1988, after several sugar company customers stopped making their own maple-flavoured syrups, that BC Sugar finally launched its own, Rogers' Canadian, followed in 1989 by a butter-flavoured version. Both have been successful.

♦

If Robert Boyd is remembered for a successful consumer product, Ballou is recalled in many anecdotes as an eccentric and difficult individual. "Golly, he was a cross to bear," sighed Forrest Rogers, in discussing the engineer during a 1975 interview.[5] The two men were predestined to quarrel. Boyd was a member of the sober-sided Plymouth Brethren sect, so devout and strict in his religious observance that it was said that he refused to read a newspaper on Sunday. He neither smoked nor drank, and was never known to swear. "When I went to work for him," said Blankenbach, who joined the company in 1929, "to some extent he was very jealous of his position. If I overstepped my authority in any way, I was very quickly put back in my place. . . . Boyd was essentially a quiet man and a gentleman with, I think, a far better brain than Ballou."

Until Ballou was hired, Boyd was the most technically qualified person at the Vancouver refinery to send to the newly acquired Raymond beet factory. He had completed one extensive report on the factory's deplorable mechanical condition and had invested much effort in wringing some efficiency from the factory. Ballou's insensitive, take-charge personality, his volatile temper and his facility at cursing quickly brought him into conflict with Boyd. When the men were together, they were prone to quarrel about anything—even about which radio station to listen to when they shared the staff house at Raymond. After two Alberta factories were operating, the men avoided being at the same factory at the same time.

Ballou was very hot-tempered. "He was a pretty hard man to work for," said Royce Craig, a member of Ballou's engineering department and later chief engineer himself. Lincoln Wood, who worked at the Raymond and Picture Butte plants, remembered Ballou as a "sergeant-major type" given to spectacular tantrums. Once during wartime, when Ballou was bumped by a military officer from a commercial flight at Lethbridge airport, Wood said, "he almost went insane." Ballou only cooled down after making a long-distance telephone call to blister someone at Trans-Canada Airlines' head office. William Hetherington recalled that Ballou, using the clout of BC Sugar's purchasing department, successfully insisted that a shoe manufacturer retread a pair of running shoes which he judged had given inadequate service. Peter Cherniavsky remembered an exasperated insurance adjuster tossing his own ballpoint pen onto Ballou's desk after the engineer filed a claim for a lost pen.[6]

Forrest Rogers first met Ballou in 1934 when Rogers still was studying chemical engineering at the University of British Columbia. During a break before classes resumed in the fall, Rogers decided to go to Raymond for some duck hunting. Ballou, a crack shot, chose to go along. After dinner on the evening before the shoot, Rogers tired of trying to make small talk with the inarticulate Ballou and announced that he was going to check his gun. When Ballou decided to do the same, he discovered that a vital spring was broken. At this, the engineer flew into such a rage that Rogers quickly retired to his room. Nevertheless, Ballou was ready for the shoot at 8 A.M. next morning, having risen much earlier and driven into Lethbridge where he had roused a gunsmith to have his gun repaired.

Once the Picture Butte plant was complete and operating well, Ballou was transferred to Vancouver, responsible for upgrading the refinery, the condition of which had deteriorated while attention was focussed on the beet sugar factories. But when war began, renovations and expansions were suspended except for those essential to the war effort, and the company had to patch and make do. This did not stop Ballou from charging ahead. According to Blankenbach: "The refinery had never had a real mechanical engineer and he started moving things around without knowing what [cane sugar] refining was all about. [He] went through the refinery and took over things that Boyd had been jealously responsible for." Because the factionalism threatened the efficiency of the refinery, Philip Rogers established a so-called Operating Committee early in 1944, chaired by Forrest Rogers.[7] It met for an hour or so each Friday morning. Despite an acrimonious atmosphere, the meetings succeeded in grappling with everyday problems and, in Blankenbach's view, clearing the air.

In December 1943 Ballou prepared an ambitious three-year plan for the reconstruction of the Vancouver refinery. In the first year, he proposed building a new boiler house and power plant. In the second year, Ballou's plan called for dismantling the old boiler house, building the new office and new raw sugar bulk storage and designing the pan, melt and packing houses—the guts of a refinery—for construction in the third year. In wartime, however, it was one thing to draw plans; it was quite another to get raw materials and government authorization to go ahead. The refinery was forced to operate three years without a complete maintenance shutdown until one was finally scheduled in April 1944.

In 1946 Ballou consolidated his proposals for refinery reconstruction into a list of forty-one items. Again, many were delayed while those that proceeded were often incremental, such as improving the machine shop, or involved making only plans and drawings. However, a new boiler house did proceed; as well, an extension was added to the pan house, a new vacuum pan was designed by Ballou's department and new packaging equipment was ordered to pack sugar in small bags.

The indefatigable Ballou's list of improvements had grown to seventy-one items by December 1947, including the packaging machinery which was to be delivered and installed over the next two years. Many of the items either reflected routine maintenance or such unspectacular improvements as new restrooms. But the total list amounted to a complete reconstruction of the refinery and all the other buildings on the site. The company's 1948 annual report seemed to confirm the need, if not the will, for a major capital program: "During the war years it was necessary to eliminate all but the most needed maintenance work, and a long-term program is now being laid out, both as regards the maintenance and bringing the present plant up to ultimate efficiency. This will eventually mean the construction of several new buildings and installation of new machinery, but it is hoped to defer the major portion of this work until conditions and prices become more stable."

The Taber factory, the final major engineering assignment of Ballou's career, was to be completed by the 1949 campaign, but labour shortages and delays in equipment deliveries frustrated that schedule and sent the completed cost from a budgetted $3.9 million to a final $5.9 million. Construction began in April 1947. A year later Ballou reported that "poor delivery of steel due to strikes is interfering with our progress." In August Philip Rogers read a less than reassuring memorandum from Ballou which advanced arguments for delaying the completion. Rogers telephoned T. George Wood to warn: "I am getting a little worried whether they are going to get it ready for 1949."[8] Delays in receiving critical tubing—the government gave priority to the oil industry—set back the completion until the fall of 1950.

The last battle between Ballou and Boyd occurred during the construction of the Taber factory. Most of the engineering was done by Stearns-Roger, but Ballou had a hand in ordering a conveyor system and certain pumps. Boyd warned that the specified equipment would be troublesome, but the engineer persisted. Boyd was correct: the factory's numerous teething problems included the conveyors and the pumps, which either were replaced or rebuilt after the 1950 campaign. Neither of the sparring technicians was around; Ballou retired after the campaign, and Boyd died early in 1951, six months before he would have retired.

14

The Workers' Best Friend

THE COMPANY INVESTS IN THE DOMINICAN REPUBLIC.

Rafael Trujillo was in the fourteenth year of his erratic thirty-one-year rule over the Dominican Republic in June 1944 when BC Sugar acquired the Ozama Sugar Company's factory and plantation about ten miles east of Ciudad Trujillo (now Santo Domingo). Sugar had been grown in the Spanish-speaking Dominican Republic—which occupied the eastern two-thirds of the island of Hispaniola with French-speaking Haiti at the other end—since cane was introduced by Christopher Columbus in 1493 on his second trip to the new world. As in Fiji in 1905, BC Sugar salvaged a failure. Under the Canadian company, Ozama introduced new varieties of sugar cane and forage grass and was the first Dominican estate to apply fertilizers systematically. The new managers from Vancouver anticipated an exotic adventure in the Caribbean but found difficult problems ranging from epidemic malaria to floods and fires. However, most of the aggravation came from the venal Trujillo dictatorship.

Forrest Rogers, sent to supervise the company's new investment, complained in his first annual review of Ozama operations that "censoring of the mail added to the difficulties by impeding correspondence with the Vancouver office."[1] Formal censorship stopped after World War II, but the mail service remained insecure. In subsequent years Rogers and other

Ozama executives used the British Embassy's diplomatic pouch or travelled to Florida or Puerto Rico to mail sensitive documents and make confidential telephone calls. Disciplined discretion kept criticism of Trujillo's government from slipping into Ozama's operating reports, sent to Vancouver weekly during the six-month harvest season and biweekly the rest of the year. The reports were typed by Dominican clerks, any of whom could be leaking details to the authorities. In the atmosphere of Trujillo's republic, it was foolhardy to risk political reprisals. BC Sugar owned Ozama for nearly eleven years: the single openly derogatory reference to Trujillo to slip inadvertently into an operating report referred to the dictator as "the big stick."

The internal post mortems, written after BC Sugar had sold Ozama to the Dominican government, were bitterly frank, however. William R. (Bill) Hetherington, an engineer from Success, Saskatchewan, who began a lifelong BC Sugar career at Ozama, remembered frustration as the "outstanding feature" of his time there.[2] Capricious government decrees and regulations made it "impossible to avoid infractions of Dominican law." Writing a footnote to the Ozama experience in 1955, six months after leaving the Dominican Republic, Hetherington concluded: "There should exist no doubt whatsoever—the foreigner is not wanted in Latin America, . . . particularly in the Dominican Republic."[3] Time mellowed such assessments. Forrest Rogers, in a nostalgic 1987 interview, shrugged off Ozama as of minor financial importance in the history of BC Sugar. But he also admitted: "To me and to various members of the company, it's a most interesting period of our lives."[4]

Buying Ozama was among the most important business decisions made by Philip Rogers during his presidency of the company. He anticipated a postwar surge in sugar prices similar to what had occurred when sugar rationing ended after World War I. In a 1944 memorandum to his board of directors, Rogers pointed out that world sugar production and consumption were in balance before the war but that production had certainly been reduced sharply since. He calculated that war damage in the Philippines, Indonesia and the Ukraine had eliminated about eight million tons or nearly a quarter of the world's production. He predicted that this shortage would inflate postwar sugar prices once free markets were restored. "In the event of inflation in sugar after the war," he reasoned, the purchase of Ozama "would prove an excellent hedge. . . ."[5]

Postwar sugar prices did jump, although the speculative excess of 1920 was not repeated because Britain (and Canada) maintained rationing and price controls far longer than most had expected. Ozama sold its 1945 crop for an average of $3.10 a hundred pounds, essentially the price mandated by the British Ministry of Food. But, as Philip Rogers had foreseen, throughout the next seven years the average never dropped below $4 and rose to $5.76 during the Korean War. What he failed to predict was that the Trujillo government's taxes ultimately would confiscate most of the profits.[6]

The Dominican Republic was not BC Sugar's first choice for investing in a Caribbean cane plantation. The company initially considered buying and merging several small Jamaican sugar estates. However, Jamaican sugar was sold chiefly to Canada under special wartime sales arrangements, the future of which was uncertain. Philip Rogers also believed Jamaica was politically unstable. Cuba, a second choice and then the world's most important cane-growing nation, was similarly unattractive. "The policy is becoming very much Cuba for the Cubans, and a large number of American companies are pulling out of the country," Rogers wrote in a memorandum to his directors.

When Canada's deputy Sugar Administrator Jack Hobbins heard that BC Sugar was looking for a Caribbean estate, he suggested that Rogers talk to the Bank of Nova Scotia, then the unhappy owner of Ozama. This plantation had been established at the turn of the century by a wealthy Dominican family whose fortunes declined when a 1924 fire destroyed the sugar mill. The bank, long active in the Caribbean, had financed a new mill in 1928 but was foreclosing in 1930 to recover its loan when a hurricane flattened Ozama, leaving the bank owed US$990,000. Instead of walking away from this debt, the bank secured control of Ozama by paying another US$515,000 for it at a public auction in 1935. It then sank an additional US$1.5 million into the plantation to return it to production in 1940. Ozama's cumulative profits of $942,000 during the five years it was run by bank-appointed admininistrators were taken by the bank. "During all of these years," Rogers wrote in his memorandum, "[Ozama] has thus not been able to expand either its land holdings or bring its factory absolutely up to date."

BC Sugar paid US$1.7 million for Ozama in the spring of 1944, buying what Hetherington later called "a down at the heels liability to the

Dominican Republic." The estate consisted of 46,329 acres, much of it wooded or grazing land needed to accommodate Ozama's 2250 work oxen, 700 cows, 800 calves, 65 horses and 20 mules. Only 7196 acres were planted to cane, with another 3000 acres designated for growing cane. The plantation's forty-six-mile narrow-gauge railway, essential for hauling the sugar cane to the crushing plant, was so poorly built and maintained that derailments and collisions, some very serious, occurred almost weekly.

Trujillo had emerged as a popular hero for his leadership during relief efforts following the 1930 hurricane that wrecked the capital district, including Ozama. By 1944 he was well on the way to being the focus of a personality cult. Santo Domingo, a name of profound religious resonance in a Catholic country, had been renamed Ciudad Trujillo in 1936. The one-time policeman had begun appropriating a bombastic string of titles running from generalissimo to father of the nation. Abroad he had a reasonably good image. Friendly to the United States, whose Marines had occupied the Dominican Republic between 1916 and 1925, Trujillo had declared war on the Axis powers immediately after Pearl Harbor. A naively laudatory profile of the republic in the *National Geographic Magazine* in 1944 maintained that the country "is emerging into a modern, progressive country of comparative prosperity."

To inspect Ozama before buying it, BC Sugar sent a team which included Philip Rogers, chief engineer F. H. Ballou, and T. George Wood. Rogers concluded that Trujillo was "a benign dictator." In an Ozama post mortem memoir penned in 1956, Forrest Rogers wrote: "While it was recognized that [Trujillo's] rule was one of complete dictatorship, it appeared that his government was based on sound principles, and the 'jefe' was then known chiefly for his excellent work in cleaning up the country, improving water supplies and sewage systems and making primary education available to all children throughout the Republic." Others shared this view. One scholar of the republic, historian Ian Bell, has written that at this time "the Republic's finances were in better shape than they had ever been, and for those who did not look too far below the surface it was a prosperous and well-administered little state."[7]

Once again, as in Fiji, BC Sugar needed to replace both personnel and equipment. Given the impoverished state of the Dominican economy, the plantation had to be largely self-sufficient: raising cattle for meat and milk as well as for field work; operating its own bakery and maintaining company stores to ensure that employees had adequate food at reasonable prices. Ozama even operated its own sawmill, producing lumber for employee housing (more than 2000 had to be accommodated during harvest) and for a peculiar employee fringe benefit—free coffins, needed because of the high infant mortality. Hetherington described these practices as "just one of the things you could do" to remunerate employees. "The pay was set by law. . . . The government published how much you paid."[8] A plantation school was run by Alice Low, whose husband, Frank, was the first agriculturalist BC Sugar posted to Ozama. When the Lows returned to Canada in 1946—he had become very ill with malaria—teaching was taken over for some time by Trish Rogers, the second daughter of Ernest Rogers.

Forrest Rogers, who moved to the Dominican Republic with his family in 1945, was not impressed with the management he found there. The manager was James Smith, a fifty-five-year-old Scottish engineer who had been born in Indonesia of a sugar plantation family and had spent most of his career in the tropics. The bank had plucked him from an unhappy early retirement in Scotland to run Ozama. In his memoir, Rogers wrote: "It eventually became apparent to us that with all his experience, he was not fitted for the post of manager, especially as he was too prone to taking advice from those under him and was afraid to stand up to others in similar positions to his." In 1947 Ian Angus was sent from Vancouver to understudy Smith. A nephew of Mrs. B. T. Rogers, Angus had joined BC Sugar after commanding a Canadian destroyer during the war. An amiable and energetic man, he was to carve out a career as BC Sugar's all-purpose troubleshooter. In the Dominican Republic, his strongest suit was superb diplomacy, especially useful for cultivating the powerful, however personally distasteful he might find them. His friendship with one of Trujillo's top enforcers, Gen. Anselmo Paulino, was useful whenever Dominican Customs tried to obstruct imports by Ozama.

Other Ozama managers besides Smith also were found wanting. At the suggestion of Dr. Frank Peto, head of BC Sugar's recently formed agriculture research department, Ozama's agricultural superintendent was replaced with Frank Low, a young Albertan with a master's degree in soil chemistry, which equipped him to undertake the major fertilizer program Peto ordered. The senior accountant, with whom Forrest Rogers found numerous shortcomings, was replaced by his assistant, A. A. Buchanan, a Canadian who continued his career with BC Sugar in Vancouver after Ozama was sold.

Forrest Rogers, Hetherington and others sent to Ozama from Canada soon learned Spanish, if only to reduce their dependence on the Dominicans they had inherited from the bank. In his memoir, Rogers recalled a worker identified only as Armanie, a "batey mayordomo" or head man in a subsection of the plantation. "As such he had charge of most activities around but outside the factory, chief of which was the storage of sugar at the river warehouses, and its subsequent transport. . . . Armanie had a glorious opportunity to take advantage of the new owners' lack of knowledge of the ajuste system," Rogers wrote, referring to the piecework system for hiring and paying labour. Once the new owners figured out that Armanie was padding the payroll, they fired him and "we were subsequently able to reduce our costs of shipping, etc."

Nothing was more dilapidated at Ozama than the plantation's railway, used for hauling cane to the mill. The six old wood- and coal-fired locomotives reminded William Hetherington of "the locomotives of the 1860's." The unluckiest—and heaviest—was locomotive No. 9, which was involved in derailments almost every week in 1945 and 1946, its front wheels being so worn that it had difficulty negotiating a switch. Once in 1945 it hit a mule, and the engineer had to stop when the carcass became jammed in the locomotive's cowcatcher—at which time the following train rammed the last car in No. 9's train.

The first train wreck Hetherington saw, two days after arriving at Ozama in February 1946, involved No. 9. It had been hauling cars loaded with sugar cane down a steep grade. At the bottom the engineer discovered that the rear half of the train had become uncoupled and the front half was pulling away. The engineer stopped and the rear half caught up with devastating force. "Remains of cane cars and about 100 tons of cane were scattered in all directions," Hetherington recalled. "Some sixteen hours were required to clear the mess."[10]

The spark arrestors on the smokestacks of the Ozama locomotives functioned poorly. In June 1946 sparks from a locomotive set fire to a heap of cane leaves, and the flames damaged a car of fertilizer on a nearby siding. Once in 1947 coals from a locomotive set fire to one of the many old, tarred timber bridges. These bridges had to be rebuilt or replaced before the company was able to introduce modern diesel locomotives, the first pair arriving in 1948. Derailments and train wrecks decreased as the railway was rebuilt. But the diesels sometimes proved too mechanically complicated for the train crews: once when a locomotive lost its oil pressure, the driver concluded the pressure gauge had failed and kept driving until the engine seized up.

Some mishaps were tragic. Early in 1946 a locomotive was pushing four cars onto a siding where two already were parked. Unknown to the engineer, an Ozama employee—a watchman responsible for guarding the fertilizer stocks—was sleeping under one of the parked cars and suffered a broken leg. A similar accident the next year resulted in the death of an Ozama field worker, who was crushed when some rail cars under which he was sleeping were moved one night. The police arrested the entire locomotive crew, and it cost the company $500 to free them from jail. Ozama's reports contain numerous other examples of accidents involving injury, extensive damage at times and even other deaths. "We spent a great deal of time and effort improving the deficiencies of the Ozama railway system," Hetherington recalled later, "but we could never completely match the ingenuity of the operators in this contest involving completely different aims."[11] He suspected that deliberate vandalism caused some of the derailments.

BC Sugar took charge of Ozama in June 1944, the beginning of what was called the "dead season" at the plantation, when the cane cutters had been laid off. (The harvest and crush started after Christmas and lasted five to six months.) The rainy season began in June; between rains, cane fields were replanted and cultivated. Unhappily for BC Sugar, the dead season in 1944 included two early floods which washed away some newly planted cane, followed by a prolonged drought which reduced cane yields. The company had estimated that it would harvest and crush about 105,000 tons of cane in 1945, about the same amount that general manager James Smith had produced the year before for the Bank of Nova Scotia. Instead, BC Sugar's first harvest at Ozama yielded a disappointing 71,156 tons of cane, producing only 65,678 bags of sugar. (Sugar was packed in 250-pound bags.)

"Even before we purchased the Company," Forrest Rogers wrote in 1956 in his Ozama memoir, "it was obvious to us that fertilization of the fields was a must and it was and still is difficult to understand why none of the companies on the Island had not adopted this practice." On Puerto Rico, the American-controlled island just east of the Dominican Republic, all the sugar cane estates were already using fertilizers. About 4000 acres of Ozama's lands were fertilized during the 1945 dead season (wartime supply shortages prevented the company from getting enough fertilizer for the entire property). The impact was dramatic: Ozama crushed 153,000 tons of cane, with the yield per acre jumping from 12.88 tons to 20.85 tons. The company stretched the scarce quantities of commercial fertilizer with bat guano, obtained first from Dominican bat caves and later from Chile. "The soil was just starving for fertilizer," said Frank Low, who drew the unpleasant task of going into the caves and supervising the Dominican labourers who were bagging the guano. "We thought we were pretty brave to go into a bat cave because there were literally millions [of bats] hanging from the roof."[12]

The Dominican plantations also lacked the more productive varieties of sugar cane being grown elsewhere. Ozama quickly joined a Barbados cane research program. Forrest Rogers also resorted to a little smuggling, spiriting a sample of Cuba's best new variety, Media Luna, from that country into the Dominican Republic. "By some clandestine method seedlings always became available," Rogers wrote.[13] New forage seeds, some varieties of which became the nation's major livestock feed, also made it past Trujillo's customs officers by irregular means: "You'd carry bits in your shoes and stuff like that to get seed in," Hetherington said.

Smuggling was not practical when the Dominican government threatened to levy duties on the first shipment of fertilizer Ozama imported. As Forrest Rogers explained, the generalissimo was wary of fertilizers: "A disastrous explosion occurred at Galveston, Texas, where a ship loading ammonium nitrate caught fire, and the Dominican Government therefore declared this material should be classed as an explosive similar to dynamite and be subject to all restrictions—which, in a dictator run country, are necessarily quite rigorous. Therefore, when our first shipment of ammonium nitrate arrived it was put under lock and key, and . . . not a pound could be removed without the permission and supervision of the army, who watched the material from the time it left the warehouse, through the mixing plant, to the final application on the fields. It was many months before these rules were relaxed, and in the meantime the lieutenant in charge of the army post at nearby San Isidro had to be given the usual hand-out everytime he came over to unlock the warehouse."[14] The company finally earned an exemption after Dr. Peto offered to conduct free fertilizer trials on one of Trujillo's farms.

Ozama employees could not avoid the handout ethic. Frank and Alice Low, married just prior to travelling to Ozama, discovered that they had to pay substantial Dominican import duties on their personal household effects, many of them wedding gifts. Low was not a slow learner: the following year when agriculturalist John Hall came to join him, he eased Hall's baggage past Dominican customs effortlessly after slipping the inspector $10. There was a Dominican army post at the entrance to the plantation. "We kept a number of them sweetened up," Hetherington remembered. During the harvest season, the soldiers were called on to supplement the plantation's own police force and firefighters in dealing with cane fires, a number of which were set by the harvest crew. Handouts also reduced the frequency of confrontations with authority in uniform. "If you didn't keep some policeman or someone happy, the first thing you'd know, he would stop all your vehicles for hours on the road," Hetherington said.

Episodes like that illustrated that the Trujillo administration was not based on such sound principles after all. The government's taxing policies—which indeed had been reasonable in 1944—came to be based on squeezing the most obvious source of wealth. In August 1946 damage caused by a major earthquake provided the rationale for a new tax to fund reconstruction: the tax was a six per cent levy on sugar and molasses sales. The sugar estates, worried that the tax would remain after the earthquake damage was repaired, fought it and finally succeeded in having it cancelled in 1947. But to gain that victory, the sugar companies surrendered to the government the entire windfall profit made on a special sale of Dominican sugar to Chile at nearly double the still-controlled price being paid by Britain and the United States, the major buyers.

In the spring of 1948 the government responded with a variety of new taxes on the sugar companies, including an increase in the export tax on sugar: it was to be 30 per cent (up from 20 per cent) of the selling price over $3.10 a pound, in U.S. dollars. Through its Dominican lawyer, Jésus María Troncoso, Ozama sought to be exempted from the new sugar taxes because it was deep into a heavy capital investment program at the plantation. The lawyer offered no encouragement that he could achieve this. Troncoso, who represented Ozama personally or through his firm during most of the time BC Sugar owned the plantation, was well connected. A charming former Dominican ambassador to the United States and son of a former Dominican president, he was at this time also governor of the country's central bank. Later, he became head of the state's sugar commission.

But Forrest Rogers found Troncoso timid. "On two or three occasions," Rogers recalled later, "I wrote letters to Trujillo, pleading with him to make life a little less awkward and a little better, not only for us but I always said for our employees and so on. I always took them to our lawyer. He invariably advised me not to send the letters." Rogers once sent a letter and showed a copy to the lawyer after it had gone. "Well, I thought really he was going to faint."[15] The letter was well received, in fact—but did not influence any presidential action.

None of the Canadians feared for their personal security, aside from one or two isolated incidents. (Angus once was clubbed over the head by a Dominican employee, apparently over a pay grievance.) But Trujillo's own citizens—even highly placed ones such as Troncoso—had reason to worry, as the fate of union leader Alberto Larancuent showed. In 1947 Trujillo decreed an increase in wages for sugar workers, allowed the establishment of a Sugar Workers Union and declared himself "The Workers' Best Friend."[16] Larancuent, who lived on the Ozama plantation, was made secretary of the union and one of his friends, an Ozama locomotive driver named José Carmona, headed the union's Ozama local. Angus, who had arrived in the fall of 1947, noted that the union leaders began taking themselves seriously, seduced by the adulation printed in the newspapers. They "were getting to the stage where occasionally they gave us difficulty in connection with labour affairs," Angus wrote later. But the government became uncomfortable with the union. At the union's first anniversary convention, Larancuent was found in his hotel room, dead with a bullet in his head. Carmona went into hiding for weeks before coming back to Ozama. The union collapsed.

The government, lacking other lucrative tax sources, was inventive in extracting money from the sugar companies. Ozama was even taxed on lumber produced at its sawmill for its own use. There were a variety of licence fees which could be and were changed by decree. Many important items were subject to duties and delays: in 1946 it took the company three weeks to clear an imported crawler tractor after a customs official measured it and decided it was wider than eight feet and was therefore a motor vehicle. Angus remembered that this transaction required a hidden payment of $300.

The various permit fees were capricious, frequently heavy and sometimes influenced by corruption. During the Korean War, the Dominicans set up an authority to control imports and exports. Each transaction required a permit which was supposed to cost $4. "The first time I went down to get a permit was to make a shipment of sugar, a boatload of sugar which was worth about $1 million," Hetherington said. "I was told in an inner room that if I wanted a permit, I was going to have to arrive with four per cent of the invoice value in cash—and I would get a receipt for $4." Accompanied by two Ozama policemen, he delivered a box stuffed with $40,000 and only then received the export permit. "For a couple of years, we just had to live with that." The sugar company was not alone with this problem. A bemused Hetherington once educated a New York auditor for a major American oil company who had trouble understanding the discrepancy between the oil company's disbursements and its receipts for permits.[17]

Only the general's sugar estates benefitted when the government introduced a new sugar policy that included a twenty-year tax holiday for new enterprises. Ozama and the other established plantations were hit with production taxes in December 1948 which tried to ensure that the government's revenues would not suffer when the world sugar price had dipped. "We were absolutely killed by taxes," Angus remembered. "You were not taxed on profits but on production."[18] Ozama, now losing money because of the taxes, appealed for special consideration and was told that in the future, the government would apply a corporate income tax from which 1949 losses could be deducted. "In actual fact," Forrest Rogers wrote in 1956, "an income tax law was decreed but the interpretation was—income tax or production tax, whichever higher. . . . The income tax law meant precisely nothing."[19] Every time the government promised to consider an income tax law, a spirited editorial campaign against income tax would suddenly appear in one of the newspapers, and Trujillo would be dissuaded. The sugar companies believed that the editorials were dictated by the government.

In 1949 the government also used the newspapers to soften public opinion for moves against foreign-owned sugar companies. The daily *El Caribe* in April published attacks accusing the sugar companies of monopolizing the supply of meat, milk and bread, to the detriment of Dominican businesses. This was particularly galling to Ozama, which had a large dairy herd and sold most of its milk to a distributor in Ciudad Trujillo who was related to the dictator. The attacks became harsher later that month when *La Nacion*, another of the capital's daily newspapers, published an article entitled "The Decadent Dominican Sugar Industry."

These articles coincided with the dictator's move into the sugar industry. In 1948 Trujillo decided to establish a small estate called Catarey. The next year the Trujillo family began a second and larger plantation at Rio Haina. Late in 1949 Trujillo's associates expressed interest in acquiring Ozama but never entered into serious negotiations even though Forrest Rogers hurried to the Dominican Republic, prepared to deal. In the meantime, the Ozama mill ground Catarey cane in 1949 and 1950 until that plantation had its own mill, and then ground Rio Haina cane in 1952 until that estate opened one of the largest mills in the country. Grinding Trujillo's cane enhanced Ozama's revenues and operating efficiencies, a benefit offset by the other disruptions caused by the Trujillo practices.

In May 1951 heavy and unseasonally early rains caused the Ozama and other rivers to rise in violent flood. The Ozama plantation had suffered during floods in 1948 when rising waters inundated 23,000 bags of sugar in a new warehouse. The floor was raised but not enough: the water in 1951 rose three feet higher than in 1948. The company had to reprocess over 16,000 flood-damaged 250-pound bags of sugar, salvaging less than half of them. The floods also washed away newly planted cane, reducing the 1952 harvest. The cause of the greater ecological damage was Rio Haina.

"There can be no doubt," Forrest Rogers wrote in 1956, "that the abnormal flood level of the rivers was due to the felling of trees in the upper reaches of the Ozama and its tributaries, where large tracts of land had been cleared and planted to cane for Central Rio Haina, the president's new sugar mill. A law of the country provided that the banks of rivers should not be denuded of trees but, of course, this did not apply to the jefe. . . ."[20]

Even after the flood damage, however, 1951 was Ozama's most profitable year: the Korean War drove world sugar prices to an average of $5.76 a hundred pounds, the highest during BC Sugar's eleven years in the Dominican Republic. Ozama's net profit in the twelve months ending 30 September 1951 was $926,858. This encouraged the company to plan costly capital improvements at Ozama, including a steam boiler and a turbo-generator to give the plantation a degree of self-sufficiency in electricity. (The generator never was installed, its cancellation a casualty of the worsening relations with Trujillo.)

The government set the wages to be paid to plantation workers and to the Haitian cane cutters who were imported each harvest. "Because the jefe, the chief himself, was in the cane business, you paid the going rate, period," Hetherington said. "No more, no less." The pay was very low, but Ozama padded it with fringe benefits such as nominally priced meat and milk from the estate's dairy. Labour shortages were constant, however. The most difficult year was 1952; Ozama was forced to leave 29,500 tons of cane uncut when the factory stopped grinding in mid-June. While the harvest had lasted 166 days, a normal length season, the mill worked below capacity or stopped altogether for the equivalent of forty days because insufficient cane was being cut to keep it busy. "Well, what was happening in 1952," Hetherington explained, "was Trujillo was buying land adjoining our property and he was having difficulty getting labour. So they sent soldiers over and just picked up our Haitians and our labourers and everything else and just hauled them away. We had no recourse."[21]

The smaller harvest of 1952 caused by the previous year's floods and compounded by the labour shortage was but one of the company's problems. Late in the year, the Dominican government decreed a major increase in the production tax on sugar and new taxes on molasses, an important by-product. The production tax was based on four cents a pound even though world sugar prices dropped below this level. Most of the sugar estates—excluding the general's, which benefitted from the twenty-year tax holiday—lost money on the 1952 harvest. Ozama salvaged some profit by selling to a New York buyer all the molasses that it was allowed to export. The published sale price was 8.25 cents a gallon. But Ozama made a deal quietly on the side: the final selling price was to be that realized by the Cuban exporters over the first seven months of

1953, if that average was higher. The average was nine cents a gallon, with the three-quarter cent difference paid directly to BC Sugar, thereby preventing the Dominicans from taxing it. A similar arrangement was made in 1954.

Early in February 1953, while the sugar estates still were contesting the new sugar taxes, a Canadian trade mission swung through the Caribbean, led by Trade Minister C. D. Howe. Ian Angus, invited to one of the Dominican government receptions for the mission, drew Howe aside to seek his aid. "Every time I moved in to talk to Howe, a Dominican would move in to eavesdrop," Angus remembered. "I started telling him they were squeezing us—and an eavesdropper moved in."[22] The trade minister quickly grasped the complaint and asked Angus to see him in Ottawa. During the next five months Ozama, in concert with the other sugar estates, argued directly with the government for tax relief. Angus did his best to win relief through the contacts he had cultivated so carefully in the government, the most notable one being General Paulino who liked Canadians because two of his sons had been educated in Montreal. Paulino had risen in the hierarchy to what Forrest Rogers described as Trujillo's "triggerman," eventually managing Rio Haina. This time, none of Angus's lobbying worked.

It was decided to seek Howe's assistance formally. Angus saw Howe at an Ottawa meeting in September that included the Canadian trade commissioner to the Dominican Republic. A firmly worded letter was written over Howe's signature asking the Dominican administration when Ozama might expect relief from its heavy tax burden. This did sway the Dominicans to back off somewhat. "It did not allow us to make any profits, but rather gave Ozama a chance to keep its head just above water financially," Forrest Rogers wrote.[23]

Trujillo next acquired three small sugar plantations and decided to redistribute his cane acreage to a group of independent cane growers in a scheme financed by the nation's Agricultural Bank. There was a catch to the generalissimo's generosity: the established plantations such as Ozama were asked to sell some of their plantations or to donate their uncultivated land to the scheme as well. Rogers considered this confiscation. In January 1954 he wrote Howe: "I am sorry to bother you once more regarding our operations in the Dominican Republic, but a situation has arisen which may assume such proportions that we may again call on you for assistance. . . ."[24] Ian Angus was told to reply that Ozama would donate no land but would consider selling uncultivated land—but only for cash.

The confrontation between the government and the foreign-owned sugar companies took a new twist in 1954. Some of the decrees were merely impractical, such as one giving its sugar commission authority to set the dates when the cane harvest would begin and end and how much each plantation would produce. Another required the plantations to pay the production tax, whether or not they were operating. Forrest Rogers saw this as a move to prevent companies from striking against the tax by refusing to grind cane and make sugar. Yet another required that most permanent employees be paid Christmas bonuses. Finally, the government ordered that all agricultural supervisors on plantations be Dominicans—a decree which the estates could evade, if temporarily, by providing full scholarships to Dominicans studying in appropriate schools abroad. Forrest Rogers looked at the range of laws and concluded that Trujillo was determined to reduce the industry to the point where it could be taken over with no compensation. Early in January 1954 Rogers made his annual visit to the plantation. On 27 January he wrote to vice-president Alan Robertson in Vancouver: "Since I arrived here I have received a letter from Mr. Howe in which he stated that he was most perturbed about the situation that I had described to him, and he was not quite sure what form of aid he could give us, but that he was discussing the problem with his colleague [External Affairs Minister Lester B.] Pearson so that they would be prepared to act when the time was ripe. This is a most encouraging letter. . . ." The American government also became concerned—some of the estates being American-owned—and intervened forcefully enough with the Dominicans that the land redistribution scheme was stopped.

In the spring Ozama's case was outlined in a strong letter the company sent directly to Trujillo (the letter that nearly gave lawyer Troncoso the heart seizure). External Affairs also delivered a stiff note to the Dominican government. Trujillo's government replied that Ozama's problems reflected the estate's own inefficiency and besides, Ottawa should mind its own business, the tax policy of any independent country being a matter of that country's sovereignty. Rogers ordered Hetherington, now managing Ozama, to cut costs and defer projects at Ozama. "As you know, we wish to keep our plant and equipment in working condition but we are forced to take advantage of every saving possible, regardless of how small."[25] The export tax on sugar was raised late in 1954.

"In Vancouver while a director's meeting was in progress in December," Forrest Rogers wrote later, "word was received through the Bank of Nova Scotia that some Cuban interests were interested in purchasing Ozama, and we were asked whether we wished to sell. There was little time spent on coming to a decision on the matter." BC Sugar asked for US$5 million. The negotiations with the Cuban—Julian de Zulueta, president of Banco Continental Cubano and a sugar plantation owner in Cuba—were so brief that the company concluded that the Cuban bid was only a ruse to draw from BC Sugar its selling price.

A curious offer to help in the sale of Ozama was made 18 January 1955 to Alan Robertson, who was approached at lunch in the Vancouver Club that day by Powell River Company president Harold Foley, a British Columbia newsprint producer. Foley introduced his brother, Lester, who ran a lumber mill near Jacksonville, Florida, and had been briefly, in 1954, the economic adviser to the U.S. embassy in the Dominican Republic. He was giving a big cocktail party for Trujillo in Florida in February and offered to "assist us in any way possible, either in an easing of taxes or a sale." Robertson passed on this offer to Forrest Rogers.[26] Whether or not this made a difference, BC Sugar soon had an offer from Azucarera Nacional, a firm known to represent Trujillo, which insisted the Cuban had offered $2.5 million for Ozama. Forrest Rogers wrote: "There was no real bargaining in the negotiations, as we realized that when he"—Trujillo's representative—"came up with an offer it would be final, and when he returned with a bid of US$3 million, plus the cost of crop expenses to the date of purchase, we had no alternative but to accept."[27]

Rogers went to the Dominican Republic personally to negotiate the sale in February. "I must say that my visit to San Domingo was a most disagreeable one, as I felt very much like the fellow who had to take the old family horse to the glue factory," he wrote Jack Hobbins. "However, with the current state of affairs in San Domingo I was not at all sorry to see the last of that country." He had to make one final trip in mid-March to transfer ownership and pick up a cheque. He summed up the experience in a letter to Sir William Rook at Czarnikow: "I must confess that we are not receiving real true value for Ozama Sugar Company [but] I think that we are very fortunate to be able to make as good a sale as we have done. Briefly, it amounts to this—that we will get back our original investment and the profits made during the past eleven years which were all re-invested in Ozama have gone for nothing. However, if we had not reinvested our past profits to improve Ozama we would never have been able to keep our heads above water during the last three years. . . ."[28] The cash was invested almost immediately in the acquisition of the Manitoba Sugar Company in Fort Garry.

The company's compensation was inadequate, since Ozama's insurance value alone was at least $4,300,000[29]—but other foreign companies were squeezed from the Dominican Republic with far less. Rogers believed the Canadian government's intervention made the difference. He thanked Howe in March: "I should add that some of my American friends in the sugar industry in San Domingo have told me that they only wish they had a 'Mr. Howe' in their State Department to go to bat for them in a similar manner."[30] The most profound impact of Ozama on BC Sugar was that it forged a team of managers into the tightly knit unit that ran the company for the next generation. "It was a great training ground," believed Peter Cherniavsky, who went to Ozama as a young engineer and ran the factory for two seasons. Ian Angus said: "It was a tremendous benefit to BC Sugar to get these fellows back who were real company men. I think it was a great strength to the company."[31]

15

Practically on the Arctic Circle

A SUGAR BEET INDUSTRY IS ESTABLISHED IN MANITOBA.

In October 1897 the Winnipeg Board of Trade set up a sugar beet committee renewing the quest for a sugar industry despite consistent failure since the first beets had been planted in the Red River Valley some fifty years earlier. At the Board's urging, nine farmers—eight of whom had grown beets commercially in Holland—planted test plots. In addition, test plantings were made at five Dominion Experimental Farms across Canada, including one at Brandon. "The results are far from encouraging," decided Dr. F. T. Shutt, a senior official of the Canada department of agriculture. The beets were low in sugar and purity, in most instances "too poor for profitable manufacture."[1]

In 1915 J. H. Ellis, a student at the Manitoba Agricultural College, initiated new beet trials in the valley, in part to grow forage for livestock. His timing was unfortunate, for it was difficult to get high quality European beet seed during the war years. Not until 1924, after Ellis obtained an adequate quantity of good seed, did the trials yield commercially acceptable beets. He recommended to the Winnipeg Board of Trade "that a sufficient acreage of beets should be grown in the most suitable portions of the Red River Valley and that an experimental carload shipment be made to an established sugar factory."[2]

In 1925 a group of Winnipeg businessmen incorporated the original Manitoba Sugar Company and proposed a $1.5 million sugar factory. In October, armed with the results of 200 test plots around southern Manitoba, the company announced that it would contract for 1000 acres of beets the next spring. Winnipeg investment dealer H. F. Osler alerted BC Sugar president Fordham Johnson, thinking to apprise him of a business opportunity. The conservative Johnson replied: "My Company would not be interested in making any investment in such a venture. With raw sugar selling as it is today, at about 2.5 cents a pound, I do not think the beet sugar industry can operate profitably." Nor did other prospective backers. The proposed company failed to raise the required capital and its plans were shelved.

Interest revived after the American Beet Sugar Company of Denver built a factory in 1926 at Grand Forks, North Dakota, close to the international boundary, providing a market to Canadian growers. Manitoba farmers—including the Trappist monastery at St. Norbert and two provincial jails—had between 400 and 500 acres of beets by 1930. They also began pressing the province to back a Manitoba sugar factory, especially after the American government in 1934 ruled that sugar from imported beets could not be sold in the United States. (The sting was removed from that ruling when the Canadian government permitted all sugar refined from Manitoba beets to be brought into Canada duty free.)

The Manitoba government and the Winnipeg Board of Trade searched diligently for investors. Heather Robertson, in her 1968 book *Sugar Farmers of Manitoba,* wrote: "A year did not pass during the dusty, wretched decade between 1930 and 1939 without some rumour or speculation of a sugar factory to be built in Manitoba. . . . It was almost as if the businessmen and politicians, desperate for something to boost the sagging economy, thought that a sugar factory could be conjured up by an act of wishful thinking. Every fly-by-night speculator who talked about sugar processing was trumpeted in the newspapers as a reliable investor."[3] In 1932 a group of Dutch businessmen tried, without success, to raise equity capital in Manitoba for a beet factory. One Dutch investor named Ferbeck made several trips to the province, once in the middle of a 1937 price war between BC Sugar and the eastern refiners, which caused him to "throw up his hands in disgust," according to Albert

Smale, a Winnipeg food broker who kept BC Sugar fully informed on each new report of a beet factory proposal.

Ernest Rogers had been wooed directly by William H. Carter, one of the ultimate backers of Manitoba Sugar. "He argues that since our Raymond factory is operating successfully, it follows that a factory in Manitoba would do likewise," Rogers wrote to W. L. Matthews in Toronto. "He overlooks the fact that the previous owners at our factory carried out all the expensive pioneering work incidental to establishing the industry on a firm footing, and lost money in so doing every year from 1925 to 1930, with the exception of 1929, when a profit of $9,000 was made."[4]

In 1934 the Grand Forks refinery, now renamed the American Crystal Sugar Company, proposed to move to Manitoba a small plant it had closed in Belmond, Iowa. However, the Canadian government would not allow the plant to be imported duty free, and the province was reluctant to lend a requested $750,000 to an American company. However, the next year the Manitoba government passed legislation offering a $600,000 bond guarantee to any firm prepared to open a factory. J. S. McDiarmid, the provincial minister of natural resources and industry, sent a copy of the bill to Ernest Rogers and invited BC Sugar to look at Manitoba. Rogers had his hands full, having just begun the second Alberta factory, but he asked T. George Wood to investigate. "When I was in Raymond," he wrote to Wood, "I mentioned the fact that it might not be desirable for our Company to possess too great a share of the sugar business in Western Canada, but on further consideration I came to the conclusion that competition for the Manitoba market between a Manitoba factory and the eastern refineries would be sufficient to offset any feelings against our company on that account. . . ." It was a prescient reflection on the danger of attracting an anti-combines prosecution.

When McDiarmid, who wanted the factory operating by 1937, pressed for a decision, Rogers responded that a rushed construction job "invariably leads to poor work at a higher cost." His engineering staff was too fully committed with designing the Picture Butte plant to design a Manitoba factory by that time. In any event, Wood's three-week investigation in Manitoba in the summer of 1935 was discouraging. "I would be reluctant to advise it as a profitable agricultural enterprise," Wood warned. Rogers, in a letter to McDiarmid, was careful to keep the door open, saying ". . . under present conditions, with the price of sugar lower than it has ever been before, we do not think there is any possibility of success in a low yield district. . . . However, if no other company enters the field, (and we can hardly see why they would under the circumstances) we may be interested once more if, and when, sugar prices return to more normal levels."

The issue of Manitoba refused to go away. In 1938, when the beet growers in Taber were pressing BC Sugar to build a third factory in Alberta, Wood surprised Rogers with a remarkable proposal. He wanted to be relieved of his duties at Canadian Sugar Factories to "promote, on a personal and friendly basis, the establishment of a competing Beet Sugar Plant in Manitoba." Wood also suggested that Rogers consider putting up half the necessary capital and letting Wood take with him six to ten key personnel from Alberta to run the plant. He believed there were two reasons why the idea should appeal to Rogers. First, it would cool down the demand from Alberta growers for another factory since the Manitoba market, which the growers presumed they could penetrate, would be filled by a new plant. Secondly, there could be no complaint of BC Sugar having a monopoly if it did not build the Manitoba factory itself. Rogers's response was frank: "I do not think our company would have anything to gain by such an arrangement." Besides, Rogers added, the price of sugar still was too low to justify another factory.

Meanwhile, Manitoba's proferred loan guarantee attracted European capitalists, including Albert Flegenheimer, a German-born American whose twenty-six factories were producing a quarter of Germany's sugar. In 1937 he was invited by the Manitoba government to Winnipeg to survey the feasibility of a beet factory. He was aware that most earlier studies argued against the project. "My father came to the opposite conclusion," says his son Ernest, now president of the Michigan Sugar Company.[5]

Because Albert Flegenheimer was a Jew, the Hitler government confiscated his factories, offering meager compensation in funds which could be spent only in Germany. He concluded a $1,130,000 contract with Hallische Maschinenfabrik in Halle (now in East Germany) for the construction and erection of a sugar factory in Manitoba.[6] Flegenheimer already had a thorough feasibility study from John Hecht, an Austrian beet sugar authority who, also a Jew, had fled to New York where he was teaching Viennese ballroom dancing in an Arthur Murray studio while looking for more appropriate work. Conventional wisdom was that Manitoba simply was too cold for sugar beets. "Manitoba? Why, don't you know that's practically on the Arctic Circle?" Hecht was told by one potential New York investor. Hecht himself was skeptical until he canvassed Manitoba farmers and realized that the long days and intense summer sunlight compensated for the shorter season. "Beets don't count the days," he admitted.[7] Hecht's report was favourable, and Flegenheimer arrived in Winnipeg in March 1939 to launch, as general manager, the Manitoba Sugar Company in partnership with Winnipeg businessmen, including contractor William Carter as president and lawyer Col. Harold Aikins as vice-president. Site preparation for the factory began in Fort Garry, a southern suburb of Winnipeg, and contracts were let for 15,000 acres of sugar beets.

Philip Rogers, who had recently become president of BC Sugar, had wanted to neutralize the competition before it was established. In November 1939 he telephoned Charles H. Houson, the president of the Canada & Dominion Sugar Company in Ontario, suggesting that the two companies jointly build a Manitoba factory. He repeated his views in a letter the next day. "I am at present rather strong on the idea of our companies entering the field and and cleaning up for some time to come the chance of competition in our most vulnerable territory." Houson disagreed: "We do not believe they [Flegenheimer et al] have anything like the money they need and it looks to us as though they are going ahead on a 'shoe-string.' "[8]

But war broke out before the German machinery for the factory could be shipped. Flegenheimer tried to have it shipped to the United States, still a neutral country, but the Canadian government refused an import permit, apparently after a clumsy and unauthorized effort by Aikins to bargain for such a permit in Ottawa. Flegenheimer and Hecht then scrambled for machinery from North American sources. "I wrote to all idle American sugar factories and have visited various factories myself," Flegenheimer wrote in a memorandum in June 1940.[9] Stearns-Roger of Denver supplied some machinery and agreed to supervise the erection. Boilers were ordered from Canadian Foster Wheeler Company, electrical motors from Canadian Westinghouse, centrifugals from Western States Machine Company in Ohio and a turbo-generator from the Elliot Company in Kansas City. It was "an industrial miracle," Hecht recalled later, that a sugar factory was actually built in Fort Garry and ready to begin its first campaign on 1 October 1940.[10]

The undelivered German machinery was to have been Flegenheimer's equity in Manitoba Sugar; the rest of his wealth was now beyond reach.[11] Consequently, the company was reorganized in November 1939 by Colonel Aikins. This chunky, tough Winnipeg lawyer, who was a director of the Imperial Bank, now assumed the presidency of Manitoba Sugar. A hero from the first war, he had an artificial leg and a false eye. He brought in three wealthy directors: H. E. Sellers, president of Federal Grain; N. L. Leach, president of Searle Grain; and E. W. Kneeland, president of Kneeland Grain. Director William Carter, briefly the original president, ran the Winnipeg Electric Company. These men held a substantial minority interest in the new company.

Flegenheimer was given a five-year contract as managing director, but Aikins had him fired in August 1940 on the pretext of a disagreement over the relationship between the company and its growers. "Had the machinery arrived, my father would have been a principal shareholder in Manitoba Sugar," Ernest Flegenheimer said. "Without it, Colonel Aikins did not want any outsiders and forced my father out."[12] Aikins was a hard man: Hecht, who had tangled with him, remarked on the colonel's compassion: "If you saw a tear, you could be sure it came from the glass eye."[13]

However, Flegenheimer had attracted investment from several European emigrés in New York. They were Baron Charles von Neuman, a Roumanian industrialist; Baron Paul Kronacher, a Belgian who had been managing director of Raffinerie Tirlemontoise but left Belgium after the Nazi invasion; and Jakob Goldschmidt, a former German bank president. Forrest Rogers, who visited the new factory in November 1940, was told by Carter—"his tongue having been somewhat loosened with Scotch"—that these financiers had between $350,000 and $400,000 invested in the company. Rogers, in a report for BC Sugar on the factory, also said that Canada Safeway Ltd. had invested $100,000 and Western Grocers Ltd., $50,000.[14] In total the new investors subscribed $1.5 million in capital, with the province of Manitoba still guaranteeing the company's $600,000 of debentures.

The company had signed contracts with 1119 growers to plant 19,968 acres of beets. That acreage included more than 4000 owned by Manitoba Sugar's shareholders and managed by Kurt Schreiber, another emigré from the Nazis. Born in Czechoslovakia, he had been the managing director of the Southern Moravian Sugar Company before coming to Canada in 1939. He joined Manitoba Sugar in 1940 and remained as the company's research agronomist until retiring in 1963. It is a measure of Schreiber's ability that a grains research project he undertook after retirement—how to coat seeds so that they could be planted in fall to germinate in spring—earned a 1975 doctorate for him, at age seventy-eight, from the University of Vienna. Schreiber was among a group of German-speaking technicians whom Flegenheimer recruited before leaving the company. Expertise in running a beet factory was hard to come by in Canada at the time: Manitoba Sugar also recruited a pair of skilled employees from Canadian Sugar Factories in Alberta, Jasper and Tom Blaskovits from Picture Butte. (Jasper later simplified his surname to Blake.)

The Fort Garry factory was fortunate that it began producing when wartime controls on sugar prices and markets protected its market in Manitoba and prevented the competitors—BC Sugar and the eastern refiners—from promptly vanquishing it. Manitoba Sugar scraped through its first year with a minor net profit—but a profit nonetheless, producing 22 million pounds of sugar.

However, the war also meant that the farmers faced a growing shortage of labour. "Suddenly, the hordes of hobos and derelicts had vanished, sucked up by industry and the armed forces," Heather Robertson noted. The novice growers also lost more than 4000 acres to insects and disease in 1940. Consequently, a number of farmers refused to renew their beet contracts, and the company was able to contract only 16,755 acres in 1941, of which, only 10,741 were harvested that unusually wet, cold autumn. Many growers lost money both years while Manitoba Sugar's profit increased.

By 1944 beet acreage in Manitoba had declined to 13,000 and, because of drought, only 9000 acres produced a crop. The factory, which had sliced 128,000 tons of beets in 1943, now had only 81,000 tons. The 1945 campaign produced even less as the growers, unable to bargain significantly higher returns from the company, began planting other crops.

That year the factory produced at half capacity and had so much extra storage space that the next year it rented some to Canadian Sugar Factories, which was back in the Manitoba market.

Postwar beet production continued to be insufficient for the factory's capacity. In 1948 only 8765 acres were harvested. J. H. Ellis, now a professor at Manitoba Agricultural College, blamed grower ineptitude. The growers in Manitoba lacked the experience that those in Alberta had acquired. In 1945 Kurt Schreiber had begun an instructional quarterly, the *Manitoba Beet Growers Bulletin,* which gave farmers much-needed advice. Still, average production in Manitoba, at 8.1 tons an acre, was only two-thirds of what Ellis believed possible.

One individual who learned first-hand the economics of growing beets was Ted Zacharkow, who joined Manitoba Sugar in 1944 as a junior office boy and rose to become its accountant and office manager. In 1948 he persuaded his skeptical brother-in-law to let him use ten acres of his farm for what turned out to be a two-year trial in beet growing. The enthusiastic Zacharkow corralled friends and family for weekend thinning and hoeing, expensively lubricated with free beer and food. A meticulous record keeper, Zacharkow noted all his expenses and his receipts. The profit for two years' labour was $28.28. "I'd had my fill of it," he admitted.[15]

In 1949 the factory resorted to desperate measures to produce enough sugar. At the cost of prohibitive freight charges, it imported and refined 10,000 tons of raw cane sugar, installing additional refining equipment which was not removed until after BC Sugar acquired the company. Alan Robertson was alerted in April, when Montreal refiner Lewis Seidensticker telephoned to warn that the sugar cargo was on its way to Manitoba. Robertson was outraged that the Sugar Administration would even allocate raw cane sugar to a beet factory when it still limited BC Sugar's market share in Manitoba. BC Sugar's Alberta subsidiary, now building its Taber factory, had contracted 32,000 acres of sugar beets, enough to produce 110 million pounds of sugar, a large quantity for the Prairies to absorb. Robertson complained angrily to administration official Tom Climo in Montreal: "Isn't it rather an extraordinary thing, Tom, to give the Manitoba Sugar Company, a beet company that has never refined a single pound of cane, 18 million pounds of sugar and put us out of that market without any chance of getting rid of our normal distribution there?" Climo defended the allocation, adding that it would be hard to tell the Fort Garry factory not to sell sugar in its own market. Robertson exploded: "Well, we were in the Manitoba market a hell of a long time before the Manitoba Sugar Company were." Climo's boss, Reginald Noble, asked BC Sugar to withdraw its cane sugar from the Manitoba market and only sell beet sugar. Philip Rogers told Sir William Rook, head of Czarnikow, in a phone conversation: "I am paying no attention to it. . . . we are going to try to sell as much in there as we can."[16]

BC Sugar fought hard, competing in the market once sugar controls were lifted late in 1949. The company was tipped off confidentially by Czarnikow's Montreal agent, Leslie Palmer, that Manitoba Sugar treasurer Emil J. Kramer had been in Montreal in early January, talking to sugar brokers. Alan Robertson thanked Palmer and noted that BC Sugar had been effective behind the scenes in stirring up opposition to Manitoba Sugar's cane refining. "As you probably know, we have been putting pretty steady pressure on them through our growers to their growers to discourage cane refining in the Manitoba plant." The scheme worked.

The 1950 Red River flood was a catastrophe for the sugar factory. When the river, less than half a mile east of the factory, began rising dangerously that spring, employees frantically built sandbag dikes to protect the site, especially the warehouse with its tons of sugar, already bagged and ready for shipment. The warehouse and factory doorways were reinforced with timbers and secured against water with sandbags. As well, the doors between the factory and the warehouse were similarly secured. But everyone overlooked one small flume used each fall to carry beets into the factory and when the river flooded, water entered the factory this way. On the morning of 7 May the entire factory was surrounded by water and remained isolated for two weeks. Office staff were relocated to the Aikins law office downtown.

The financial disruption caused by the flood made it even more difficult for the factory to find the money for urgent capital improvements. William Hetherington, when he took over as general manager in August 1955, was distressed at some of the shortcomings. For example, in 1940 the company scrimped by omitting a pulp dryer from its design. But midway through the construction of the factory, it was realized that piles of wet pulp would quickly smell offensively rank. "They had to find enough money somewhere or other to come through with a pulp dryer," Hetherington said. "And they didn't have much money so they put a wooden shack over the building and the darned thing kept catching fire."[17] BC Sugar had to spend $75,000 to replace that shack.

Nor had Manitoba Sugar established a reputation for quality. Customers who had been forced to overlook poor sugar during rationing now looked for other sources. Hetherington found that the Fort Garry factory "was doing a very poor job at refining"; it was leaving molasses traces in the sugar, causing cloudiness and discolouration in clear soft drinks and in some other foods. Candy maker Paulin Chambers complained when it used the factory's sugar to make white peppermints. "They would turn a little yellow if the sugar wasn't well refined," Hetherington said. "It was just a question of poor technique in the factory. That was one of the things that BC Sugar was able to improve tremendously in Manitoba."[18]

Manitoba Sugar's difficulties between 1940 and its 1956 takeover by BC Sugar were exacerbated by rivalry among the owners, which found its way into the factory.[19] There were three factions contending for authority. The Winnipeg shareholders, while holding only about 20 per cent of the company, were led by the steely Colonel Aikins, who remained president until 1952 and was succeeded by his law partner, Sir Charles Tupper. Despite his busy law practice and his other interests, Aikins usually came to the factory at least three times a week. Also looking out for the Winnipeg group's interests was sales manager John McDiarmid, Jr., son of the politician who had promoted the factory in the 1930s. Baron von Neuman's interests were guarded by the company treasurer Kramer, who jealously insisted that all the paperwork flow across his desk. (He sought the general manager's position when BC Sugar took over but left when Hetherington got it.) Baron Paul Kronacher was represented by a Belgian, René Abras, a knowledgeable beet factory technician who arrived after the war and who, despite an extremely poor grasp of English, was made general manager. Siding with the Kronacher group was plant superintendent Adolf Zenzinger, a tall and austere First World War German army officer. The shareholder cliques failed to agree on selling their shares to each other, creating the opportunity for BC Sugar to negotiate for control.

"In my opinion," Zacharkow asserts, "the best thing that ever happened to Manitoba Sugar was when B.C. took us over. You knew where you were at and what direction you were going. You did not know that with the others running it because of the infighting."[20]

16

They Disorganize the Market

THE COMPANY TANGLES WITH THE COMBINES BRANCH.

After wartime sugar controls ended in 1947, the Manitoba market became "a cut-throat race," in the words of Alan Robertson, BC Sugar's vice-president and sales manager. Not only had the Eastern refiners re-entered the market but, after Canadian Sugar Factories opened the Taber factory in 1950, an additional forty million to fifty million pounds of sugar were being offered to Prairie consumers. Robertson's strategy was to cut prices until the Eastern refiners found Manitoba unattractive and pulled back. "It was open to BC Sugar to do nothing and when Eastern sugar is dumped on the Prairie market, to abandon Manitoba and part or all of Saskatchewan [and] close down one or two of its Alberta plants," the company explained in a brief prepared later when it came under a protracted Anti-Combines investigation. Because price wars flared continually in Manitoba and eastern Saskatchewan during the early 1950s, the Department of Justice in Ottawa pounced when BC Sugar finally did acquire Manitoba Sugar in 1955. The anti-combines investigators believed they had a clear example of a large company gobbling a small one to eliminate nettlesome competition.

Manitoba Sugar at this time was obtaining from Eastern refineries all of the speciality sugars it was not producing at Fort Garry. BC Sugar decided to capture this business by offering to package speciality products for the Fort Garry factory under Manitoba Sugar's label. Forrest Rogers recounted what happened next: "This of course involved correspondence with [Manitoba Sugar secretary Emil J.] Kramer and was close to success when Kramer suggested to Alan that we might go one step further and buy out the company, in other words von Neuman had got fed up and in his old age was anxious to sell."[1] The idea appealed to Rogers. "We felt that by owning Manitoba Sugar Company we would strengthen our competitive position with our eastern competitors," he told the Combines tribunal later.[2]

A change in the control of Manitoba Sugar became possible in mid-1954 after the death of Colonel Aikins, the former president, whose estate included 5700 of Manitoba Sugar's 34,000 common shares. Aikins had been a member of a Winnipeg group of shareholders, with a total of 11,000 shares, bound under a pooling agreement not to sell to anyone but each other before June 1956. Aikins had formed the pool to prevent von Neuman, who owned 13,200 shares from buying more. But by 1954 the elderly and conservative von Neuman, convinced that the Eastern refiners would become devastating competitors after the St. Lawrence Seaway opened in 1957, had decided to sell his shares.

The pooling agreement blocked BC Sugar from buying Aikins's shares and those of others in the Winnipeg group. But in April 1955 BC Sugar paid about $1 million to buy von Neuman's shares (for $75 a share) and a handful of others, for a solid 40 per cent interest. (When it finally bought the other 60 per cent several years later, the remaining shareholders succeeded in levering $100 a share from BC Sugar. It was a generous payment. Robertson believed, when he tried to buy John Hecht's 114-share block in 1955, that the stock was "actually worth $60 on a book value basis.")

Forrest Rogers, en route to Europe for a two-month holiday, concluded the purchase of von Neuman's shares in person in New York with the baron and his son. This surprised Kronacher, who only owned 4000 Manitoba Sugar shares and had wanted to buy von Neuman's position. He soon was creating dissension, either directly or through René Abras, his factory management representative. Robertson relayed all the gossip in letters to the vacationing Forrest Rogers: "Abras is running around like Dracula, as Joe [Kramer] says, trying to start intrigues. . . ." Kronacher tracked Rogers down in Vienna with a telephoned proposal that they operate Manitoba Sugar in partnership. Rogers was not interested but agreed reluctantly to have lunch with the Belgian in London in June. From Vancouver, Robertson passed on the warning from one of Manitoba Sugar's Winnipeg shareholders, lawyer John MacAulay, that Kronacher was slippery. "Funnily enough," Robertson wrote, "MacAulay sounded a note of warning to anybody dealing with Kronacher and said that he (MacAulay) never saw Kronacher by himself but always had somebody with him as a witness. The reason being that Kronacher is liable to claim having been given certain guarantees when such is not the case and a witness is a definite protection." Robertson regretted that he could not be in London at Rogers's side.[3] Over lunch, Kronacher offered a bizarre proposal: the Belgian, in return for retaining a 30 per cent interest in Manitoba Sugar, wanted BC Sugar to finance 50 per cent of a cane sugar plantation he was developing in the Belgian Congo. He also suggested that William Hetherington, who was just returning from running BC Sugar's recently sold Dominican plantation, become the manager in the Congo. Rogers, irritated to be pursued on his vacation to consider such a scheme, turned it down. "That was the last I ever saw of Kronacher and when I got back to Vancouver I charged up my expenses for the London visit to [BC Sugar] because it had been no holiday for me," Rogers wrote later.[4]

With the co-operation of Manitoba Sugar's Winnipeg shareholders, Forrest Rogers became the company's president in July 1955, and BC Sugar took over management of the Fort Garry factory. There was outraged reaction in the House of Commons. M. J. Coldwell, leader of the Co-operative Commonwealth Federation and a member from Regina, protested that this combination would neutralize the competition that had been assuring low sugar prices on the Prairies. He called for an Anti-Combines investigation, and Justice Minister Stuart Garson, a Liberal, acquiesced in late July 1955.

Combines investigators, accompanied by an RCMP officer, descended on Manitoba Sugar, seizing a vast quantity of documents in what Hetherington, the new assistant general manager, described as a fishing expedition highly disruptive to a company carrying on business. "We had to get an order from a judge to be able to go down and take the records and photostat them," Hetherington said. "I spent all one weekend in a lawyer's office uptown, photostating over 4000 documents that we needed for the continuing operation of our business. They didn't come in with anything specific—they just came in and went through everything and walked away with boxes of records. It was a hell of a job refiling the stuff too when we eventually got it back."[5] BC Sugar's Vancouver office also was raided twice.

The quasi-judicial hearing before the Combines tribunal in Winnipeg in 1956 was one of the most difficult experiences in Forrest Rogers's business career. Born in 1912, the youngest of seven Rogers children, Forrest's career could be said to date from 1914 when, as he recalled later, his father showed him the cube machine at the refinery. Unlike his brothers, he was educated entirely in the West, at Brentwood College on Vancouver Island and at the University of British Columbia where he received a degree in chemical engineering. (He was the only one of the four boys to complete university.) Forrest became a full-time employee of BC Sugar in 1935 and quickly accepted the responsibilities thrust on him by Ernest's death and later, by Philip's illness, until in 1953, he became president. While he was president for the next twenty years and chairman until 1977, Forrest found the Combines investigation as distasteful as anything he would experience. "I think Forrie was uncomfortable," said Hetherington. "He was never a comfortable public personality anyway. He wasn't on the stand for too long because Alan Robertson had done most of the negotiating for the purchase of the shares of the company."[6] The Restrictive Trade Practices Commission presumed that BC Sugar's takeover could have no motive other than eliminating competition. Some of Robertson's testimony would have reinforced that view. "They disorganize the market," Robertson said of Manitoba Sugar. "You never know what they are doing. . . . In the first place, they might go bust. . . . They would have a lot of distress sugar floating around. In the second place, eastern refiners might buy them up." Forrest Rogers tried to persuade the investigators that BC Sugar was acting from reasons which were as valid as they were lawful. "Apart from the fact that we had some money to invest from our operations in Santo Domingo, there are two basic motives." First, he argued that the Western sugar producers, united under one owner, would better be able to fight off the anticipated competition from the new Redpath refinery then being built in Toronto.

Secondly, BC Sugar believed it could operate Manitoba Sugar much more efficiently and more profitably. "We were actually somewhat surprised to find out how correct we were," Rogers said.

The company came away from the hearings believing it had made a convincing case. Therefore, when Kronacher decided to sell his shares late in 1956, before the Combines tribunal had published its report, BC Sugar bought them, firmly establishing its control. At the time, there were seven sugar companies with eleven refineries or factories across Canada. BC sugar now operated all five western plants: the refinery in Vancouver, three beet factories in southern Alberta and the newly acquired Fort Garry plant. Hetherington said: "There was no directive or anything of that nature that suggested the company could not buy additional shares. However, we were roundly criticized in the press for having as they called it 'flaunted' the government." The Restrictive Trade Practices Commission report, which Garson released in January 1957, criticized BC Sugar for "completely eliminating the competition of its most important rival in the market in Western Canada" and recommended prosecution. "It is our opinion that the proposed merger should be renounced. We believe that the public interest would be best served if Manitoba Sugar operated as an independent company with no share interest in it or control over it held, directly or indirectly, by any other Canadian sugar refining company."[7]

BC Sugar sought to avoid prosecution. "There was a lot of discussion obviously what the company's position would be if we had had to divest ourselves of our interest," Hetherington said. "Quite frankly we would have been in a situation of having a fire sale." Hetherington now began to receive feelers from other companies, including Beatrice Foods, the American giant. All were sniffing a bargain.[8]

In October 1957 BC Sugar advised its 1600 shareholders that it was considering giving them the Manitoba Sugar shares in proportion to their interest in BC Sugar. An American sugar refiner, Harry Havemeyer, whose grandfather had once employed B. T. Rogers, was added to Manitoba Sugar's board. These moves would have diffused voting control, but they did not meet Ottawa's concern about diminished competition. The share distribution did not proceed, and in July 1958 E. Davie Fulton, the Justice Minister of the new Conservative government, decided to take BC Sugar to court. Horace Havemeyer Jr., Harry's brother, passed on to

Forrest Rogers the opinion of another Canadian refiner that "your chances of success in this case were minor." Since the Havemeyers had begun accumulating BC Sugar shares since 1956, they were acutely interested in the outcome.[9] Ironically, while the case was argued before the Manitoba Court of Queen's Bench in 1960, increasing volumes of Ontario sugar poured into the Manitoba market. That led Rogers to suggest in a letter to Horace Havemeyer that "only a lunatic" would accuse BC Sugar of having gained a monopoly in Manitoba.[10]

The case, the first brought before a Manitoba court since the Combines Investigation Act was passed in 1923, was one in a succession of such prosecutions which the federal government launched after World War II. BC Sugar retained John J. Robinette, a partner in the Toronto law firm of McCarthy & McCarthy and one of Canada's most distinguished defence lawyers. Initially a criminal lawyer, the versatile Robinette added corporate law to his repertoire in the 1950s. His first major defence was on behalf of one of several companies that manufactured and distributed dental products and that had been charged with having conspired to lessen competition unduly. All of the accused companies were acquitted by the Supreme Court of Ontario. Subsequently, Robinette was retained by one of the companies in an Anti-Combines prosecution of the fine paper industry; in a 1953 action against the tire industry; and a 1955 action against wire and cable producers. Only in the fine paper case did the government succeed in its prosecution. In 1959 Robinette was one of two leading counsel representing Canadian Breweries Ltd. in its successful defence of charges under the Combines Investigation Act. BC Sugar had retained the best Combines lawyer in the land. His fee was $35,000, about half of BC Sugar's $80,000 legal expenses generated by the Restrictive Trade Practices Commission hearing and the subsequent court case.[11]

Robinette had been admitted to the Manitoba bar just so he could argue the case. Hetherington's first impression of the Toronto lawyer left him with misgivings. In later years a tall, spare man, Robinette then was overweight. "He was a cheerful fellow," Hetherington recalled. "And you wondered if he was doing anything or not. But when he got up to the lectern and started talking, he never missed a nickel's worth of anything. He had absorbed everything. . . . and he went for 36 hours and he did a masterful job." The case was argued entirely from documents, the government filing 590 exhibits. "The documents were voluminous, running to thousands of pages," Chief Justice E. K. Williams remarked in his judgement. "The earliest of the seized documents is dated October 7, 1926, and in the documents there are references to events happening before that date." Forrest Rogers wrote later: "Robinette built his case around evidence introduced by the Crown, so nobody from our company was required to enter the witness box to identify material and thus we were not faced with cross examination."[12] In a letter to Horace Havemeyer in April 1960, Rogers recounted that Robinette had taken only an hour and a half to introduce his documentary evidence "and rather upset the prosecutor, who had apparently relished the idea of cross-examining Alan and me at some length."[13]

Robinette's genius was in turning the Crown's evidence against the government. Forrest Rogers later recalled a conversation he had had with the lawyer between the first and second seizures of documents from BC Sugar offices. Robinette casually asked whether his client had considered shutting Manitoba Sugar after buying it. "I told him that that was economically ridiculous, to which he answered, 'Can you prove that?' I then returned to Vancouver and asked Allan Dunlop to make a financial study of this suggestion. His study was most complete in detail and left no doubt that closure of MSC would be completely stupid. Then out of the blue the RCMP descended once again and stole papers out of our files, including Dunlop's report on the stupidity of closing down MSC."[14] When the Crown entered this study among its evidence, Robinette seized on it as a key to the defence.

"The essence of the case," Robinette wrote later, "was that charges against the company were under the merger or monopoly sections of the then Combines Investigation Act and not under the sections dealing with conspiracy."[15] The act proscribes a variety of business practices, perhaps the most serious being price-fixing (which was the conspiracy pinned on the fine paper companies). "There was no conspiracy or agreement between the accused and the Manitoba company," Chief Justice Williams found. He was irritated that the government tried to insinuate price-fixing in its evidence. Price-fixing would not stick because it was not being done. "The introduction of this argument by the Crown points up what in my respectful opinion is a fundamental weakness of this branch of the case," Williams wrote. "Not only must it be remembered that the price of sugar is, in the final analysis, a world price, but also that sugar is a world product."[16]

The indictment did accuse BC Sugar—by having acquired Manitoba Sugar—of engaging in a "merger, trust or monopoly which has operated or was likely to operate to the detriment or against the interest of the public." The combine which allegedly resulted from the acquisition enabled BC Sugar to control "substantially or completely" the sugar business across Western Canada. These were also serious charges: violations of the Combines Act are regarded as criminal violations. If BC Sugar had been convicted, it would not only have been fined but Forrest Rogers and Alan Robertson could have been sent to jail. Yet if the sugar prices were not being fixed, it was difficult to find the public detriment in BC Sugar's acquisition of Manitoba Sugar. There was no question that BC Sugar had consolidated its dominance of the sugar business in Western Canada by acquiring Manitoba Sugar. But its actions were entirely legal, there being nothing in the Combines Act, Williams noted, to stop a company from buying a competitor.

"In the popular sense of the word, the accused might be said to have had and to have a monopoly of sugar refining in British Columbia and Alberta," wrote Williams. "Apparently no one else manifested a real desire at any time to enter the sugar refining business in British Columbia and Alberta. There may have been many reasons, probably all economic, why this was not done. It was open, and still is open, to any one to do so."

"The Crown," Williams concluded, "has not satisfied me beyond a reasonable doubt, even if all the evidence it tendered were admissible, that the merger in question destroyed or even limited competition. . . . The Crown has not satisfied me beyond a reasonable doubt that the 'merger, trust or monopoly has operated or was likely to operate to the detriment or against the interest of the public'. . . ."[17]

The Crown filed a notice of appeal to the Manitoba Court of Appeal. The company fought to have the appeal withdrawn because the Combines investigation and the subsequent trial already had delayed the major capital investment so urgently needed at the sugar factory. "We went to the Manitoba government," said Hetherington, who had come to know provincial attorney-general Sterling Lyon personally. "And we went to the Ottawa government. . . ." Justice Minister Fulton was told

BC Sugar had had enough with a case that was not going to serve the public interest if it proceeded. The Manitoba beet growers chimed in with the same message. "We cannot understand the reasoning or fathom the motives that are prolonging the uncertainty that has surrounded our industry for nearly five years," the growers' association said in a brief to the province. "Is it possible the Manitoba sugar industry is being made to suffer in order that the Department of Justice may carry out extended tests of its combines laws?" Willow Forrester, then the association's president, also went to Ottawa to see Fulton. The Justice Minister began the interview by assuring Forrester that the case would go to the Supreme Court. But by the end of the meeting, Forrester had convinced Fulton that Manitoba Sugar's future as an independent factory was dubious.[18] The Justice Minister also had other pressure. "It was not until years later that I learned that the judge himself had persuaded Ottawa to call a halt," Rogers wrote in his 1983 memoir.[19] In late January 1961, Fulton dropped the appeal.

The Combines investigation and the subsequent trial had interrupted the modernization of the Fort Garry factory. "From the time they started working on this Combines case until the time we were completely cleared of it, it was over four years," Hetherington said. "We had plans on the drawing boards for things like bulk storage bins and packaging equipment and a very big expenditure to bring the factory up to modern standards." All of these improvements remained in abeyance, BC Sugar understandably being unwilling to commit funds to a company that it might have been forced to sell. "The whole development of Manitoba Sugar was retarded by the Combines case," Hetherington insisted. "When we were clear of it, why we were able to go right ahead."[20]

17

We Were a Great Offender

THE COMPANY TAKES CHARGE OF THE FORT GARRY SUGAR BEET FACTORY.

In the summer of 1962, when the first three of the Fort Garry factory's towering bulk sugar siloes were erected, Neon Products proposed blazing Manitoba Sugar Company's name across them with a sign 6 feet high and 125 feet long. The sign's advertising value appealed to William Hetherington, who recommended it to the Vancouver headquarters. Forrest Rogers shot back a veto. "I agree with you that the public in general doesn't seem to know where our factory is," he wrote, "but perhaps that is just as well, in view of the stench that arises from the settling ponds."

The factory then was in the midst of its epic struggle to bring its effluent discharge under control. BC Sugar, when taking over the factory in 1955, had underrated the pollution problem despite being warned by Sir Charles Tupper, Manitoba Sugar's outgoing president, that patching up grower relations and tackling pollution were the most pressing challenges. BC Sugar vice-president Alan Robertson had relayed Tupper's warning to Forrest Rogers: ". . . the City of Winnipeg claim that the Manitoba Sugar Company had been polluting the Red River for fifteen years and want a cash settlement of $230,000 for this past pollution. . . . I suppose something will eventually be worked out on this but it is not one of our immediate problems."[1]

Hetherington's first priority after becoming Manitoba Sugar's assistant general manager on 1 August 1955 was repairing the factory's dismal relations with the growers. "I always figured that was the easiest part of the job because when things are so bad, anything you do has got to be better," he said. "The difficulties between the company and growers were so severe that the growers had threatened to boycott growing beets."[2]

The outgoing management's adversarial and mean-spirited approach had fostered intense distrust of the company among the growers. John MacAulay, who remained on the board of directors after BC Sugar assumed management, had urged Robertson to dismiss Emil J. Kramer, the treasurer, because the growers "hated him with a bitter hate." Robertson, who was considering dumping general manager René Abras and promoting Kramer, confronted the treasurer about his relationship with the growers. "He quite agreed," Robertson told Forrest Rogers, "but he said that as his instructions came from [Baron] Kronacher to be immovably tough, he had no alternative but to be bitchy."

The baron also had given devious instructions. In 1954 Manitoba Sugar tried to form a rival beet growers' association and win a concession-laced contract while the two top officers of the Manitoba Beet Growers Association were in Denver at a conference. The resulting breakdown of beet contract negotiations forced Manitoba Minister of Agriculture R. D. Robertson, at the request of the growers, to mediate directly with Kronacher. "He is a very difficult man to have a discussion with," Robertson told the growers. "He feels he represents the ruling class."[3] Although Robertson extracted no concessions from the baron, he prevented the growers from striking. With perfect weather, they produced their largest crop yet, 140,000 tons of beets. Robertson again had to intervene when the 1955 contract was negotiated. This time the growers won the right to have their own accountant audit the company's figures.

The growers were now so unhappy that, in February 1955, they began examining the feasibility of building a competing sugar factory in southern Manitoba. This investigation and the audit of Manitoba Sugar both were shelved once BC Sugar took over management of the factory because Hetherington, at the direction of Forrest Rogers, moved decisively to improve grower relations, among other measures by showing them the factory's accounts. "Nobody had ever showed the growers the books before," Hetherington said.[4]

Author Heather Robertson described the changed atmosphere for the 1956 beet negotiations: "BC Sugar settled the matter in a few days and offered the growers the best share of the profits they had ever received; in fact, the farmers got what they had been asking for all these years." The beet contract was completely rewritten. "The old contract was a very complicated affair," BC Sugar's Alan Robertson later told the Combines inquiry. "It was so complicated, in fact, that 90 per cent of the growers did not like it because they could not understand it. Frankly, it took a long time for us to understand it."[5]

The good relations endured. A joint company-grower research committee was set up in 1975. The Manitoba Beet Growers Association has participated in numerous capital programs including the installation of packaging machinery, the installation of equipment to produce liquid sugar, and the construction of two additional storage siloes (which fortunately came just in time to handle the immense 1975 crop). Typical of the Manitoba growers' business-minded attitude was the way they promoted the consumption of their beet sugar. The farmers were growing larger crops, but a significant amount of eastern refined cane sugar continued to sell in Manitoba at premium prices. This reflected the old bias against beet sugar: even the wives of growers were found to be buying cane sugar for making preserves.[6] The bias was aggravated by the inconsistent quality of the sugar the factory had been making. Strangely, this technical deficiency was at odds with Manitoba Sugar's crisp white and blue consumer packages which were so much more attractive than the dowdy brown kraft bags BC Sugar was still using. Hetherington immediately began pressing Vancouver to update its packaging: "It is my observation that packaging for the whole sugar industry has not received the attention that it gets in other industries," he told Forrest Rogers in September 1956.

In 1957 the Manitoba Beet Growers Association hired as publicist a retired University of Manitoba English professor, Clark R. Hopper. He prepared a twenty-five-minute film on Manitoba-grown sugar that was shown in schools and to other audiences around the province. He wrote and distributed a series of pamphlets and made speeches whenever he could find an audience. He had school home economics departments try beet sugar in cooking and preserving, demonstrating that it was the equal of cane sugar. In one of his most effective pitches, he provided a dozen sugar beet seeds to any school child who wanted to grow them, thus influencing the sugar buying habits of the parents through their children. As well, in 1957, the growers and the company agreed that 164 4H club members in Manitoba each would get contracts to grow one acre of sugar beets.[7] Hopper retired from his second career in 1966, after having the growers' association sponsor Heather Robertson to write *Sugar Farmers of Manitoba.*

The condition of the Fort Garry factory when BC Sugar bought it reflected its having been built and run on a shoestring. Nine days after settling into his Winnipeg job, Hetherington recommended an immediate study of the warehouse and packing room. "From my observations this is possibly the most difficult and inefficient part of the whole factory operation," he wrote Forrest Rogers. "It is hardly necessary to point out the inadequacy of our sugar handling equipment." Peter Cherniavsky, then the general superintendent of the refinery in Vancouver, had already completed a comparison of Manitoba's packaging costs with those in the Alberta factories and was startled to find the Manitoba costs "so consistently much higher that we had to doubt their accuracy." Some of Hetherington's more urgent requirements—conveyor systems and pallets for the warehouse—were provided, but he had to wait until 1961, after the Combines case had ended and BC Sugar's ownership was secure, before a new shipping warehouse was built.

The factory's working conditions also were poor. A provincial safety inspector, after a 1955 tour, produced a long list of deficiencies. The new owners formed a safety committee in January 1956, and established a budget for improvements. Early that year Hetherington also fired Roy McLellan, the plant superintendent who had been there when BC Sugar took over. A Scot whose lucrative sideline was appearing on stage as magician Raymond Ash, McLellan did not take orders well from his new superiors. He was replaced by Ross Humphreys, a soon-to-retire superintendent from Picture Butte. Manitoba Sugar also advertised in Winnipeg for another engineer. William Willison, a mechanical engineer from Qu'Appelle, Saskatchewan, who was then unhappy in his job with a Winnipeg meat packer, remembered that the advertisement ran for some time before he applied. "The old Manitoba Sugar did not have a good reputation," Willison said later, explaining his hesitation.[8] When he started as plant engineer in February 1956, he was also surprised at the condition of the plant. Except for the terrazzo in the washrooms, the factory's interior floors were wood and were far more difficult to keep clean than was prudent for a food processing plant. "There is an almost complete absence of such safety guards and devices in the factory and many very hazardous working conditions exist," Willison complained to BC Sugar's chief engineer Royce Craig in Vancouver. In May Willison was authorized to install safety guards.

As Sir Charles Tupper had warned, the Fort Garry factory was under increasing pressure from the Greater Winnipeg Sanitation District to bring its waste water discharge under control. Since 1940 the factory during the campaign had been discharging directly into the Red River about four million gallons of effluent daily, mainly the waste water that had been used to transport and wash sugar beets. It was so laden with mud and plant materials that the discharge had begun to build a small island which the company had to remove. As well, the factory's waste process waters contained plant material and minor amounts of sugar. This rich broth created a heavy oxygen demand which competed with other life in the slow, meandering river. In 1954 the Sanitation District's tough and conscientious manager, N. S. (Nate) Bubbis, ordered Manitoba Sugar to clean up and start paying for each gallon discharged from the factory. The fee potentially amounted to $20,000 a year. Unimpressed with the progress, Bubbis in July 1955 gave the factory only a temporary one-year permit to discharge its effluent.[9] Pollution abatement was a new science when BC Sugar bought the factory. As Willison noted later, the meat packing plants were directing into the river effluent far more objectionable than mud, sugar and beet residue.[10]

Hetherington gave Bubbis a firm undertaking to deal with the factory's discharge. "There was no question we were a great offender," Hetherington said.[11] After the 1955 campaign, Bubbis told the factory that it was not getting a temporary licence that fall unless further measures were taken. Acting on information supplied him by the vengeful former plant superintendent Roy McLellan, he also accused the company of having discharged more into the river during the campaign than had been admitted. Hetherington was outraged since he had uncovered a production deception in the plant which he blamed on McLellan and which added to the unmeasured discharge into the river. Chief chemist William Blankenbach came from Vancouver to install measuring devices in the factory. In April he and Hetherington met Bubbis and soothed the official's suspicions. "He was tough but straight," Hetherington remembered Bubbis. "We had a good relationship."

Hetherington reported new demands to Vancouver in May 1957. Forrest Rogers grumbled: "It is rather disturbing to think that there seems to be no end to the improvements that Mr. Bubbis may require as the years go by."[12] The company doubled the capacity of its settling ponds, but neither Hetherington nor the city saw this as a long-term solution. "They would have no objection to 'lagoons' but believe we would run into 'odour' troubles with the municipality," Hetherington reported to Vancouver. The odour of fermentation and decomposition in the settling ponds became, in fact, the most persistent social problem for the factory. It had been built at a site once so far from downtown Winnipeg that the employees hunted ducks on the property in the fall. But in the 1950s, residential development in the suburb of Fort Garry brought neighbours who found the pungent odours hard to take. In 1961 Hetherington reported to Forrest Rogers: "Last year over forty complaints were registered with the Municipality in respect of our odours and waste discharge and it was only through the co-operation of municipal officials and councillors that we were saved more trouble than was actually encountered." Manitoba Sugar now also came in for criticism in the newspapers as a drought reduced the flow of the river and aggravated the discharge problem. A waste water management system installed that year was of some help, but measurements of the factory effluent's BOD (biological oxygen demand) remained high in 1962 and 1963 before Manitoba Sugar was able to get the upper hand on the problem. Two developments about the same time accounted for this.

After the conclusion of the Combines case, BC Sugar had begun the urgently required modernization of the Manitoba factory. This included in 1963 the replacement of the diffusion battery in which batches of sliced beets were soaked. This process generated a great deal of waste water. The new continuous diffuser was designed to recover what had been waste liquids. The impact was significant: Peter Cherniavsky estimated it halved the factory's pollution load on the Red River. The BOD count dropped by 20 per cent in 1964 and then plunged dramatically to a low reading well within the city's requirements.

The dramatic plunge reflected the second development, the installation of a flume water recirculation system for the 1965 campaign. On a working vacation in Britain, Hetherington had visited a beet factory at Poppleton, near York, that had developed a method of re-using the water required for transporting and washing beets. Hetherington's rough sketches and ideas were turned over to Willison and Blankenbach who adapted the British method to Manitoba. A heavy dose of lime added to the water speeded the settling of solids and made it feasible to recycle the flume water. The mud was settled in ponds on factory property and not discharged into the river. The effluent reduction was so significant that, by the nomination of the Sanitation District, Manitoba Sugar in 1966 won a prestigious pollution abatement award from the Canada Institute on Pollution Control. "They have done a tremendous job," Alex Penman—who had succeeded Bubbis—told the Winnipeg *Tribune* which reported in May 1967 that the Red River's industrial pollution load now was under control. It had cost the company $1.5 million to install the system. (A decade later, the same system was installed at the Taber beet factory in Alberta to reduce effluent dischange into the Oldman River.)

If Fort Garry's BOD count was under control, the odour problem was not. During May 1970 the municipal health officials received nineteen complaints "with respect to strong odours similar to those of a hog farm" from the factory property. The source was the ponds where the mud from the wash water had settled and been left to dry. Late spring rains created puddles, and warming temperatures caused smelly bacterial action. Chlorine treatments were effective only until the next rain created more puddles. Hetherington promised municipal officials that, after the next campaign, the company would bulldoze the sludge from the ponds while it was frozen and either spread it elsewhere on the factory property or haul it away. Malcolm Faviell, the refinery's chief chemist, in June 1970 advised Hetherington: "As this odour problem is likely to be a perennial one of considerable public interest, I would recommend that we have it solved promptly and permanently. . . ." Removal of frozen sludge proved expensive, with earthmoving equipment continually breaking down in the harsh winter conditions. But as experience was gained in handling the frozen mud, cleaning the ponds during the winter proved to be the practical solution to a difficult problem.

The 1970 odour complaints caught the attention of a Manitoba government agency, the Clean Environment Commission, which had found that the factory did not have a licence covering emissions into the air. A beet factory's pulp dryer generates a large vapour plume, particularly on crisp wintery days. The toasty odour is not unpleasant, but the pulp dust may settle to earth as a fine residue. Willison once was taking an inspector on a tour around the factory yard when an unexpected wind shift dumped dust on the yard. Willison barely kept a straight face as he watched dust accumulate in the brim of the inspector's Homburg.[13] The company did not regard the dust as dangerous; however, it was a social irritant, especially when it fell on neighbourhood laundry. At the instruction of the commission, the factory installed a recirculation system to reduce its emissions.

The achievement to make the factory a good neighbour in an urban setting has been impressive. In 1977, when the Manitoba system was being adapted to Taber, Peter Cherniavsky noted: "We bought the Manitoba Sugar Company in 1955 at which time pollution abatement was in its infancy. Much of the technology had not been developed so it was at least 10 years before we had essentially developed a system to meet the required standards."

18

We Have a Hornet's Nest on Our Hands

THE PAINFUL CLOSURE OF TWO FACTORIES.

Ernest Rogers needed only four months to buy the Raymond sugar factory in 1931. But in 1959, when the factory began losing money consistently, it took Forrest Rogers four confrontational years to close it.

Throughout the 1950s, while the acreage of sugar beets had expanded east and north of Lethbridge, there had been a gradual decline in the number of beet growers supplying the Raymond plant, chiefly because the alkaline soil in parts of the area was not ideal for the crop. Only 150 growers remained in the area in 1963, down from 230 in 1945. The Raymond factory, old and small, had become the high-cost factory among the three plants under the Canadian Sugar Factories umbrella. In the 1958 campaign, the manufacturing cost for a 100-pound bag of sugar was 60 per cent greater at Raymond than at Taber.[1] The irony was that Raymond that year had sliced 144,000 tons of beets, its largest slice since 1949.[2] Even at a high rate of processing, the factory no longer was efficient. In 1959 the company developed a plan for moving Raymond's operations and employees to the Taber and Picture Butte plants, leaving only a warehouse and packaging plant run by a handful of employees. Forrest Rogers circulated this study among senior executives in Vancouver and Alberta, adding in his covering letter: "I think it is very likely that by the start of the next campaign we will have reached the conclusion that it is no longer economical to operate the Raymond factory and we may then wish to make a public statement to that effect."

Immediate resistance to closing Raymond came from Frank Taylor, the plant's original agricultural superintendent, and now the general manager of Canadian Sugar Factories. An austere and widely respected Mormon, Taylor for many years was a member of Raymond's town council and had served one term as mayor. The thirty-four beet campaigns he had gone through at the Raymond factory, as he wrote Rogers on 2 May 1959, "represent quite a part of my life's interest." The news that BC Sugar planned to close Raymond did not come as a surprise since the community was full of what Taylor termed "dame rumour." Taylor poured his emotions into four and a half foolscap pages of argument against closing the plant, handwritten to prevent any more details leaking to the community through his secretary.[3] During the next four years, Taylor and Ian Angus, his successor at Canadian Sugar Factories, were to write many longhand letters to Rogers.

Other senior employees also argued against closing Raymond. J. Gerald Snow, the general agricultural superintendent of Canadian Sugar Factories and another devout Mormon, not only repeated some of Taylor's arguments but also dipped into international politics to make his case. "The present unsettled world political situation," Snow wrote, with the Cold War in mind, "could again explode in violence and overnight expansion of domestic sugar sources and increased production from then existing plants become matters of vital national urgency that only a beet industry having reserve capacity could meet."

Ian Angus, when he was transferred in 1953 from Ozama to Raymond as Taylor's assistant, owed his loyalties to Vancouver, not to the local community and the Mormon church. His differing priorities emerged a week after Taylor's in fourteen foolscap pages addressed "Dear Forrie": "There is no doubt in my mind that the day of the 1500 ton old mill is gone, and there have been enough figures exchanged to prove this point. The definite closing announcement, in spite of the local chit chat of recent months will be a shock to the employees and their families, the community of Raymond, and also the province of Alberta." He advised Rogers to lay careful groundwork with the government, the growers' association and the press before the announcement; and to arm all senior company officials with the same explanations. "I believe we should be ready at the time to tell Growers and other interested parties that the company will be prepared to increase daily production at Taber and Picture Butte as the market warrants," Angus wrote.[4]

He recommended offering employees affected by the closure early retirement or transfers and suggested that very few outright terminations would be necessary. He also recommended that the head office of Canadian Sugar Factories be moved to Taber when Raymond was closed, making a clean break. As it happened, a number of the Raymond employees were scheduled to retire during the following four years. Allan Dunlop, BC Sugar's treasurer, asked whether it might not be preferable to operate Raymond several more years and let retirement resolve some of the personnel problems. In June Rogers told Angus that Raymond would operate during the 1959 and 1960 campaigns, giving time to expand both Picture Butte and especially the newer Taber factory.

While BC Sugar considered what to do, the rumour that Raymond was about to close reached T. George Wood, who had retired as Canadian Sugar Factories' general manager in 1953. Wood called Angus to report that he was being asked constantly about Raymond's future and, as a former company officer, he wanted to know what to say. "Without waiting for an answer," Angus complained to Rogers, "he elaborated on the influence of the *Church* and Raymond Community in sponsoring the industry." Wood challenged BC Sugar to show foresight "as Mr. Ernest Rogers had when he went to the Alberta government when others were messing around and said 'We will build a plant.' Mr. Wood foresaw that there will be a lot of political pressure to build a factory in Saskatchewan when the [Gardiner] dam etc is completed and we should consider running the Raymond plant until the plant could be moved to Saskatchewan." (Wood's observation was perceptive: in 1960 Forrest Rogers was asked by Saskatchewan Premier T. C. Douglas to investigate the beet-growing potential near the dam.)

After a meeting in October 1960 in which community leaders tried to dissuade Rogers from closing the factory, Wood warned Angus that "we have a Hornet's nest on our hands." The reference was to the Mormon community in southern Alberta which was bringing its influence to bear on provincial politicians. Wood, who had wept with emotion in Angus's office, then asked for an appointment with BC Sugar's board in Vancouver. "I find myself torn and sleepless, between two loyalties," Wood wrote to Forrest Rogers: one to the company with which he had worked for thirty years and on whose board (CSF) he still was a director, the other "to this community by social and religious ties."[5]

The Raymond Chamber of Commerce late in October sent a brief to Forrest Rogers which stated: "The immediate area of the Raymond Factory is the cradle of the Sugar Beet Industry in Western Canada. Our Pioneers went through hardship to prove that Sugar Beets could be successfully grown here." Besides arguing to keep the factory open, the brief also suggested that if BC Sugar were to withdraw from Raymond, it should sell the factory to the community as a going concern. "We have such faith in the Sugar Beet Industry that we are prepared to go ALL THE WAY in our Determination that sugar will continue to be manufactured in Raymond."

All this pressure finally got to Rogers: early in November BC Sugar deferred closure while further studies were made. But Rogers warned the Chamber of Commerce that "it may ultimately develop that there is no other course open to us than to cease operations." Raymond's costs ballooned to double those of Taber in subsequent campaigns until finally in January 1963, Rogers announced that the factory would have to close at the end of that year's beet campaign. This time, the company retained a professional publicist, Douglas Heal, a public relations counsellor from the Vancouver office of James Lovick and Company, to manage the announcement. Carefully drafted letters were sent to everyone who would be concerned, from T. George Wood and Frank Taylor to provincial and federal politicians. Ian Angus delivered personally to *Lethbridge Herald* editor Cleo Mowers a copy of the company's announcement and discussed the story with him. Angus then delivered another copy to Lalovee Jensen, the president of the Alberta Sugar Beet Growers and explained the company's position. Heal's strategy prevented an immediate outcry. Jensen even assured Rogers: "Let me say that you will have no criticism from the growers. . . ." Jensen, having accepted that the plant would close, had extracted concessions from the company protecting the interests of growers (such as compensation for the additional cost of shipping beets to Taber or Picture Butte).

But not all the critics and growers were silent. Alma E. Hancock, the mayor of Raymond, fired an intemperate letter to Rogers in Vancouver, snidely referring to BC Sugar's supposed monopoly position and upbraiding Rogers for having told community leaders that there "was no room for morals in business." Rogers, so incensed that his lawyer toned down his reply before it was sent, corrected Hancock: "I told your delegation that 'there is no room for sentiment in business.' "

The mayor, joining forces with a newly formed Save the Sugar Factories Committee, appealed to the Alberta government to intervene. Forrest Rogers, who also met with cabinet ministers, discovered that Industry Minister Russell Patrick did not trust Hancock. Patrick reluctantly agreed to speak to the Raymond Chamber of Commerce in February on the issue of the sugar factory. His remarks were not what Raymond wanted to hear: "We discussed the matter in Cabinet but we can't tell any industry that they have to do this or they have to do that. That's the whole point of free enterprise."[6] Rogers was grateful for this support.

Ian Angus scribbled a note on 12 February 1963 to Rogers that "the word from the street in Raymond this morning is that the Hancock letter to you is only the opening round." One concern was that the mayor intended to seek a federal Social Credit nomination, campaigning on reopening the Combines investigation to which BC Sugar had been subjected after buying the Manitoba Sugar Company in 1956. The threat had some substance. The Social Credit party, largely on the strength of Réal Caouette's populist leadership, seemed poised for a national political breakthrough.

BC Sugar in March defused accusations that it was abandoning its committment to the beet sugar industry by announcing, jointly with the growers' association, that it planned to contract 44,800 acres of beets in the 1963 campaign, well up from the previous year's 41,500 acres. It also announced a $1 million program to expand the Picture Butte factory, raising its daily capacity from 1800 tons to 2500 tons. The *Lethbridge Herald* editorialized approvingly: "Million dollar investments are not made by companies that intend to stay around for only a year or two." Harry Strom, the Alberta minister of agriculture and a beet grower himself, commended the company in the legislature. Clearly, BC Sugar was winning the public relations battle this time.

However, Mayor Hancock continued to fight for the survival of the Raymond plant. In one letter to Rogers, Hancock hinted darkly that he was accumulating a file which would be of interest to any parliamentary committee or other inquiry looking into the sugar industry. He may well have been doing so, for in mid-June, he wrote the Manitoba Sugar Company in Winnipeg for details on its beet operations. William Hetherington, the vice-president, passed the letter on to Rogers in Vancouver.

Hancock also sent letters inquiring about beet sugar operations to Spreckels Sugar Company in San Francisco and to Canada & Dominion Sugar Company in Chatham, Ontario. The mayor overlooked the camaraderie existing in the sugar industry, for both companies sent copies of correspondence to Ian Angus. A Canada & Dominion vice-president, W. H. Punchard, suggested that Angus might wish to review his reply—which included the information that his company had just closed permanently the beet factory that it had operated at Wallaceburg, Ontario—before he sent it to the mayor.

Meanwhile, the Save the Sugar Factories Committee formed Raymond Co-operative Industries Ltd. and attempted to raise money to buy the Raymond plant. When BC Sugar declined to entertain such an offer, the committee's leader, Rulon Dahl, travelled to the United States, looking for either an American refiner willing to open a Raymond plant or for a processing plant which might be relocated to Raymond. Since American sugar refiners—including companies controlled by the Mormon church—also were closing smaller, older factories, Dahl attracted no immediate support. Mayor Hancock—who had decided against running federally—implied in a letter to Rogers that support had been found. "We are fully prepared to buy the Raymond Factory," he assured Rogers. "In fact, if you so desire we can arrange the purchase of all three of the Alberta Sugar Factories, for we know where the capital can be obtained for this purpose." Dahl had come to believe that the Mormon church would finance a Raymond plant with assistance from the Alberta government, whose treasurer, E. W. Hinman, himself a Mormon, had taken part in some meetings of the Dahl group.

T. George Wood once more tried to change Rogers's mind. "As you know, I have never been reconciled to this proposal," he wrote to Rogers in October 1963. He received an unexpected reply: "I would like to advise you very confidentially that in view of the very serious world shortage of sugar and the consequent high prices we are giving consideration to keeping the Raymond factory going as long as these conditions prevail." The world price of sugar suddenly had soared to its highest level since 1920, making it difficult—at least temporarily—for Rogers to maintain that Raymond was unprofitable. Rogers also looked momentarily at another solution: converting the factory to the production of glucose, a sweetener made from starch. "It would be a great relief to everyone to find some useful use for the Raymond factory," he confided to Ian Angus when he asked him to study the idea. The study indicated that the project would not be viable.

Dahl, having enlisted the Mormon Church to his cause, arranged an early November meeting in Calgary between representatives of the company and the Church, but Rogers and Angus were not swayed. Then he asked the Alberta cabinet to order BC Sugar to desist until there was further study. He also sent a telegram to Ottawa asking for a similar order from the federal government. But neither government was prepared to intervene. Alberta's Russell Patrick remained committed to the position that the province would not interfere in business, and Dahl was forced to give up. The Raymond factory ended its final campaign at ten minutes before eight on the evening of 15 November 1963, after slicing 83,809 tons of beets.[7] Forrest Rogers wrote to a friend the following spring, "T. George Wood was most opposed to closing Raymond and I once had heard him say that as he had watched every campaign from the first, he wanted to see the plant continue to operate as long as he was around. Unfortunately for him this statement turned out to be somewhat prophetic, as he died of a heart attack just a few months after the plant sliced its last beet."[8]

After that campaign, most of the employees were moved to Lethbridge, Picture Butte or Taber, with the assistance of relocation allowances and housing loans. The Raymond facilities were used for a number of years to pack specialty sugars and for sugar storage. Finally, in 1986, the buildings were sold to Parrish & Heimbecker Ltd., which renovated the bins for grain storage and dismantled the factory smokestack that BC Sugar had been asked by the community to leave standing as a landmark. The number of beet growers continued to decline until in 1988 only one beet contract remained in the Raymond district.

♦

Never one to vacillate, Peter Cherniavsky handled the closure of the Picture Butte factory in 1977 swiftly. In August he briefed BC Sugar's board of directors who had to approve the decision. "In a nutshell, we have far too much capacity for our markets," Cherniavsky told his directors. "The refinery alone is capable of doubling its output at virtually no increase in capital cost and Taber can quite satisfactorily run 120 days instead of its projected 70-80 days this year." By 7 November he told the employees at Picture Butte that the factory would close at the end of that campaign, the victim of low sugar prices and a provincial demand that an estimated $1 million be spent on the factory's pollution abatement.

Picture Butte was a well-engineered factory in 1936 when it was opened. Kept up-to-date, it outperformed the new Taber factory initially in 1950 and for several years until Taber's start-up problems were overcome. In 1961 a pulp drier was added to Picture Butte. In 1963 the original diffusion battery was replaced with a 2500-ton-a-day continuous diffuser similar to the one just installed in Manitoba Sugar's factory. The heart of a factory, the diffuser is the equipment in which sliced beets, or cossettes as they are called, are immersed in hot water to extract the sugar. The new diffuser prolonged Picture Butte's life because it reduced labour costs, increased sugar recovery and cut the volume of waste water discharged into the Oldman River.

The Oldman's water quality became an issue after the provincial government in 1968 ordered both the city of Lethbridge and the town of Taber to install secondary treatment for their sewage. When the Picture Butte and Taber factories began the 1969 campaign, both the *Calgary Herald* and the *Lethbridge Herald* ran front-page articles suggesting that the waste discharge was degrading the river. In January 1970 an anti-pollution group was formed in Lethbridge, and a delegation of high school biology students, in a brief to the Lethbridge city council, criticized Canadian Sugar Factories for the state of the river.

The company did not believe that the mud and plant matter discharged from the factories posed a significant problem for the swift-flowing river. However, in 1975 the province asked that the factories strive for zero discharge of pollutants. BC Sugar vice-president William Hetherington protested: "To achieve zero discharge requires an investment of several million dollars with no economic return for the industry and, in our opinion, no significant environmental benefit." He warned the provincial department of the environment that the Picture Butte factory could be forced to close. The company agreed to incorporate extensive water recycling and treatment facilities in a $4-million upgrading of the Taber factory initiated in 1977. The company maintained that this installation would reduce effluent discharge sufficiently to obviate a comparable expenditure at Picture Butte. The government thought otherwise. The "final straw"—as Cherniavsky saw it—was a letter from a provincial official in July, implying that the factory was unlikely to get a licence for discharging its waste water into the Oldman River without spending heavily on a treatment system.[9]

The economics of Picture Butte already had been undermined because the tonnage of beets produced in the contiguous Lethbridge Northern Irrigation District had been declining since 1960 and now was only 17 per cent of the total sliced by the factory. This figure was significant because Canadian Sugar Factories paid the cost of hauling beets to the factories from the piling grounds to which the growers delivered them, and Picture Butte's hauling costs were rising. In addition, the soaring natural gas prices in the 1970s caused a tripling in the cost of fuel to produce sugar at the factory. Taber also was under similar cost pressures but, as the sole factory, would improve its margin dramatically by slicing a higher tonnage of beets during a longer campaign. The Taber factory had had the capacity to handle the entire Alberta crop since 1965 when the factory's original diffuser was replaced with a larger one. Some thought had been given to moving the Picture Butte factory to Saskatchewan when Hetherington—at the Saskatchewan government's request—surveyed the sugar beet potential around the Gardiner Dam, a venture that never proceeded because insufficient acreage was brought under irrigation.[10]

The announcement of Picture Butte's closure was planned carefully. On the morning of 7 November, Cherniavsky, Hetherington and Canadian Sugar Factories' general manager W. A. Willison briefed senior Alberta cabinet ministers in Edmonton. According to Hetherington, "the attitude of the government ministers was friendly and understanding." The planned next step was to announce the decision simultaneously that afternoon to the employees at the factory and personally to Picture Butte mayor Ted Crapnell. Unfortunately, the news leaked from the Edmonton meeting and Crapnell, a doctor, already had heard it from a patient. Willison said that the mayor was "steaming" when they met in his office. As the sugar company executives departed, Crapnell yanked a picture of the factory from his wall and told the delegation that they might as well take it, too.[11]

Dr. John Walker, a Southern Alberta member of the legislature, assumed leadership of the Picture Butte Action Committee. In a letter to Cherniavsky, he charged that the company was moving to close the entire beet industry and suggested that BC Sugar be prosecuted for being an apparent monopoly. Cherniavsky responded: "We would ask you how this could be associated with the question of whether the Alberta industry be a one plant or a two-plant operation." On 19 December, two days after emerging empty-handed from a meeting with Cherniavsky in Vancouver, Walker's committee and the town of Picture Butte got a ten-day injunction from the Alberta Supreme Court to prevent the removal of any equipment from the factory. The committee later tried but failed to convert that to a permanent injunction.

In a letter to Dr. Hugh Horner, Alberta's deputy premier, Cherniavsky dismissed as "absolute nonsense" the notion that the company intended to withdraw entirely from processing sugar beets. "We are currently spending $4 million on Taber improvements," Cherniavsky wrote. "We intend to develop with one efficient plant rather than die with an inefficient two-plant operation. . . . We have invested $13.5 million in beet sugar capital improvements on the Prairies in the last five years." He went on to remind Horner that BC Sugar had other investments in Alberta as well, including oil and gas and packaging. The deputy premier's reply was vintage Horner: "Those opportunities have come about because of the policies of this government to have a bouyant economic situation here. In view of that, and the other matters that are so important, perhaps more of your head office executive should be located in Alberta where you could have a better understanding of the policies and the climate that affords an aggressive company many opportunities in Alberta." (The next summer Canadian Sugar Factories, which now had just one factory, changed its name to Alberta Sugar Company.)

When Horner invited BC Sugar executives and individuals from the Picture Butte Action Committee to a February meeting in his office, Cherniavsky agreed to go but told Horner that no "constructive purpose" would be served by inviting Walker's committee, considering their legal attack on BC Sugar: "The action was later discontinued, but was a costly nuisance to the Company and tended to unsettle our employees while we were in the process of arranging alternative employment at Taber." (Most of the sixty-six hourly paid workers were taken on at Taber.) Horner took Cherniavsky's advice: "As per your suggestion, interested parties from the Picture Butte area have not been invited. . . ." The meeting with the deputy premier and several other cabinet ministers went well, and Horner issued a statement afterwards supporting BC Sugar.

The growers also had been briefed in early November on the company's decision. "Strong and violent objections were registered and the growers vowed to continue the fight even though we advised that the decision was irrevocable and non-negotiable," Hetherington wrote in an internal memorandum. The growers were reluctant to haul their beets farther to Taber and they worried about the sugar loss that might occur to beets in storage during a longer one-factory campaign. The company agreed that the average haul might increase from five to fifteen miles but pointed out that Manitoba growers coped with hauls of fifty to seventy miles at their own expense. The company also argued that the sugar loss could be minimized if beets were delivered to storage in good condition. In the spring of 1978, when beet contract talks began, the growers threatened to boycott Canadian Sugar Factories unless the company guaranteed to process all beets within a ninety-day campaign—something which would have been impossible with just Taber running. When the company threatened to contract for beets directly with individual growers, the growers' association backed down and contracted for the 1978 crop. Taber, in fact, needed 121 days to complete that year's campaign.

Cherniavsky had tried to head off federal interference in the Picture Butte decision by going to Ottawa in mid-November 1977 and explaining his decisions to ministers there. However, in February 1978 Agriculture Minister Eugene Whelan, who had compaigned ineffectively a decade earlier for the revival of Ontario's sugar beet industry and now was being lobbied hard by Alberta growers, wrote to Cherniavsky: "I do not agree with the unilateral action of BC Sugar either. The fact that such an important decision as closing down a factory was not discussed with the Growers Association is surprising." Cherniavsky was out of the country and was unable to reply in detail until 24 May. At that time he wrote, "Hopefully, many of the unfortunate speculations and statements by ill-informed persons will now disappear and sensible progress will be attained."[12] Together with Hetherington and Willison, he met with senior executives of the growers' association in Calgary on 30 May to talk about improving the relations between growers and the company.

Major components of the factory were disassembled and moved to Fort Garry, including the centrifugals, and two of three beet slicers. But the Picture Butte factory's last hurrah occurred in 1981 when its diffuser was scavenged for parts to repair Taber's diffuser, which had broken down after an iron bar fell into its moving parts, a catastrophe that prolonged the campaign an unprecedented 191½ days.

19

A Row of Spinach

HOW BACK-BREAKING LABOUR WAS ELIMINATED FROM BEET GROWING.

Dr. Peter Bergen, the Alberta Sugar Company's director of agronomy, changed the thrust of his research after being asked a simple question at a growers' field day in 1970. He had organized the demonstration of a new John Deere electronic beet thinner on a lush stand of beets at the Taber factory's farm. "We had planted the seed every three inches and the beets had come up almost that well," Bergen said. "It was just ideal for an electronic thinner to work."[1] With the thinner performing flawlessly, Bergen invited Taber's general manager Dwight Purdy and operating superintendent Herb Hayward, both engineers, to witness the demonstration with the growers. "I was just thrilled by the work it was doing," Bergen recalled. "Herb said, 'What percentage of the beets are you removing with this machine?' I said, 'About half of them.' He said: 'Why don't you just plant half as much seed?' "

Bergen, who had been focussing on mechanization to reduce labour, had not asked himself that question. The following year he planted a demonstration field with half the usual quantity of seed. It proved as productive and required far less labour. Thus, another step had been taken to reduce the toil of growing sugar beets. "I keep looking at this irony," he said later. "For years, people have slaved and sweat under the hot sun to remove excess plants when, why did they put so much seed there in the first place? . . . Most people my age that I speak to who worked in the beet fields have not pleasant memories of it," Bergen said. "I'm sure had I grown up on a beet farm I would not have taken on sugar beet research."

J. Gerald Snow, in his memoir *Jus' Ramblin'*, described beet farming as "a stoop-labour industry."[2] Snow, a native of Raymond, was thirteen when the Raymond factory opened in 1925. "My first experience with the sugar beet business was on the end of a hoe, out thinning beets," he said, recalling casual summer jobs. "At that time, they always planted about eighteen pounds of seed to the acre and when it came up, it was like a row of spinach. You had to chop out probably two hundred plants to leave one that you wanted."[3] The seeds in that era were of variable fertility, and farmers overplanted to assure an adequate stand.

When the Utah–Idaho Sugar Company built the Raymond factory, casual beet field labour was provided by immigrants recruited by Canadian Pacific from central Europe. Canada's open immigration policy ended when the Depression began. "By then," Snow said, "a lot of those people had graduated from being on the end of a hoe handle to owning farms." The Depression created a new pool of labour: drifting unemployed workers who reacted to low wages and poor living conditions by forming a beet workers' union. When Snow, trained to be a school teacher, was hired by Canadian Sugar Factories in 1935, he was shown a file of agitators' propaganda against the company as a warning about what he was up against as a field man. The Communist-led Beet Workers' Industrial Union organized strikes against the growers in 1935 and 1936.

Under BC Sugar ownership, Canadian Sugar Factories began to mechanize field work by buying and operating the beet drills needed to till and plant. Snow, who had twenty-five to thirty-five drills under his command, scheduled them among growers and demonstrated their use. "During this period there were many new growers who knew nothing of beet operations," he recalled in his memoir. After 1940 the drills were rented and then sold to the growers. The first real reduction in back-breaking labour, Snow believed, was the development in 1942 of a loader to replace the beet fork with which newly harvested beets had been shovelled onto wagons. Canadian Sugar Factories had a Lethbridge machine shop build several loaders modelled on an American design. In the postwar period, both local inventors and the major implement manufacturers developed improved machines to harvest the beets and to remove the tops until, by 1960, the beet harvest had been completely mechanized. But it still remained necessary, between planting and harvesting, to thin the stands.

During World War II, demands of the war effort depleted Alberta's farm work force until by 1941 it had shrunk 44 per cent from its prewar level. While labour shortages forced a drastic reduction of sugar beet farming in Ontario, growers of Alberta and Manitoba were able to tap a new, unexpected pool of workers: the 21,000 citizens of Japanese extraction who were evacuated from British Columbia. Alberta Sugar Beet Growers Association president Philip Baker later gave himself the credit for the idea of relocating some of those families in 1942 as beet farm labour.[4] By that summer there were 2495 evacuees in Alberta and 1021 in Manitoba.

The Japanese families found the primitive living conditions appalling: housing was poor, and there seldom was adequate water for bathing. Had they had a choice, the Japanese would have moved on. Forrest E. La Violette, a McGill University sociologist who studied the Japanese evacuation, reported: "Because many of the farmers looked on the Japanese as prisoners of war or slave labour to be exploited, it was not long before there were hundreds of complaints to the [B.C.] Security Commission [the agency that supervised the evacuation], and requests for permission to leave the farms and move into the cities."[5] In 1943 the federal government gave the growers lumber and other materials with which to improve housing. The growers also discovered what a reliable work force fate had dealt them. An unnamed Alberta government official later told La Violette: "Soon the farmers learned that this was the best help that they had ever had and that the Japanese . . . were the finest people with whom to deal."

Before the 1943 season, Philip Rogers wrote one of the company's Toronto shareholders: "Field labour is again the bottle-neck, and as only a few more Japanese families are available, we intend experimenting with prisoner-of-war labour and conscientious objectors." The Lethbridge area prisoner-of-war camps were filled primarily with veterans of Rommel's Afrika Korps and with captured submariners. By 1945 several thousand prisoners were working in the fields, some housed all summer in large tent camps throughout the farming areas and some even living in farmers' accommodations. Still, the Japanese workers were far more numerous. Arledge Hill, a sugar company field man at the time, said of the Japanese: "They saved our bacon."[6] Without this involuntary field labour, neither the Alberta nor the Manitoba beet growers would have been able, as they did, to increase their acreage, and sugar rationing in Canada would have been more severe.

Prisoner repatriation after the war again left the growers short of workers. It happened that T. George Wood, while in Montreal for a 1947 meeting with the Sugar Administration, encountered an official of the United Nations Refugee Relief Administration and learned that the displaced persons camps in the British Zone of Germany were full of "Baltic peasant farmers, from Latvia, etc., who fled the Russian advances." Wood wrote Philip Rogers that UNRRA would pay to transport as many as 5000 people to Canadian beet farms.[7] Thus, in the decade after the war, the growers again drew on European immigrants for casual labour. Between 1948 and 1953 Snow and James Lynn, the manager of the federal government's employment office in Lethbridge, regularly met the immigrant boats in Montreal or Quebec and returned with trainloads of immigrants whom they had interviewed and assigned to growers by the time they reached Lethbridge.

When the stream of European immigrants dried up, the growers in 1953 recruited 120 native workers from Indian bands in northern Alberta and northern Saskatchewan. The growers also pressed Ottawa to allow them to bring in Mexican field labour from the United States. When Ottawa refused, they recruited natives more aggressively. In 1964 they recruited 2700 native Indians who did about 60 per cent of all the hand labour.[8]

By this time the company and the growers were pursuing a permanent solution to the chronic labour shortage: monogerm seed. Prior to the development of this seed, all commercial sugar beet seed had two to four germs in each seed pod, each germinating multiple plants that then had to be thinned. The discoverers (in 1934) of monogerm seed were a pair of Russian beet scientists, Dr. Viacheslav F. Savitsky and his wife, Helen, who, as political refugees, had fled the Soviet Union in 1947 and secured employment with the Beet Sugar Development Foundation of Salt Lake City. In Russia, they had found that the monogerm characteristic did not express itself in robust plants but in inbred runts, precisely the sorts of plants growers chopped from otherwise healthy stands. In a search of beet seed stands in the western United States in 1948, they found similar monogerm mutants in a commercial field in Oregon. In the ensuing decade of crossbreeding, the Savitskys succeeding in placing the monogerm character into vigorous beet varieties. Because technical information was being shared freely in the industry, other researchers also soon were hard at work on the same quest. One of these was Dr. Frank Peto, BC Sugar's director of agriculture research.

Peto was born in Emerson, Manitoba, and earned a doctorate in cytogenetics from the University of Wales. He was employed as a National Research Council plant researcher from 1933 until 1940 when, as one of the very few Canadians who knew anything about beet seed, he was seconded by the NRC to Buckerfields Ltd., the Vancouver seed company. With European beet seed supplies cut off by the war, Buckerfields had been asked to grow seed in Ladner, in the Fraser delta. (Because a beet plant produces seed only in its second year, seeds could not be grown on the Prairies where plants in the ground would not survive over the winter.) Since BC Sugar was buying most of the seed for its Alberta growers, the company took over the seed project in 1944. That fall, seed was harvested from 238 acres, with the single largest grower—125 acres—being George Reifel, a Vancouver businessman (whose seed farm later was converted to a bird sanctuary).

Peto, the first BC Sugar employee with a doctorate, soon hired John Hall (with a master of science degree) as his field man. When BC Sugar bought the Ozama plantation in the Dominican Republic, Peto hired Frank Low (a master of science in soil chemistry) to work with sugar cane there. The agriculture department Peto built around these individuals quickly established its reputation within the company by boosting Ozama's sugar cane production by 62 per cent with the application of fertilizers.

Research was done both in Ladner and in Alberta. In 1948 a demonstration farm was included in plans for the Taber factory. According to that year's annual report of Peto's department, the farm would be "managed so that it becomes revenue-bearing or at least self-supporting. Its function shall not duplicate that of the Dominion Experimental Farm, but rather function as a final proving ground of the most modern methods of culture." Its books would be kept separate from the company's newly established Sugar Beet Experimental Station, which the company supported for "the breeding of superior sugar beet varieties." Peto had hired a plant breeder named Wesley Smith, sending him for two months to study the beet breeding work being done by the Great Western Sugar Company at Longmont, Colorado. New European varieties once again were available in 1949 and Peto included some in the tests, along with a new hybrid variety developed by Great Western. An active research program was pursued, developing the first scientifically reliable data in Alberta on variety performance.

The twin objectives of the research were the evaluation of new beet varieties and the search for labour-saving monogerm varieties. Peto, on learning in 1949 of the Savitsky methodology, promptly hired a crew of women to search Ladner-area beet seed farms for monogerm plants. They found only one plant and that one was a compromise: half its seed pods had monogerm seeds. Finally in 1953 Peto obtained some true monogerm seed from the United States. The first crosses with the American seed to develop monogerm varieties suitable to Alberta and Manitoba were made by John Hall, and the project was taken over by Bergen when Hall was transferred to Manitoba as agricultural superintendent. Bergen's research formed the basis for his thesis when the company sponsored him in 1960 to get his doctorate from the University of Alberta. "My Ph.D. project was actually designed to answer some of those questions that had been coming up in my breeding program," Bergen said.[9]

The first field trials of monogerm seed began in Alberta in 1959, and the company began releasing its varieties to growers in 1961. A company variety called CS42, introduced in 1966, was being planted by all Alberta growers and nearly all growers in Manitoba within two years. John Vaselenak, who was then the growers' association agricultural chairman, wrote: "The breeding of monogerm seed, no doubt, is the most significant change that has ever taken place in the beet industry. . . . Monogerm seed is the key to low labour cost beet production."[10] In 1974 the company introduced CS43, a better variety that yielded more sugar per acre.

But Peto's agricultural research program was dwarfed by that of the major commercial breeders. "I went down to Great Western Sugar in Colorado to see their breeding program," Frank Low said. "They had nine or ten Ph.D.'s. There was no way we could compete with companies

Peter Cherniavsky, the company's chairman, with the historic brick façade of the refinery behind him. (DEBORAH MACNEILL PHOTOGRAPH)

BRITISH COLUMBIA SUGAR REFINING CO

Top: An aerial view of the Taber, Alberta, sugar beet factory.

Left: An aerial view of BC Sugar's Vancouver refinery today.

The refinery's female employees (circa 1911) bagged refined sugar and sewed up the bags; they joined the first strike against the company in 1917 when they were not offered a wage increase.

Facing page: Prior to the introduction of bulk transport, raw sugar was received in 200 to 250 pound jute bags.

Top: Chief chemist Robert Boyd developed one of BC Sugar's most successful consumer products, Rogers' Golden Syrup, in 1913.

Facing page, top: The BC Sugar office staff, circa 1915.

Facing page, bottom: BC Sugar's laboratory in 1916 with (*rear to front*) chief chemist Robert Boyd and assistants Ernest Abbott and Margaret MacKenzie.

Top: The mill at Ozama Sugar Company in the Dominican Republic was dilapidated in 1944, when BC Sugar bought it, but a completely salvaged operation eleven years later when it was sold to the Dominican government.

Bottom: The Ozama River, shown here with sugar-laden barges, often flooded the Caribbean plantation.

Ozama's steam locomotives were notorious for disastrous derailments, sometimes causing loss of life.

The sugar beet factory at Picture Butte, Alberta, after its 1936 completion.

The Raymond factory, bought in 1931, led the company into a confrontation with the Mormon Church when the factory later had to be closed.

Energetic entrepreneur Morris Belkin became BC Sugar's partner when the sugar company invested in his packaging company. (JOHN SCHREINER PHOTOGRAPH)

J. C. Anderson, founder, president and chief executive officer of Anderson Exploration Ltd. (DAN O'CONNELL)

Top: Firm-handed William Hetherington imposed harmony on the warring factions he found at Manitoba Sugar Company when he became general manager in 1955. (ROBINSON PHOTOGRAPHY, WINNIPEG)

Bottom: Manitoba Sugar's lawyer-president Col. H. S. Aikins was so tough that it was said the only tears he shed came from his glass eye.

Top: T. George Wood, the able administrator who managed the company's sugar beet factories in Alberta, tried but failed to save the Raymond factory from closing in 1963.

Bottom: Fred Ballou, the company's hot-tempered, eccentric first chief engineer, managed to upgrade the refinery while feuding with his associates.

William (Bill) Brown, company president since 1988, is identified with BC Sugar's diversification into chemical production.

that were working on a scale like that."[11] In the 1970s the large European seed companies, with even greater research resources, re-entered the North American markets. This quickly spelled an end to the practice whereby each sugar company had been the exclusive source of beet seed to its growers. Now the growers wanted to buy the best seed, whatever the source. Manitoba growers began buying German seed in 1977. In 1980 a small amount of a superior seed developed by Hilleshoeg, a major Swedish company, became available to Alberta growers and by 1982 had entirely replaced CS43. Since then, European companies have supplied nearly all the seed for Prairies growers. The company continues to evaluate varieties in field trials but has discontinued seed breeding programs.

The availability of European seed also spelled the end to growing seed commercially in Ladner. The Fraser Delta never had been ideal for beet seed, and the industry might not have started but for wartime needs. The threat of frost required the company to keep a two-year supply of seed on hand in case a crop failed. The birds that used the delta as a flyway also caused problems. Frank Low recalled one farmer losing a field of young beets to ducks which ate the crowns of the new plants. Gulls looking for worms pulled up many young plants in another farmer's fields. The company's losses in seed growing mounted once the growers began buying monogerm seed—since they were buying far fewer pounds of seed to do the same job. Finally in 1977, over Peto's objections, the company sold its Ladner seed plant to a commercial grower, who also failed to make it pay. Three years later the plant was sold to a local fertilizer distributor.

Once the growers began using monogerm seed, they discovered another problem: weeds. Formerly, hoeing and thinning had dealt with weeds as a matter of course. The company and the growers had relied on the Canada Department of Agriculture to work on weed control at its experimental farms. In the mid-1960s the company decided, Bergen recalled, that "if we depended on the government to do it, it would just take too long." Bergen began evaluating herbicides, integrating this research with other work to reduce the cost of growing beets. "One of the things I really started working on was planting to final stand. Dropping a seed every six inches. I had initiated that in the early Seventies but I kept working on that harder then and coupling that with weed control." Bergen had concluded that "if we were to depend on hand labour in the fields, we had very limited life as an industry. If we could mechanize it so we did not need hand labour in the fields, then we could survive."

Bergen began reduced seeding trials with monogerm seed in 1970. "Following the European example, I initiated reduced seeding (one to one and a quarter pounds per acre) experiments. . . . After three successive years of success in my experiments we promoted the practice as practical for the farmers. In 1973 two per cent of the commercial acreage was planted-to-stand with this low rate of seeding. This gradually increased to 95 per cent in 1987."

In 1976 Bergen decided that the company would grow beets on its demonstration farm in Alberta with no hand labour. This had been tried in Michigan and Europe but not yet in Canada. "We were the first to grow beets without thinning but still using hand labour for weeding. Then we were the first to grow beets, zero labour, in Alberta." The research through the 1980s has now brought beet growing to the point where most farmers have adopted so-called zero-labour practices: one person on a machine can handle what once called for an army of hand labour.

Added together, the innovations in plant breeding, machinery and agricultural practices have helped the beet industry survive. Since Bergen joined what was once Frank Peto's department in 1956, average yields have doubled to between eighteen and twenty tonnes of beets an acre. Bergen believes the next development will be an increase in the quantity of sugar produced in each tonne as new varieties are introduced and as the payment system is changed to offer more incentive to grow high-sugar beets.

Since 1986 the growers have been sharing the cost of sugar beet research with the company. That change was made partly to relieve the factory of certain costs, and also to create further direct interest by the growers in agricultural research. "Throughout the years that I have been here," Bergen said, "agricultural research has had—as far as money goes—the support it needed to solve the problems. . . . When an issue comes up and there is a problem that needs to be looked at, I have yet to experience where management would say, 'No we don't want to do that.' "

20

Like a Flea Biting an Elephant

AN UNSUCCESSFUL DIVERSIFICATION.

The explosive achievement of plant science in the 1960s was captured in that apt phrase "The Green Revolution." Beginning in 1945 the Rockefeller Foundation sponsored research at the International Maize and Wheat Improvement Center in Mexico by a team under Dr. Norman E. Borlaug that produced a dramatic breakthrough in the breeding of high-yielding cereals and other grains. The yield improvements were so large that the defeat of hunger shimmered as an attainable ideal. In countries as far apart as Mexico and India, farmers began planting the highly productive varieties. Among those swept up in the global excitement over Borlaug's work was Dr. Frank Peto, BC Sugar's director of agriculture research.

In 1966 a Manitoba plant breeder and seed dealer, Jerry Twomey, was soliciting backing in Canada for a new American company, the International Institute for Biological Research (which later changed its name to World Seeds, Inc.). A friend of Peto's, Twomey pitched such firms as Consolidated Mining & Smelting Company as well as BC Sugar to take Canadian rights for growing and exporting the newly developed seeds. "I feel that our Company should have the first chance," Peto said in a memo to Forrest Rogers in November 1966. "The real basis for our personal confidence in the ultimate success of an export venture of good seed of superior varieties accompanied by fertilizer is that our Company has seen this effect in the Dominican Republic. We did see an overall doubling of sugar per acre . . . and a trebling if agronomic improvement and land utilization were included."[1]

William Hetherington, vice-president of Manitoba Sugar in Winnipeg at the time, was skeptical. "If it's so good, why have we been asked to participate?" he wrote in a prescient November memorandum to his Vancouver colleagues. "In the initial phases, the economic attractiveness of the whole deal seems to indicate that there must be a joker in it somewhere." Even more hesitant was Reginald H. Tupper, a BC Sugar director and the company's lawyer. "While I favour diversification," he wrote Forrest Rogers in December 1966, "I think that in time this can be done with less speculation than is now proposed and in a fashion that would give us complete control and our money's worth." Neither was as persuasive as Peto, then at the peak of his influence within the company.

When Peto convinced BC Sugar's board to back World Seeds, he was running a research department that had four plant breeders (two with doctorates), several university-trained agronomists and nineteen field men. He believed that this staff, along with the company's fertilizer distribution network on the Prairies, could be the basis for commercializing new seeds in Canada. The objective was ambitious because, then as now, plant breeding in Canada was essentially the exclusive preserve of the Canada Department of Agriculture, its provincial counterparts and the universities. Canadian research had produced the world's best breadmaking wheats. The quality standard against which all new breadmaking wheat varieties were measured was (and still is) Marquis, which was released to growers in 1910. But these wheats were significantly less productive than those developed by Borlaug and his Green Revolution emulators. Critics of the Canadian plant breeding establishment had begun to argue that Canada was falling well behind in grains research and that Canada's share of world wheat markets was threatened.

The founder of World Seeds was John Strohm, then a fifty-four-year-old agricultural journalist from Woodstock, Illinois. BC Sugar took the precaution to have its bank check out Strohm, discovering that his net worth was about $1 million. His executive vice-president was Dr. Earl Collister, a plant geneticist who had been director of the High Plains Research Foundation in Plainview, Texas. The vice-president was Arthur

Greenberg, a Grand Forks, North Dakota, farmer operating 6000 acres and also something of an amateur plant breeder. Both World Seed's chief plant breeder and its plant pathologist were Mexican scientists who had worked with Borlaug. The consulting geneticist was a Canadian, Dr. Charles Jenkins, who had worked at the University of Manitoba on the development of triticale, a high-yielding cereal created by crossing durum wheat with rye. World Seeds needed capital to commercialize several grains under development: in spite of its president's net worth, the company only had $6500 in cash when it concluded its agreement with the sugar company. Strohm believed that one variety, a high-yield red spring wheat (later called Red River 68), was ready to be reproduced for release to the seed trade.

BC Sugar planned to incorporate World Seeds Canada Ltd., to reproduce in Canada the varieties already developed in the United States and to do further plant breeding. Peto's department would do the breeding and Prairie beet growers would grow the new cereal grains under contract. This made sense since beet farmers had to rotate their crops to prevent beet disease and to control weeds. These contract growers would reproduce World Seeds' super varieties, and the seed then would be exported to countries whose farmers needed more productive varieties. It would be, BC Sugar said in a brief to Agriculture Minister J. J. Greene in Ottawa, "a new way in which Canada can help the starving people of this world, without seriously encumbering the treasury and the Canadian taxpayer." It was only necessary that the Canadian government change the regulations that prevented private plant breeders in Canada from importing and growing unlicensed wheat varieties. Strohm and his American associates were relying on BC Sugar to get the regulations changed.

In January 1967, after BC Sugar agreed to pay US$214,000 for a 50 per cent interest in World Seeds, Cherniavsky, then BC Sugar's vice-president and general superintendent, and Frank Peto began calling on key figures in the West's agriculture establishment. Dr. C. F. Bentley, dean of agriculture at the University of Alberta, agreed to support World Seeds among his peers but would not commit the university to field trials. Dr. D. R. Knott, the plant breeder at the University of Saskatchewan, reacted with hostility on learning that Charles Jenkins was involved with World Seeds. Knott told Cherniavsky that "Jenkins was crooked."[2] Jenkins, impatient to speed the development of triticale (which was not released by the University of Manitoba to farmers until 1970) had bolted to World Seeds with some seed material. Hetherington, doing some research on World Seeds from his base at Manitoba Sugar in Winnipeg, had warned his colleagues in Vancouver that Jenkins's removal of seeds from the university showed "somewhat dubious" ethics and that he was controversial in the academic circles whose co-operation the company sought.[3] Jenkins was not the only controversial individual in World Seeds. In April 1967 Cherniavsky was disturbed to learn from the University of Manitoba that two Mexican scientists employed by the new company were suspected of having taken Rockefeller Foundation seed material with them when they left to join World Seeds.

At the end of January 1967, a BC Sugar delegation made the first of four trips that year to Ottawa, spending three days lobbying both the department of agriculture and various members of the federal cabinet including Agriculture Minister Greene, Finance Minister Mitchell Sharp and Trade and Commerce Minister Robert Winters. The company wanted the Seeds Act to be amended so that seed breeding of unlicensed varieties could be done by private, commercial firms. Cherniavsky's memo about this trip said: "Sharp seemed to grasp the essentials very quickly and Greene was somewhat defensive regarding his department. 'Surely my men have been testing and know of these varieties and if they are good would draw them to my attention.' " The delegation received a much better reception from R. M. Esdale, the chief of the grain division in Trade and Commerce. Esdale, who encouraged them to extend their research beyond cereal grains to oilseeds, observed that Canada's hard red spring wheats, for all their superior milling qualities, were losing market share to cheaper grades in countries where bread was not the dietary staple. Cherniavsky emerged sanguine from these meetings: "It must be emphasized that at no time did we meet any antagonism toward World Seeds Canada. . . . Our only known obstacles to date are the regulations under the Seeds Act."

On the heels of the Ottawa visit, BC Sugar reiterated its case in a January 1967 brief which Forrest Rogers sent to Greene and other ministers: "The Company's intention this year is to propagate for commercial seed approximately 1,000 acres of one dwarf bearded variety of spring wheat and to export this seed. At the same time, the company wishes to test dwarf varieties ranging from bread wheats to feed wheats at four different locations in Western Canada. . . . We would also arrange with agricultural officials in selected developing countries to run trials of the new high yielding dwarfs in comparison with their own domestic varieties. Orders would be solicited for future delivery, in large quantities, of any variety they selected."

When the department of agriculture stalled, Cherniavsky and Peto returned to Ottawa early in May, seeking permission to import 100 bushels of Red River 68 for planting in Canada by the company's contract growers. With the help of a British Columbia senator, John Nichol, they secured top-level meetings with many of the important decision-makers, including Greene's executive assistant, David Thomson. After that visit, Greene wrote: "I have asked the department officials to work out the details and advise you of the conditions under which the department will permit imports until provided for in the Seeds Regulations."

But in May the department's plant products division rejected imports of Red River 68 because it failed the key condition for the dissemination of an unlicensed variety. In apppearance it looked too much like the approved bread wheat varieties, posing the danger that it could leak into general agriculture, adulterate the traditional varieties and wreck the reliability of Canada's grading system. Ottawa also objected to a lack of information on the pedigree of Red River 68. Rogers wrote Greene: "I must say that I feel very frustrated at not being able to carry out our original plans, as I felt that what we have proposed to do would in the long run prove very beneficial to our Company and eventually to Canada as a whole."[4] Nichol, when he learned what had happened, was sympathic but not helpful. "Since I do not know wheat seed from bird gravel, I am hardly one to make an assessment as to the wisdom of the regulations in questions," he wrote.[5]

Meanwhile, quantities of Red River 68 seed, which had been grown the previous year in California for World Seeds, were planted in the spring of 1967 in North Dakota. In June, with the young plants barely out of the ground, the ever-confident Strohm already began offering quantities to seed dealers in the state at $15 a bushel. This was premature since the variety still awaited North Dakota certification and tests for its baking quality.

The research arm of the Canada Department of Agriculture finally agreed to co-operate that summer in carefully controlled variety trials. A number of World Seeds varieties, which Peto had imported through the University of British Columbia, were grown alongside established Canadian varieties to ascertain yields. In December 1967 Cherniavsky, Peto and Angus were in Ottawa, this time to report on the yield trials and to lobby the government again. Agriculture Minister Greene repeated his reliance on the advice of his scientists, notably J. Ansel Anderson, the department's director of agricultural research, who happened to be an old friend of Peto's and who had authorized the yield trials.

Peto, who had looked forward to meeting Anderson again, was stunned to find him hostile. He "took me to task for the memo we had sent the Minister of Agriculture and claimed it was highly inaccurate," Peto confided in notes on the meeting. "He gave us a long dissertation on his experience, his dealings in Russia, Germany, the U.K., etc. and his 25 years in charge as Cereal Chemist in the Grain Research Laboratory—Winnipeg. I tried to argue the relative merits of our World Seeds baking and milling results vs the latest Canadian variety 'Manitou' but Anderson in no uncertain language shot me down. Anderson has a huge empire under his command, and one only has to walk through the research centre with its tremendous staff of Ph.Ds and many laboratories to realize the immensity of the organization. In other words, we are 'like a flea biting an elephant.' "[6] He came away from this meeting with the feeling that the Canada Department of Agriculture, jealous of its own turf, was shaken to discover that a group of private researchers were charging ahead of them in developing high-yielding, short-stalked wheats.

In January 1968 a new tactic was tried: the company sought the support of the Prairie governments to pressure Ottawa to amend the Seeds Act. "Investigation shows that the yields of Canadian hard spring wheat due to improvement in varieties has not increased appreciably over the past *twenty-five or more years.* Developments in the line of high yielding feed wheats have not been in evidence," BC Sugar argued in a brief to the provinces.[7] The company proposed an elaborate new grading system with controls to ensure that the traditional hard red spring wheats would not become mixed in the market place with newer high-yield varieties. But the three provinces all deferred to the federal government.

Meanwhile, Forrest Rogers, disturbed at the way money was being spent by World Seeds, visited its research farm in Salinas, California, early in 1968 to reorganize personnel and to get rid of several temperamental scientists. BC Sugar's troubleshooter, Ian Angus, was assigned to establish budget discipline. Angus discovered that in November 1967 Greenberg had leased a light aircraft for personal travel at $5,000 a month; and that there were plans being laid to send Jenkins on a trip around the world to gather plant materials. That was very much in Strohm's style: he and one of the Mexican breeders at World Seeds already had spent three weeks on a premature world sales trip. Greenberg was told to get rid of the plane (an order he ignored), and Jenkins's trip was cancelled. On 15 January 1968 Jenkins resigned, protesting his diminished authority after Rogers's reorganization and asking for six months' salary. He also asked to be allowed to acquire "early genetic materials and varietal collections brought with me from the University of Manitoba." He cooled down but ultimately left in August.

The American partners now began trying to sell the company. In February 1968 World Seeds was offered for US$3 million to an American firm, International Milling Company. In May Strohm tried to sell a one-third interest in World Seeds for $2.5 million to Continental Grain Company of New York. In August Strohm, accompanied by Cherniavsky and Greenberg, met with Occidental Oil Company of Houston, who were in the fertilizer business and who seemed prepared to buy World Seeds with Occidental shares. Cherniavsky came away from the meeting believing the oil company was interested. However, nothing more came from this.

On 1 July 1968 Rogers was surprised to receive a letter from Strohm which began: "Forrie, would B.C. Sugar be interested in getting out of World Seeds, with all of its loans paid back, plus some profit on the transaction?" He asked for a two-month option to find another partner. The alternative, he added, would be additional financing from BC Sugar.[8] Even Strohm recognized that that was unlikely: "BC Sugar looks at this 'as a banker would' when it comes to lending World Seeds money," he complained. Rogers circulated Strohm's letter to his directors: "Mr. Strohm has proved to be no manager, but very definitely a promoter with dreams of great success always just around the corner." Rogers said he was inclined to grant the option "if there is any indication that Strohm and his partners can actually exercise it. Otherwise we seem to bounce from one financial crisis to another and from what I now know of our American partners there seems little likelihood that this state of affairs will cease in the near future."

World Seeds had 174,000 bushels of Red River 68 in storage, now essentially unsaleable as a breeding variety. Reports in the farm press in November 1967 that Minnesota's Crop Quality Council had recommended against releasing Red River 68 made it difficult to sell it to farmer-growers at any price, let alone Strohm's hoped-for $15 a bushel. The Council feared that the wheat's strong gluten content would produce bread dough too binding to be worked easily in the bakery. The Manitoba Department of Agriculture, taking its cue from Minnesota, advised its farmers to shun Red River 68. Subsequently, the Board of Grain Commissioners said it did not meet the milling and baking standards set by the Canada Grains Act.

By the end of 1968 BC Sugar had had enough. Arthur Greenberg, the Grand Forks farmer, paid $1,000 in November 1968 for a three-month option to buy BC Sugar's 50 per cent of World Seeds. BC Sugar asked for US$1,250,000—enough to repay BC Sugar's investment and even leave the sugar company with a small profit.[9] When a deal was finally struck, Greenberg and Strohm were to pay only US$339,000. They tried hard to maintain some relationship with BC Sugar, arguing that "World Seeds and its stockholders desire to retain the goodwill of BC Sugar and its officers." But the company wanted nothing more to do with its American partners and relinquished its interest in mid-1969.

BC Sugar's shareholders were told: "Your directors are naturally disappointed that this course of action had to be taken as they had hoped that this would prove to be an interesting and profitable diversification for the company; however, it became abundantly clear that Canadian governmental regulations would make it difficult, if not impossible, to accomplish our objectives within Canada. . . ." The loss on this investment, including a write-off of most of the loans, was $649,731.

Frank Peto wanted to continue developing new wheats even while his company was trying to unwind from World Seeds. In February 1969, for example, he was in Edmonton, maintaining in interviews that Canadian farmers were growing the wrong varieties. He told the *Edmonton Journal*: "It's both economically unsound and morally wrong for Canada to continue producing the Cadillac of world wheat while most of the world wants low-priced food." BC Sugar, in 1969, set up a cereal and seed division to go it alone in the seed business. At BC Sugar's research farm at Ladner, Peto continued wheat trials, concentrating now on a variety of Mexican origin called Pitic 62. This high-yielding wheat was not a bread wheat but a non-controversial feed wheat aimed at feeding livestock. Yet this variety faced direct competition from Glenlea, a new feed wheat developed in Manitoba. Pitic was licensed but only with considerable difficulty and delay.

By the end of the year Forrest Rogers decided to withdraw totally from cereal seed breeding in Canada. In a letter to John Strohm, Rogers explained: "It is abundantly clear that there are too many bureaucratic bodies abundantly opposed to private plant breeding and even if we come up with a really superior material, licensing would be delayed so long by the authorities that there would be no financial reward for us." A disappointed Frank Peto retired shortly thereafter.

21

We Parted Very Amicably

THE COMPANY BEGINS TO DIVERSIFY.

Indirectly, the Hitler terror was behind BC Sugar's initial diversification. By 1937 Nazi persecution of Germany's Jewish population led Jews and other intellectuals and business people there and in neighbouring Austria to immigrate to more secure countries. One of these was John Bettelheim, better-known by the name he adopted in Canada, John Bene (pronounced Bennay). Born in 1910, he graduated in mechanical engineering from the University of Budapest and had become a talented young designer and operator of plywood and veneer plants by the time the Nazi menace emerged.

Bene came to Canada in 1937, on a visitors' permit, looking for work. By the time he reached Vancouver, his permit was close to expiry and he still had no employment. But he did have friends: the Rogers family. Musician Jan Cherniavsky, who had married B. T. Rogers's daughter Elspeth, was close to one of Bene's uncles in Vienna. It is probable that either Philip or Ernest, enthusiastic travellers who had visited Vienna during the 1930s, also had met Bene and his family. Bene now visited the Rogers and told them of his difficulty finding suitable work.

Bene was invited to a cocktail party hosted by Ernest Rogers, who recited Bene's plight to another of the guests, Minister of National Defence Ian Mackenzie. The minister, moved by the story, telephoned

Trade and Commerce Minister C. D. Howe in Ottawa, who arranged that Bene be given a new permit and a year in which to establish a plywood plant. The following year Bene, back in Vancouver once again, was introduced by a banker to two other recent Austrian refugees, John Prentice and J. G. (Poldi) Bentley, who had been successful textile manufacturers in Europe.[1] They put their capital behind Bene's technical expertise to establish Pacific Veneer Company, the forerunner to the pulp and lumber giant, Canfor Corporation.

When Bene, after a falling-out with his partners in 1944, formed Western Plywood Company, he turned for financial backing to Philip Rogers and BC Sugar. The plywood company was incorporated in July 1944, with BC Sugar investing $100,000 in 1000 preferred shares and 5000 common shares. Subsequently, that holding was tripled, giving BC Sugar a one-third interest. Furthermore, the sugar company's influence was even greater since three of the positions on Western's original five-person board of directors were held by Philip and Forrest Rogers and Alan Robertson, BC Sugar's vice-president. (The others were Bene and his partner, Dr. Leslie Schaffer).[2] Philip and Forrest Rogers later personally assumed the equity investment, and the company's role changed: it acted either as a lender to Western or as a backer of its bank loans. Unlike later diversifications, Western Plywood never appeared in any of BC Sugar's annual reports.

Western's first plywood plant, built in Vancouver at the foot of Fraser Street, began producing in November 1945 and was making money by the end of its first year. It continued to grow profitably throughout its history as an independent company.

John Bene was "very, very expansion-minded," said Geoffrey Tullidge, who joined Western in 1947 as the senior sales executive.[3] In 1945 Bene took the company into a joint venture, called International Plywoods Ltd., with Canadian International Paper Ltd. to design and operate a birch plywood mill at Gatineau, Quebec. The mill cost $500,000, with Western's $125,000 portion provided by loans from BC Sugar. The venture ended profitably in 1948 when CIP purchased that interest for about $410,000.

Bene sought BC Sugar's aid in the spring of 1952 when Western Plywood was offered a large stand of choice timber at Harrison Lake for $440,000. Bene, whose company was short of its own wood supply, had tried to buy this stand before and did not want to miss the opportunity now, despite being low on cash. "At the present time," he lamented in a letter to Philip Rogers, "we do not feel that we can commit the company to such a heavy capital investment. I was wondering whether the Refinery might be interested in purchasing the timber and we would in turn commit ourselves to buy the logs and pay for them at a premium over the market." Rogers demurred. "As far as this Company assuming the liability temporarily," he replied, "I am afraid that this is rather beyond our policy, particularly as we have before us very heavy capital expenditures on our own plants."[4]

When the next expansion opportunity came along—purchase of Murray Plywoods Ltd., with a Vancouver plant next door to Western's—Bene financed it in part by a public stock offering and in part by borrowing from the Bank of Montreal, BC Sugar's bank. With the acquisition of Murray, Western now was making about 20 per cent of all British Columbia's plywood. Bene raised more bank financing, began building a plywood plant near Edmonton, bought another small plant in British Columbia and a 600-acre cottonwood plantation in the Fraser Valley. Western's sales topped $18 million in 1956 but, in its rapid expansion, it had piled up $3.6 million in debts.[5] The next summer BC Sugar's financial trouble-shooter Ian Angus moved into Western temporarily to install some cost-cutting.

In 1959, to support new expansion, Western began negotiating with Georgia-Pacific Corporation of Portland for a partnership in which the American company would invest $3 million in the Canadian company. At the last moment, Georgia-Pacific changed its mind. "That left us in a pretty bad spot," remembered Tullidge. "There had been some big ideas of expansion and some commitments." Then Bene succeeded in getting U.S. Plywood of New York to buy control of Western, and the company, reorganized as Weldwood of Canada, developed into a substantial manufacturer of pulp, lumber and plywood in western Canada. Bene left the company to take up a career as an international consultant, devoting much time to the Canadian International Development Agency.

BC Sugar retained no direct connection with Weldwood, but Forrest Rogers remained a director until he retired from that board in 1983. Tullidge believes that BC Sugar's own directors, at least briefly, considered taking a major stake in Western Plywood in 1959 but opted for the status quo.

There is no question that the sugar company had the means to make acquisitions. In early 1962, with no immediate acquisition in sight, the directors began to worry that BC Sugar's cash reserves would attract a takeover raid by someone who would then strip the assets. To forestall this, the company declared a dividend to its shareholders of 800,000 $20 preferred shares, with shareholders getting one preferred for one common share. During the next three years the company then redeemed about 500,000 of these for cash at par value and bought others on the stock market.

By 1966 Forrest Rogers again was ready to expand the company by considering the acquisition of a sugar refinery in eastern Canada. After rejecting Cartier Sugar, a small Montreal refiner, he took a serious look at the long-established St. Lawrence Sugar, also in Montreal, controlled by the McConnell family. In early July he asked J. R. McConnell (also publisher of the *Montreal Star*) to send annual reports and other data covering the refinery's operations for the previous decade. Rogers had already run the idea by David Henry, the director of the Combines Investigation Branch in Ottawa. Rogers wrote McConnell: "Mr. Henry advised me that should our company acquire St. Lawrence Sugar Refiners Ltd. his department would not automatically institute an investigation, although of course he might be required to do something if a complaint were lodged with his department."[6] Henry did not have to do anything because Rogers ultimately did not proceed with this acquisition. Although the investment in World Seeds the following year was unsuccessful, it did not discourage Rogers for long: the company backed Belkin Packaging in 1970.

This was not the first time the company had been in the packaging business. The B.C. Cooperage & Jute Company was incorporated by B. T. Rogers in October 1892 to take over the business of Eastman & Clerin, a firm which had been making sugar barrels for the refinery. Rogers intended to expand into the manufacture of salmon cases, barrels for beer, cement and fish; and to add equipment for making jute sacks, which were then being imported from India or being purchased from eastern Canada. The shareholders, who subscribed a total of $27,100, included several who had backed BC Sugar (William Van Horne, Lord Strathcona, Ernst Gerbracht and several Anguses). The cooperage proved a source of many headaches; in 1893 Rogers concluded that Eastman was an incompetent manager and fired him. Shortly thereafter a fire destroyed the plant. Rebuilt, it was run for many years by B. T.'s brother Lawrence until it was sold after B. T. died.[7]

Unlike the cooperage, the investment in Belkin was not made to assure a supply of packaging materials. The company wanted to diversify beyond the sugar business, where growth was being stifled by new artificial sweeteners, sugar substitutes from corn, and some public hostility to the use of refined sugar, often based on faddish diets. Peter Cherniavsky, who was being groomed to succeed Forrest Rogers, argued persuasively that it was dangerous to trust the company's future to sugar alone.

The seed business venture, while not successful, had alerted the business world that BC Sugar was interested in diversifying. Consequently, a number of opportunities were presented, often by H. R. Whittall, a vice-chairman of Richardson Securities and a director of the sugar company, but it was some time before a suitable candidate was found. Allan Dunlop, BC Sugar's chief financial officer at the time, said that many candidates already trading publicly were rejected because the company would not invest in any firms in which BC Sugar shareholders themselves could invest directly. "You can look for a long time before you find something suitable if you are going in on that kind of basis," said Dunlop, who believed the principle was sound.[8] BC Sugar also maintained the principle of not competing with its customers, which ruled out other possibilities. When soft drink bottlers—big buyers of sugar—began using cans in the early 1960s, the refinery had the opportunity to install a contract canning line. "But," explained Cherniavsky, "that would have been seen as competing with our own customers and so we stayed away from it. . . . Perhaps that was a mistake."[9] The right opportunity came along in June 1970 when a Vancouver businessman named Morris Belkin, needing capital to complete an acquisition of his own, sold half his company to BC Sugar for $9.5 million. To finance this purchase, the sugar company floated a bond issue—the first time in BC Sugar's history that any expansion or acquisition had been funded with long-term debt.

Belkin was an entrepreneur of the old school, determined and single-minded, who insisted on running his own show. "I thought he was a super guy," Cherniavsky said. "He had an idea every bloody minute and it was really a question of holding him down." He was born in Calgary, son of a Russian-born meat merchant whose business had suffered badly in the 1930s. The family was so hard up that when Morris Belkin travelled to university in Vancouver, he arranged a free ride on a cattle car in exchange for tending the animals.[10] Belkin earned an arts degree at the University of British Columbia in 1944. He became interested in the printing business while working on the student newspaper, which was being printed by the *Point Grey News Gazette*. When the *News Gazette* slipped into receivership shortly after Belkin graduated, he raised the money to buy the printing company. He then converted the presses to the production of paper boxes and was in on the ground floor of the postwar boom in consumer packaging. A subsidiary company, Belkin Paper Box Ltd., soon became more important than the printing division. By January 1957 Belkin's company, once housed in a small Kerrisdale print shop, had moved into a major plant in Richmond that boasted the first two-colour lithographic press in Western Canada. Five years later, after yet another expansion, the company's name was changed to Belkin Packaging Ltd.[11] It was selling its products across Canada by 1970.

It was Morris Belkin's need for a reliable supply of paperboard—raw material for packaging—that led to the partnership with BC Sugar. Because of wartime quotas and later because of intense demand among carton manufacturers, as a new entrant to the business he often found himself scrambling to buy from American suppliers, which put him at a price disadvantage vis à vis his Canadian competitors. In 1969 he decided to build his own paperboard mill. Then the Vancouver forest products firm MacMillan Bloedel Ltd., expanding into Europe and the United States, offered to sell him its Burnaby mill. Belkin was prevented from raising the money in a public share issue by a stock market slump late in 1969, forcing his financial advisor, Richardson Securities' Whittall, to look for a well-financed partner. Whittall recommended Belkin to BC Sugar, whose executives quickly perceived that this investment would add "substantially to the Company's growth potential," as the 1970 annual report noted. The Belkin acquisition raised BC Sugar's annual revenues from $50 million in 1970 to $71 million in 1971.

With solid sponsorship, Morris Belkin—like John Bene before him—quickly built his company. By 1973 it had opened a new corrugated box manufacturing plant in Richmond and had begun producing, under licence, paper milk cartons—now familiar but then an innovative product. "Your company's investment in Belkin Packaging Ltd. again proved its worth, since sales and profits increased substantially," Forrest Rogers wrote in the 1972 annual report. Because the Belkin profits were being ploughed back into that company, Rogers added, "it should be pointed out to shareholders that as yet no cash dividends have been received from this source." BC Sugar shareholders were accustomed to generous and constant dividends and had to be reminded that companies in a rapid growth stage, such as Belkin, have other priorities for their cash flow. Three years later the capacity of the paperboard mill had been doubled and Belkin, looking to Eastern Canada, bought Somerville Industries Ltd., a carton maker which already had nine plants in the East. This acquisition more than doubled Belkin's sales in 1977. By the following year, BC Sugar was reporting that its Belkin interest was contributing more to total company revenues than the refinery's sugar sales.

However, Belkin contributed far less to BC Sugar's profits. Sugar, while less than half the company's revenues, provided close to 90 per cent of the company's net earnings in 1979.[12] Morris Belkin's comment in BC Sugar's 1979 annual report—"net earnings for last year were somewhat disappointing"—was an understatement. "Well, that was disturbing in an industry that was going through a very rough time, no question about it," Cherniavsky recalled. "We didn't like it and we didn't like all the debt." At one point Belkin's debt was about $100 million. "Although the debt wasn't ours, we would of course have had a moral responsibility had something gone wrong with Belkin."[13]

The modest profits of the packaging operations also aggravated the clash of styles that occasionally led to a prickly relationship between Belkin and his partners at BC Sugar. "He was impossible to work with, to be very honest," remembered Allan Dunlop. "Oh, I liked Morris. He had a lot of great ideas. [But] he thought he could run the whole show." Cherniavsky also had become uncomfortable with Belkin's "one-man band" style: "As long as the company was small, it was okay. But the bigger Belkin got, the more difficult it became" to manage. This was reflected in a letter that Cherniavsky wrote to Belkin in May 1978: "It is interesting to look back over the years and see what has happened to your Company since we became your partner. In B.C. it has gone from one site to three, with very substantial investments in corrugated, paperboard and milk cartons. Then the Alberta plant and, of course, the acquisition of Somerville. All in all, quite a record in spite of the difficulties in recent times, although we think some of the major problems are now behind us—you are to be commended." Then Cherniavsky made the real point: "What all this points to is the necessity of strengthening your management team."[14]

Cherniavsky also was concerned that, should Belkin become incapacited or die, BC Sugar would find itself running a large company in partnership with an estate or a trustee, a commercially stultifying situation. When Belkin refused to amend the partnership agreement to get around this potential problem, Cherniavsky asked him to buy BC Sugar's share of the packaging company. In April 1980 Belkin offered $17.5 million. Cherniavsky argued that, based on the packaging company's ability to generate cash, it was worth considerably more. Belkin stubbornly stood by his view of the company's worth. Finally, in July 1980, BC Sugar sold its 50 per cent of Belkin for $18 million, about double what it had paid a decade earlier. "We parted very amicably," Cherniavsky remembered, and they remained friends. Belkin died in 1988.

22

They Bet on People

BC SUGAR ENTERS THE OIL AND GAS BUSINESS.

Oilman J. C. Anderson was called away to the telephone shortly after the 9 A.M. start of his first meeting in November 1975 with the BC Sugar team that had come to Calgary to invest in his oil and gas business. "When I came back in," Anderson remembered, "I said 'I am sorry I had to excuse myself there for a minute but we are perforating a well this morning and there was some question about where we were going to perforate it.' And one of them asked, 'What is perforating a well?' "[1] The tall, drawling Nebraska-born petroleum engineer sighed in resignation and spent the rest of the morning giving a lesson in the jargon of petroleum exploration, explaining among other things that perforating a well means opening the walls of the drill hole to the surrounding rock to access oil or gas.

His new partners, however, were quick learners. By the end of the day, Anderson and Peter Cherniavsky shook hands on a verbal agreement to take BC Sugar into the petroleum business. "I won't say the decision was finally made that day," Anderson said. He warned Cherniavsky that it would take another six months for him to restructure his business so that BC Sugar could make its investment. "And one of Peter's concerns was: 'Christ, what if you go out and make a big discovery—then the price is going to change.' " It was an understandable concern: Anderson had become an overnight legend five years earlier when his company discovered Alberta's mammoth Dunvegan gas field in an area where four other exploration teams had found nothing. "I said to Peter: 'Our deal is that the price ain't going to change. That's it.' And it was all verbal up until six months later [when] we signed the paper." Anderson was impressed by the trust his new partners placed in him. He said: "They bet on people which I think is good—providing you are betting on the right people."

BC Sugar moved into the oil business amid the dramatic rises in energy prices in the 1970s. Many energy-dependent Canadian businesses had been alarmed in mid-decade by a National Energy Board warning that production from existing natural gas wells would decline after 1976. Anderson recalled the mood: "Then the vogue was, 'Christ, we are going to run out of oil and gas' which I always thought was a crazy thing—being in the business." BC Sugar was then operating two sugar beet factories in Alberta and one in Manitoba which, among them, consumed annually two billion cubic feet of natural gas. Cherniavsky believed that the company was dangerously exposed to rising gas prices and declining supplies and began looking for a partner in the energy business in Alberta.

Anderson also was seeking a partner. An American citizen, he needed to bring a substantial Canadian shareholder into his business to comply with Foreign Investment Review Agency restrictions on non-Canadian investment in energy production. A University of Texas graduate, he arrived in Calgary in 1966, transferred by Amoco to Canada as their chief engineer here. He soon concluded that Alberta was an exploration frontier and, with $400,000 backing from his brother Robert, and other American investors, struck out on his own in 1968. Their investment paid off when he found Dunvegan, a northern Alberta gas field that has been producing since 1973 and will continue to produce into the next century.

Anderson was as adept at creative financing as at exploration. Alberta & Southern Gas Company in 1970 agreed to a gas purchase contract that included an interest-free development loan based on the quantity of gas Anderson discovered. By 1972 he had received $11 million from this agreement, an unusual one in the oil industry. "We built all these assets by our wits, so to speak," he recounted. But to keep expanding, he now needed to Canadianize his company. He structured a deal in which the prospective investor in his company would garner significant tax savings by writing off petroleum exploration costs against other income. He was refused by the first Canadian non-oil company to which he showed his investment package. "They did not understand it," he believed. A friend at the brokerage firm of Richardson Greenshields of Canada Inc., whom Anderson consulted, spread the word that the oilman was looking for a partner. Richard Whittall, the long-time BC Sugar director who had earlier introduced the company to Morris Belkin, successfully encouraged the sugar company to back Anderson.[2]

In May 1976 BC Sugar agreed to invest $15 million—$5 million immediately and $10 million during the next four years—in a new company, Fairweather Gas Ltd., to be owned 60 per cent by BC Sugar and 40 per cent by Anderson's company. (The name Fairweather was suggested by Cherniavsky in a tribute to family history: it was the maiden name of his great-grandmother, Mary Fairweather, who was the mother of Mrs. B. T. Rogers.) Fairweather got a 3.8 per cent interest in production from the Dunvegan gas field and quickly drilled additional wells in 1977 to increase its production. The objective was to give Fairweather a running start: sales from its gas production not only funded more exploration but also provided dividends to BC Sugar. Forrest Rogers and Cherniavsky told their shareholders in 1976 that the sugar company expected "an immediate cash return on its investment."[3]

Fairweather drilled one hundred gas wells in 1977, completing seventy-three of them as producers. However, the rising energy prices triggered so much exploration in Western Canada that, instead of the shortage forecast by the National Energy Board, a surplus of gas resulted. Now Fairweather found itself with interests in more than one hundred Alberta gas wells that were shut in to await revived markets. The Dunvegan field, unable to sell all its production, throttled back to less than two-thirds of its 1977 and 1978 output. Fairweather, which now had natural gas reserves of 91 billion cubic feet and oil reserves of 720,000 barrels, drilled fewer gas wells in 1978 and shifted its focus to oil.

By 30 September 1980, when Fairweather's original joint venture agreement with Anderson expired, some $2.7 million of BC Sugar's committment still had not been spent. In spite of the slowdown in drilling and marketing, the investment had paid off. BC Sugar had received about $1 million in dividends from Fairweather and also had benefitted from Fairweather's exploration tax credits, which reduced the tax bite on the profitable sugar business. J. C. Anderson later calculated that the sugar company, for a net investment of about $6.5 million, ended up owning 60 per cent of a gas company whose estimated value by 1980 was between $35 million and $40 million. Fairweather had participated in 230 successful wells and could have drilled more had it been able to sell more gas. The joint venture agreement was extended, for BC Sugar was in the energy business to stay.

Once Anderson's company was Canadianized, he planned to expand through acquisitions. At first, rising oil and gas prices inflated the cost of acquisition targets. It was not until 1981 that the right opportunity came along: Fairweather paid $209 million to buy two Alberta oil and gas companies, Alamo Petroleum Ltd. and AMAX Petroleum of Canada Ltd., both owned by AMAX Inc. of Greenwich, Connecticut. J. C. Anderson knew these companies well. All of Alamo's oil and gas reserves had been discovered by Anderson's exploration company in joint venture drilling programs, and 65 per cent of the combined reserves of Alamo and AMAX were under contract and were being produced. This purchase, which raised Fairweather's interest in the Dunvegan field to 47.5 per cent, was a big bite for the small energy company. The plan was to replace the large bank loan that provided the initial financing with privately raised equity capital, a routine way of doing business. As soon as the deal was closed in July 1981, Anderson began looking for an investor. He shortly received a big setback when the federal government introduced the National Energy Policy in September 1981. "Instead of taking me two or three months to do the private placement," he said, "it ended up taking about two and one half years which we ultimately did on November 1, 1983."[4]

The negative impact of the NEP on the market value of petroleum companies, combined with the very high interest rates of 1981, required a total re-organization of the oil and gas investments now controlled by Anderson and BC Sugar. All the investments—including Fairweather, Alamo and AMAX—were merged in October 1982 into Anderson Exploration Ltd. with BC Sugar owning 53 per cent.[5] Paying the interest on the company's bank debt caused Anderson to lose nearly $8 million in 1983. The debt was retired by a $110 million equity refinancing in

November 1983 which brought in Kerr Addison Mines Ltd. of Toronto as a one-third owner, reducing BC Sugar's interest to 38.7 per cent (J. C. Anderson and associates held the rest).[6]

Cherniavsky noted in BC Sugar's 1982 annual report that the sugar company had invested, in total, $73 million in the petroleum business since 1976. Most of that money came either from revenues of the sugar business or from a redeployment of the capital after the Belkin sale. BC Sugar itself had had to take on only $21.5 million additional debt, raising its long-term debt to $25.2 million. Shareholders' equity was nearly three times that, giving the company a safely conservative balance sheet. But the company's long-term shareholders were even more conservative and needed additional reassurance. In the 1983 annual report BC Sugar published a table showing its remarkable record of having paid dividends without interruption for ninety years. Cherniavsky observed proudly that the oil and gas investments had been made "in a manner that did not jeopardize dividends. It is the company's intention that any future investments will be made out of resources available after payment of dividends."

The wisdom of reassuring shareholders on dividends was confirmed in 1986 when circumstances in the oil and gas business resulted in BC Sugar reporting a loss for the first time in more than sixty years. Because oil and gas prices had declined from earlier highs, the accounting profession—as a matter of general auditing policy—insisted that investments in oil and gas reserves comply with a "ceiling test." Anderson Exploration Ltd. reduced by $41 million the value of its gas reserves, anticipating that, after the November deregulation of gas prices that year, the selling price of gas would drop (it did) and so would the value of reserves. This write-down in value produced a loss for Anderson and ultimately a loss for BC Sugar—but only on paper. No actual cash losses were suffered. As usual, BC Sugar paid a regular cash dividend ($1.20 a share) even though it reported a net loss of $36.6 million or $5.99 a share.

The long-term plan after the AMAX and Alamo purchase in 1981 had been to convert Anderson into a publicly traded petroleum company in which BC Sugar would hold a significant but minority stake. This goal was frustrated by a series of events—the NEP, the slump in oil and gas prices, the gas surplus—that depressed the value of petroleum stocks. When the stock market climate finally seemed appropriate in 1987,

Anderson Exploration spent nearly $300,000 on the highly sophisticated evaluation of reserves that a public offering would require. Then in October 1987 the stock market crashed; it was no longer possible to have a successful public offering of a company worth perhaps as much as $300 million.

At BC Sugar's first annual meeting after investing in oil and gas, enthusiastic shareholders had asked whether they could invest directly in Fairweather. But by 1988 shareholders were asking why the value of the petroleum company was not being reflected in higher values for BC Sugar shares. Nor was Cherniavsky pleased that BC Sugar's shares clearly were undervalued: it was a dangerous situation that could have attracted an uninvited takeover bid for BC Sugar from a corporate raider. Across North America during the 1980s, many historic companies had been taken over this way, only to be dismembered by new owners intent on selling the pieces for more than had been paid for the whole. This was not a fate Cherniavsky desired for the company founded by his grandfather. Thus, in May 1988, the company declared a special dividend of about half of its shares in Anderson Exploration (still retaining a 20 per cent interest, however). BC Sugar's 4000 shareholders received 3,420,000 Anderson shares (one for each two BC Sugar shares they owned). Anderson was then listed on the Toronto Stock Exchange in July and by year end the shares were trading for about $13. That put the total value of the dividend at $44 million, the largest special dividend ever paid in the company's history.

23

You Couldn't Milk the Public

THE VOLATILITY OF THE WORLD SUGAR PRICE.

In December 1974 BC Sugar disclosed the record $8.8 million profit during a rare press conference convened by Forrest Rogers and Peter Cherniavsky in Vancouver. "We hope you fellows can get the message across," chairman Rogers implored reporters. "The company has never in its 85-year history had a press conference to announce its earnings."

If earnings were high, so were sugar prices. The world raw sugar price in November of that year peaked at an all-time high of 65 cents (U.S.) a pound, four times its price a year earlier. In Eastern Canada, Redpath Industries Ltd. tried to deflect criticism with full-page newspaper advertisements declaring: "Due to forces beyond our control, our sugar price is ridiculous." Across the country, restaurants began removing sugar bowls to thwart pilferage. In Vancouver, the Super-Valu food chain put up signs asking their customers to refrain from buying unneeded sugar. The Food Prices Review Board, established by the federal government in 1973 to monitor food prices, received more complaints about sugar than about any other commodity.

In Ottawa, Consumer and Corporate Affairs Minister André Ouellet threatened to establish a national sugar-buying corporation. In Winnipeg Ouellet's provincial counterpart Ian Turnbull wanted to force down the price of Manitoba-produced beet sugar and prevent it from being exported from the province. Only the beet growers were openly elated. "We don't think the price is excessive at all," Alberta Sugar Beet Growers Association president Lalovee Jensen told the *Edmonton Journal* in February 1974. "In fact, we'll have to work like the Dickens to keep up with the costs involved with this crop."

Unusually high sugar prices trigger unusual controversy because they occur so infrequently in a world that normally has overabundant sugar production. Typically, price spikes are caused by war or threat of war. The outbreak of the Korean War in 1950 sent prices spiralling for a year.[1] The next spike was caused by fears that the Suez Crisis and the Hungarian Revolution in the fall of 1956 could lead to war. The 1963 price spike occurred when the United States orchestrated an economic boycott against Cuba. World Sugar production had been lagging behind growth in consumption because raw sugar prices had been unusually depressed during the previous five years. A small European sugar crop that year coincided with the disruption in sugar trading caused by the boycott. A return to normal crops the next year quickly dropped sugar prices until, by mid-1965, they were at their lowest in twenty-four years and still falling. Those depressed world prices of the late 1960s helped cause the 1974 spike. Sugar production again began lagging demand, reducing the pool of freely traded raw sugar until that pool was vulnerable to supply disruption.

Only a small portion of total world sugar production is traded on the open market. The rest is consumed where it is produced or traded under bilateral agreements. It is the freely traded sugar that establishes world prices. In 1971 the Soviet Union's beet crop was below average quantity and, for the first time in years, the Russians entered the open market to buy one million tons of sugar. This unexpected order sent world sugar prices up by nearly 25 per cent in one month. That year, and again in 1973, lower than expected crops in Europe as well as in Russia kept moving sugar prices ever higher until, at the end of the year, the International Sugar Agreement collapsed. While international agreements never stabilized prices very successfully, they did enforce a degree of discipline, which now was gone entirely. In January 1974 sugar prices began their sharpest rise in history.

The year was a trial under fire for Peter Cherniavsky, who had become president and managing director in January 1973 when his uncle Forrest

Rogers retired. The grandson of B. T. Rogers, Cherniavsky was born in London, England, on 5 November 1926. His father, pianist Jan Cherniavsky, was one of the celebrated Ukrainian-born Cherniavsky Trio, brother-musicians who played before the Czar's court in prerevolutionary Russia and, after 1917, became well-known both in Europe and North America. A chance meeting on a passenger ship from Fiji to Vancouver led to a classic shipboard romance between one of the musicians, Mischel Cherniavsky, and Mary Rogers, B. T.'s strong-willed eldest daughter. The disapproving Rogers sent Mary to New York to separate the pair, only to have the romance flourish when the musical trio went there to perform. Mischel's brother, Jan, then courted Mary's younger sister, Elspeth. After B. T.'s death both daughters married, with the approval of their music-loving mother.[2]

Peter Cherniavsky was raised and educated in private schools in England and British Columbia before enrolling in mechanical engineering at the University of British Columbia in the fall of 1943. By that time, he was already working for the sugar company, having started in August 1942 as a laboratory boy at 25 cents an hour and then as a machinist's helper for an additional 10 cents an hour. In the summer of 1944 he was sent to the beet factory at Raymond where he was assigned to weed and thin the factory's neglected field of beets. "It was the hardest work I've ever done in my life,"[3] he remembered. His elders were testing him: when he finished the field, it was ploughed up to make way for a railway spur that, he discovered with bitter disappointment, had been planned since the spring. Yet when he became a permanent employee of BC Sugar after graduating in 1948, he asked to go to Raymond for that fall's campaign. One of the attractions for the young employee, who loved hunting, was hinted at in a memorandum Philip Rogers sent to T. George Wood: "I think that Cherniavsky would prefer to have Mondays off rather than Sundays on account of the ducks and pheasants. . . ." A cherished keepsake from that 1948 campaign was a letter that Wood wrote to Philip Rogers: "Peter has made a good impression here, and we think he has a fine personality as a young man. We shall be glad at any time to have him back with us, if that is desired."[4] He was in Alberta for the first campaign at Taber in 1950 and subsequently spent nearly two years as factory superintendent at Ozama. Cherniavsky became general superintendent of the Vancouver refinery in 1954 and, during the next two decades, established a sure-handed technical grasp of all BC Sugar operations. He had the happy facility of learning quickly on the job—and 1974 provided plenty of lessons.

The collapse of the International Sugar Agreement plunged Cherniavsky into the chaotic experience of trying to order sugar cargoes when sellers were holding out for higher prices. The company's major source, Australia's Colonial Sugar, was unable to meet Cherniavsky's requests for additional raws because of a small 1973 cane crop in the state of Queensland. Cuban raws were available, but the asking price rose several times before BC Sugar concluded the purchase of a cargo. A small cargo was purchased from Nicaragua, but the offer of Mexican sugar proved to be an illusion. Throughout the year, the soaring price of raws pushed up the retail price.

Cherniavsky and his fellow executives decided on a pricing policy that would not expose BC Sugar to accusations of profiteering. H. Allan Dunlop, the company's chief financial officer, said in an interview: "We were all agreed that you couldn't milk the public. We felt that in the long run . . . we would pay some penalty for it."[5] In Vancouver the refinery cut its margin to the bone, operating with a pre-tax loss of $46,000 in the fiscal year ended September 1974.

The beet sugar factories, however, were making what Dunlop called "fantastic" profits now that the world sugar price was far above the cost of producing beet sugar. It was beet sugar that enabled the company to show that 1974 record profit, which occasioned the press conference, and an even greater $9.2 million profit in 1975. In August BC Sugar decided to refrain from further increases in beet sugar prices on the Prairies while holding its existing customers to 105 per cent of their purchases of the previous year. Since the company was the sole supplier in the territory served, it felt it had an obligation to keep prices stable.

The company's selling policy did not please everyone. That fall, BC Sugar declined to give a prospective new customer—a soft drink bottler in Thunder Bay, Ontario—sugar at the reduced price available to an established customer in Kenora. The Thunder Bay bottler complained bitterly. Mindful of the company's 1955 confrontation with the Combines branch and of the price-fixing case then underway in Eastern Canada,[6] Peter Cherniavsky sought advice from law firms in Vancouver and Toronto to confirm that the company could sell only to existing customers and at prices lower than that which prevailed in the market. His Vancouver lawyer, E. F. Horsey of Bull, Housser & Tupper, advised against seeking an advance ruling from the Combines branch. Horsey wrote: "If you wait until questions are raised, then your answer should be sufficient to satisfy both them and any complainant." The question never arose.[7]

By late summer the rocketting prices created the impression among consumers that there was a serious sugar shortage. W. A. Davies, BC Sugar's general sales manager, invited a *Vancouver Sun* photographer to snap reassuring pictures of the huge piles of sugar stored at the refinery, available for sale.

Relief to consumers came in mid-1975 after new crops of sugar around the world began rebuilding the free-market pool of raw sugar. Prices not only moderated but plunged as new supplies hit the market. In the 1976 annual report, Cherniavsky told his shareholders sugar had "plummeted to unrealistically low levels." The world market was down to about 8 cents a pound, lower than it had been when the International Sugar Agreement fell apart. "Only a few years ago," Cherniavsky reported, "this would have been considered to be a satisfactory price, but various recent studies indicate that the most efficient world producers of raw sugar incur costs of production well in excess of 10 cents a pound."[8] Sugar prices bottomed out in the early 1980s, jeopardizing the very future of the company's sugar beet operations.

24

Sanity Is Not Prevailing

THE 1975 STRIKE AND WAGE AND PRICE CONTROLS.

The fuse for the ten-month-long strike that began on 2 June 1975 at the Vancouver refinery was lit when, in 1971, the company agreed for the first time to take job applications from individuals sent by the union and to give them equal consideration with other applicants. With this, the union had taken the first step towards establishing a hiring hall for the refinery and thus controlling the company's most vital personnel decisions. In 1975 the union asked that the company hire *only* individuals referred to it by the union. BC Sugar judged this proposal completely unacceptable. This impasse led to a strike that cost the company about $50 million in lost sugar sales and cost the employees millions in lost earnings.

The refinery's employees had organized in mid-1944 into the Industrial Union of Sugar Workers which later became local 517 of the Retail, Wholesale and Department Store Union, an international organization capable of providing the required service support to the refinery union. By 1975 local 517, with about 250 members, was one of the union's largest British Columbia units, accounting for nearly 10 per cent of its province-wide membership. Employers found Retail, Wholesale a tough organization. Dave Ritchie was a veteran management negotiator in Vancouver at the time for other food companies organized by the union.

"The tactics of the union for a good number of years were that they'd come into the bargaining session and threaten you to give them what they asked or face a strike," Ritchie said. "In the food business, you don't go on strike. If you do, you're not in business."[1] In 1976 the Employers Council of British Columbia attempted to strengthen the resolve of employers dealing with this union by grouping them into a mutual support committee.[2] Several companies—among them a Seagram's distillery in New Westminster—had closed British Columbia plants, blaming the union's demands. By the fall of 1975 BC Sugar president Peter Cherniavsky was wondering "if we are next on their list?"

Over the years at BC Sugar there remained more than a touch of the decent, if paternal, atmosphere created by Ernest Rogers's management when the work week was reduced without a pay cut and when a medical plan and a pension were established. In 1940 the refinery workers petitioned that the night shift be paid more than the day shift, and Philip Rogers agreed to do so after only a cursory survey of four other companies. G.B. (Gib) Murdoch, who started in 1937 in the laboratory and rose to assistant superintendent before retiring in 1985, recalled the company's atmosphere when he joined. Substantial hot meals were served daily in the company's dining rooms at the refinery. Male plant workers could buy their meals for as little as 25 cents while the office staff and female production workers received meals free of charge. The refinery often employed two or three generations of the same family. Gib's father, a Scottish coal miner who immigrated to Vancouver in 1929, worked briefly for BC Sugar, paving the way for three of his sons (the others were William and John) to join the company. "They believed if your dad or your brother was a good worker, you also were going to be a good worker," Gib Murdoch said. "It was rather a family-oriented company to start with. When the union came in, a lot of things changed. With the union, it seemed to bring in a 'we and them' attitude."[3]

Ray Haynes, when he became Retail, Wholesale's business agent in the mid-1950s, still found a close-knit familial loyalty to the company among members of local 517. For many years, agreements were concluded without the union's asking for mediation or taking a strike vote. "I remember it was quite a shocking thing when we went to mediation," Haynes said. He believed the bargaining unit became more militant after the company allowed the wages of its trades people to fall well behind those in construction and forestry. Initially, the company deflected the union's demands for higher trades rates because the refinery's more numerous production workers were reluctant to force the issue. Haynes finally threatened to urge the tradesmen to leave local 517 and join militant craft unions. "I think I was serious but I'm not positive," he said. "In any case it worked—we put through a substantial increase for the tradesmen."[4]

The first collective agreement negotiated by Retail, Wholesale, in 1947, was a slim sixteen-page document dealing with wages, vacations and other limited objectives.[5] At first, the payment of union dues was voluntary. In 1950, however, the union began to entrench its position through a contract clause obligating refinery employees who had joined the union to remain union members as a condition of employment. Ultimately, the union—like most other unions—won the right to make membership a job requirement.[6]

The union never was shy in pressing demands on a company that it felt could afford to be generous. "They made it clear they were not talking inability to pay," Haynes remembered. Vacation entitlements were continually improved; in 1953, for example, four-week vacations were granted to employees with twenty-five years' service. Four weeks vacation was extended to fifteen-year employees by 1965 and to twelve-year employees in 1967, with even longer vacations for the more senior. A fully paid sick benefits plan and a shared-cost medical care plan were negotiated in 1965, expanding programs that the company had inaugurated years before.

In the 1973 contract, immediately prior to the strike, local 517 negotiated some of the most extensive benefit gains in its history. The company agreed to pay all medical care premiums; to initiate a company-paid dental plan; to introduce an early retirement program; to pay triple time for work on nine statutory holidays; and to provide employees with an accumulated paid time-off benefit based on hours worked, at one hour's pay per week. These had been difficult negotiations, however, with the employees engaging in work slowdowns. There was more unrest the following year when the company, with its record profits, voluntarily offered modest wage increases to offset the price inflation then raging. The refinery employees responded with a brief sitdown strike, forcing a significant wage increase of about 60 cents an hour.

When bargaining for the refinery's 1975 contract began on 12 February at Vancouver's Sheraton Plaza Hotel, the union's menu of proposals consisted of forty-one items without wage demands. The company also made some proposals, among them asking that Friday afternoon be payday in order to reduce absenteeism. Both bargaining committees agreed to study the proposals—a routine beginning.[7]

But in the second meeting on 24 February, the difficult issue came into focus: the union again insisted on providing the candidates for refinery jobs. Whether the refinery workers cared about this point is questionable. Union hiring halls are common practice in certain transient jobs—involving construction workers and longshoremen, for instance, but rare in factories where employees and employers expect to have a long-term relationship.

BC Sugar's opposition to this provision was based on a matter of fundamental principle. The company's minutes from the fifth bargaining meeting of 17 April state: "Companies cannot give up the right to hire qualified, able and willing workers." The union indicated that it would refer only union members for jobs and that the employer could reject applicants sent by the union. The company countered by proposing that it would advise the union when it was screening new applicants. When the union rejected this offer, the company repeated that "there can be *no* acceptance of a hiring hall arrangement."

When the eighth meeting on 2 May became heated, Allen T. Peterson, the union's international representative, met privately with the company's chief negotiator, J. L. Gallagher. BC Sugar wanted the union to understand that the company was no longer the pliable BC Sugar of old. The minutes stated: "The Company intends to maintain this position even against coercion or other pressures. This may represent a different posture from previous years."

The union and the company sparred throughout May, with the union refusing the company's request for a mediator. On 26 May, with a cargo of raw sugar due, the employees refused the company's request to work overtime to unload it. Instead, the union served strike notice on 29 May. It was only with difficulty that the company got a crew to complete the unloading of the sugar boat.

The bargaining meeting on 1 June lasted an acrimonious thirty-five minutes. The company had suspended a laboratory assistant for insubordination: he had left the laboratory and was in the shipping area where a work slowdown was underway. The union insisted on the man's reinstatement. The tension in the plant was now so great that the plant superintendent William Murdoch suffered a mild heart attack. His brother Gib drove him to the hospital to avoid having an ambulance call at the refinery. "We didn't want to create a scene," he said.[8]

The next day the company gave the union a formal proposal for a settlement, including an offer to increase wages by 80 cents an hour in the first year and 70 cents in the second. The offer, which would look good months later when federal controls made it unattainable, received scant consideration. A sitdown strike began in the employees' lounge at two o'clock, and the union's negotiating team failed to show up for a scheduled meeting that evening. For the remainder of the week, employees came to work at their usual times, punched in—and then spent their shifts in the lounge. Those operating critical processes stayed on the job, and the refinery was "sweetened off"—that is, closed without damage to the equipment.[9]

"As we approached the end of the week, we didn't know what to do," Stanley George, the refinery's operating manager, said. "There were no meetings or anything else. The employees were friendly, nobody was bitter at each other." The company, to ensure it could close the refinery securely once the employees left, served lockout notice to the union. Both parties now exchanged letters offering to resume negotiations when work returned to normal at the refinery. "Now in my opinion," George said, "the union fully expected a repeat of '74—that within a few hours, a day at the most, the company would come running and say O.K. guys, let's get together and get this thing settled up. Well, there were several demands that the company just plain couldn't agree to." Peterson, in a letter to J. S. North, BC Sugar's personnel manager, complained: "Apparently, sanity is not prevailing." It was the one point on which both company and union could agree. The refinery stopped producing sugar on the first weekend in June.

The refinery's British Columbia customers were caught by surprise, and many stores were without sugar by the end of the week. While Alberta wholesalers diverted beet sugar to southeastern British Columbia, BC Sugar discouraged Canadian Sugar Factories, its subsidiary, from taking British Columbia orders. CSF had barely enough sugar for Alberta and Saskatchewan. That movement dried up in any case after 16 July when the British Columbia Federation of Labour issued a "hot" declaration on the products of BC Sugar and its subsidiaries, making it probable that other union employees would decline to handle any beet sugar. BC Sugar then referred its customers to sugar companies in Eastern Canada and the United States. Months later, when the strike ended, several American suppliers—notably the Utah–Idaho sugar company—attempted to retain some of the British Columbia market, retreating only in the face of tough price competition from BC Sugar.

On 2 July the M.V. *Saltnes* arrived from Australia with 17 500 tonnes of raw sugar. She anchored in the harbour until the captain, anxious to depart with a waiting cargo of grain, decided on 16 July to unload into barges. The next morning local 517 members bedecked a small boat with "locked-out" signs and circled the *Saltnes* until longshoremen refused to cross the floating picket line. They only returned to resume unloading a month later after the owners secured a Labour Relations Board injunction against the picketing.

Early in October rumours circulated that federal wage and price controls were being planned. Concluding that controls would only make it harder to settle the dispute, BC Sugar hurriedly made local 517 a new, somewhat fatter, version of the June offer. "They [the union] asked for 250 copies which we rushed and had printed and got to them Friday afternoon [10 October], figuring they would have a meeting over the weekend . . . ," Stanley George said. "They didn't schedule their meeting until Tuesday [14 October] and by that time it was ball game over." That Monday, Thanksgiving Day, Prime Minister Trudeau had announced the formation of an Anti-Inflation Board with powers to impose wage and price controls. (In any event, the union rejected the offer.)

In a letter directly to the employees, Peter Cherniavsky urged that a quick settlement be reached and taken to the new board that was enforcing the guidelines. The strategy would be to seek an exception for the refinery contract since the bargaining had begun six months earlier. At the same time, the company improved its wage proposal. Whereas the company wanted its employees back to work while seeking AIB approval of these wage terms, the union refused, arguing that a continuing stoppage would lever a quicker and more favourable decision from the board.

The employees thus found themselves in the peculiar stance of striking against the federal government.

British Columbia's 1975 labour climate was particularly stormy. In October the union-backed New Democratic government, under David Barrett, found it necessary to legislate an end to three crippling strikes. Cherniavsky wired Barrett, asking that the sugar refinery also be included in the controversial back-to-work legislation, but the government declined, unwilling to add Retail, Wholesale to the list of unions enraged by the law.

By now, Cherniavsky was so frustrated that he even considered appealing to the New York headquarters of Retail, Wholesale. He would have received a sympathetic hearing—though little else—since even the international headquarters was disturbed with the headstrong militancy of its British Columbia unit. Instead, he met in early November with Barrett's labour minister, Bill King, who immediately ordered veteran mediator Ken Albertini into the dispute. Albertini had already encountered the union's inflexibility during an unsuccessful September mediation, and was pessimistic. When he gave Peterson the company's list of unresolved items, the union bargainer tore it up and stalked from the meeting. (Peterson was well-known among his colleagues for such behaviour. "He sometimes had trouble closing a deal," a former union colleague said. "He'd get so goddamn mad and excited that he'd never recognize the employer would settle. I think he was a shade over his head, mostly because of his emotionalism.") Another fruitless meeting was held in December between Peterson and Gallagher, BC Sugar's negotiator, at which Peterson threatened that "the refinery may just not be reopened."[10]

When talks resumed on 7 January 1976, BC Sugar and the union agreed on a settlement that included a wage increase of $1.30 an hour retroactive to March 1975, and a further 8 per cent on 1 March 1976. The offered first year increase was well in excess of the AIB guideline of 8 per cent in the initial year of new contracts. But local 517 refused to return to work until the Anti-Inflation Board had ruled on the settlement.

On 26 February the AIB said no and ordered rolling the settlement back to 10 per cent in the year beginning 1 March 1975 and 8 per cent in the second year. The AIB's ruling was rejected at a union meeting where employees criticized their own union leaders for the blunder of not having grabbed the wage increase offered just before the guidelines were announced. Employee David Berger told the *Vancouver Sun* that there had been "a dirty trick on us all the way down the line."

The company and the union now resumed bargaining in the AIB's Vancouver offices, where the real negotiation was between Peterson and a senior AIB officer, David Chapman. The union finally authorized a return to work on 22 March, Peterson admitting to the *Sun*: "After 10 months our 250 members cannot continue indefinitely the fight against the federal government." In April the AIB approved a settlement, including wages and benefits, of 14 per cent in the first year and 8 per cent in the second.

Industrial harmony returned slowly during the next several contract renewals, although the union in 1978 tried again—still without success—to win a hiring hall. In these negotiations, the company adapted a practice from an American refiner and began issuing, directly to the employees, impartial bulletins summarizing each bargaining meeting. Peterson's outrage that the company would communicate directly led the union to object to the British Columbia Labour Relations Board that this was an unfair labour practice. LRB chairman Paul Weiler disagreed, ruling that: "We want to state emphatically that the trade-union is not granted a lock on the minds of the employees when it obtains the certification to represent them. Anybody can communicate with the employees, including their employer."[11]

Various other measures also were adopted to improve the climate and the communications between the company and its employees. A regular company magazine, *Sugar Scoop*, was begun in late 1976. In a private initiative that cut across union and management lines, a group of employees formed the Refinery Employees Boating Association, leasing an unused portion of the company wharf for a marina. When the association borrowed $33,000 in 1978 from the Bank of Montreal for its facilities, the company guaranteed the loan. Perhaps one of the most important steps, made at Peter Cherniavsky's suggestion in 1978, was the inauguration of an employee share ownership plan. A decade later, employees own nearly 10 per cent of BC Sugar's common stock.

25

The Pie Was Too Small

UNEASY RELATIONS BETWEEN THE COMPANY AND THE BEET GROWERS.

Alberta's sugar beet farmers thought that BC Sugar was bluffing when the company threatened to close the Taber sugar factory during the 1985 contract negotiations. When the closure was announced on 11 May, the 600 growers were stunned and angry—and afraid that it was over for their industry. "I was pretty scared," said John Zeinstra, a director of the Alberta Sugar Beet Growers' Marketing Board. "It was okay when I was with the other guys but it really hit me when I drove home." That year no sugar beets were grown in Alberta for the first time since 1925.

After the company bought the Raymond sugar factory in 1931, it found that the factory had been signing firm contracts before spring planting that guaranteed what the growers would receive for beets after harvest, regardless of what happened to the price of sugar in the meantime. Those terms contributed to Raymond's losses. Ernest Rogers had the factory negotiate a new contract giving the growers a percentage share of the ultimate sugar sales. The growers then worked on raising their percentage until, in the 1936 contract, it was agreed that each party would receive 50 per cent of the revenue from the sale of refined sugar after deducting processing and marketing expenses. (The growers continually improved the contract until, by 1984, they were receiving 63 per cent of the refined sugar revenue, 50 per cent of the revenue from the sale of beet molasses and 27 per cent from the sale of beet pulp.) Walter F. Boras, president of the growers' association in 1985, called the contract the "envy of North America."

The growers had had determined leadership. Philip Baker, who negotiated the 1936 share contract and was president of the growers' association for nineteen years, was described by those who bargained with him as a "table pounder."[1] A large, man with a booming voice, Baker was the physical opposite of Canadian Sugar Factories' stubby district manager T. George Wood, who was always on the other side of the table. Wood, jealous of his authority, resented Baker's coming between him and the growers. Baker's initial success came because he exploited the apprehension that the company had about Alberta's newly elected Social Credit government under William Aberhart. The growers (who were themselves facing labour disruption from the new Beet Workers' Industrial Union) asked government help to pressure the company for a more generous contract, finally proposing that Aberhart appoint a royal commission if the 50-50 contract was refused. Ernest Rogers told Wood to agree to the new contract rather than risk having a public inquiry put notions into the premier's head.[2] When sugar prices weakened in the mid-1950s, the company tried to regain a larger share of the net revenues. It took three weeks of hard negotiation in 1954 for the company to secure a modest improvement of its share when sugar prices were low.

Lalovee Jensen succeeded Baker in 1955. "He had more finesse and tact," remembered Arledge Hill, a former company agricultural superintendent "but he was firm, too, and he got a lot of concessions from the sugar company."[3] Jensen's bargaining style frustrated the company: he would simply refuse to discuss any matter that he considered non-negotiable.[4] Wood's right-hand man, the usually mild-mannered Frank Taylor, once snapped during a tense bargaining session that he had made one of his biggest mistakes when he had given Jensen a beet contract in 1938.[5]

The economics of beet growing were eroded in the late 1950s by the rising cost of farming. Under the new Agricultural Stabilization Act of 1958, sugar beets became eligible for deficiency payments in years when the return to farmers was considered below production cost. This policy, announced late in 1961, set a floor price for beets of $15 a ton, no matter how low the world price of sugar dropped. Between 1958 and 1961, Canadian beet growers collected a total of $4.5 million in deficiency payments. The Alberta Sugar Beet Growers' 1962 annual report stated: "Something has been designed which has been instrumental in keeping us in business." No deficiency payments were required in 1962 or 1963, but during the next seven years, another $13.6 million was paid. Even that support failed to encourage enough Ontario beet production to sustain Canada & Dominion's Chatham factory, which closed in 1968.

In 1973, when world raw sugar prices rose sharply, the sharing contract rewarded growers with record returns.[6] The subsequent decline in sugar prices again made deficiency payments necessary in 1976, 1977, 1981 and 1982. Then, unexpectedly, the federal government stopped making the payments. By 1984 the growers realized their lowest price in eight years, a return estimated to be only two-thirds the average cost of production. The growers began pressing Ottawa for a national sugar policy that supported sugar beets. At the same time, they also looked to the sugar company to improve the return to the growers.

However, BC Sugar was operating the Taber and Fort Garry factories at a loss, despite having modernized both to ensure their being among North America's most energy-efficient factories. A major internal study in February 1984 found that the beet factories no longer were viable, given depressed sugar prices.[7] The federal and provincial governments were advised in the fall of 1984 that both factories likely would have to close. The growers received this information when the executive of the Alberta and Manitoba associations met in January 1985 with Peter Cherniavsky in Vancouver. Paul Thibodeau, then a vice-president of the Alberta association, recounted: "We were told that we should go to the federal and provincial governments to get some assistance if we wanted to grow a crop in 1985."[8]

Cherniavsky's antagonist as the confrontation developed was a farmer from Iron Springs, Alberta: Walter Boras, the son of a Yugoslav immigrant, who had become the beet growers' association president the previous year. A voluble activist, he articulated grower suspicions towards the company that developed after Picture Butte closed. The hint then that the company might by-pass the association and contract for beets directly with individual growers eventually led the association in 1983 to convert itself into a marketing board. Unlike other boards, this one could not set a price for sugar or control production. It did, however, have control over licensing a grower—a prerequisite for planting sugar beets. (The company had argued with the Alberta government against this move.)

The perennial suspicion—that BC Sugar intended to replace beet sugar entirely with cane sugar—raised its head again when a study of the western sweetener market commissioned by the growers in 1982 concluded that BC Sugar was shipping increasing quantities of cane sugar to the Prairies. BC Sugar contended that the study was riddled with error, but the growers accepted it as fact. In February 1985 the Alberta growers sent a brief to the federal and provincial governments, charging: "We as beet growers have a refiner who is also the seller of our share of the sugar (63 per cent) but who, at the same time, through its parent company is also our competitor, in the same market." Boras, in a newspaper interview, said that BC Sugar was "using the profit jar of the sugar industry" to support diversification into other businesses.[9]

The company gave its proposals for a new beet contract to the growers at a Calgary meeting in March. The bottom line was that the growers could expect a drastically reduced return on the 1985 crop of about $22 a tonne. (The company later guaranteed $25 a tonne, exclusive of any government subsidies to growers.) At the first negotiating meeting six days later, the company repeated its warning that the Taber plant would not operate that year if the proposals were turned down. G. M. (Joe) Guccione, Alberta Sugar's general manager, said later: "The pie was too small for the two of us and had to be made bigger."[10]

The previous month the beet growers had hurried to Ottawa to press for federal duties against raw cane sugar that they believed was being dumped onto the Canadian market. They argued that, since Ottawa had made deficiency payments for sugar beets in fifteen of the last twenty-four years, obviously the price of sugar was too low.[11] They proposed a federal sugar floor price equal to 25 cents a pound, with the revenue coming from a duty on imported raw cane sugar, then selling for about 4 cents a pound. This duty would have cushioned beet growers comfortably above their estimated production cost, then 18 cents. This proposal was ultimately rejected by Ottawa.

By early April the company and the Alberta growers were deadlocked.

It was a different story in Manitoba, where the growers and the company had maintained a more harmonious relationship. The Manitoba growers did believe the company's warning that the Fort Garry factory was in danger of closing and, once mothballed, was unlikely to reopen. They concluded a contract aimed at sustaining the factory and, once temporary federal and provincial grower subsidies were announced, the beet crop was planted in May.

A beet subsidy of $10 a tonne first was offered by the Alberta government in an effort to break the deadlock. Initially the federal government refused to top this subsidy. Agriculture Minister John Wise relented after Walter Boras led a fifty-two-person delegation of growers and community leaders to Ottawa for two days of intensive lobbying. Ottawa agreed to pay an additional $6 to $8 a tonne. The growers now resumed bargaining with BC Sugar, with those in Manitoba crafting a new contract.

However, negotiations became increasingly provocative. By the 29 April meeting, Boras suggested it was perhaps time for the growers to build their own factory. Boras also wondered whether the company intended to by-pass the marketing board to contract directly with individual farmers. A number of growers were indeed prepared to do just that rather than risk losing the 1985 crop, provided that the company would sell them the seed.

The final bargaining session began on the afternoon of 10 May in Lethbridge, continuing until 10:20 P.M. "We were very close to an agreement," Guccione said later. Grower John Zeinstra agreed. Both sides made concessions, but the company was adamant that any new contract must alter fundamentally the way revenues were shared, and the growers were just as adamant that the historic contract be retained. Cherniavsky in Vancouver, after being briefed on the talks, called off the next morning's meeting and announced that the Taber factory would close. The company dropped any idea of contracting directly after some growers received threats of violence if they planted. "It was not pleasant," Guccione said, recalling the mood.[12] The growers then scrambled for other crops to plant on the 30,000 acres meant for beets. Most sowed soft wheat, only to witness a collapse in the market price of what already was a low-value crop.

Both the company and the growers now looked to the federal government for a support program that would enlarge the pie and save an industry. The growers retained an Ottawa lobbyist, Peter Clarke, and Boras later said that he made seventeen trips to Ottawa during the crisis. Wheat Board minister Charles Mayer, a Manitoba farmer, had been assigned in March 1985 to produce a report on which Ottawa could base a sugar policy. While a new policy was awaited, eastern Canada's remaining beet factory—Raffinerie de Sucre du Quebec at Ste-Hilaire—closed permanently in 1985. In Alberta, the communities in the beet growing area became increasingly concerned until, in January 1986, the *Lethbridge Herald,* CKTA radio in Taber and CHEC radio in Lethbridge organized a petition to Ottawa. Presented in late January, it had 18,000 signatures.

As a result, the federal government agreed that the support price for sugar beets in 1986 was to be $45 a metric tonne, and a ten-year support program was announced. With these measures in place, the growers sat down with the company in April 1986 to negotiate. "Again this year negotiations proved to be very, very difficult," vice-president Paul Thibodeau wrote later in the growers' association's 1986 annual report. But Guccione, who sat across the table, found that the year's suspension of factory operations "had cleared the air." The first-ever three-year contract between the growers and the company emerged after seven meetings. The new contract returned to the company all the revenues from by-products and a greater share of the refined sugar revenues. The growers undertook to pay a larger share of beet hauling charges and to pay for half the agricultural research done by the company.

The support program in force is the National Tripartite Price Stabilization Program. Each of the three parties to the program—growers, federal government and relevant provincial governments—contributes to a fund that will support beet growing in years when world sugar prices are low. The first tripartite program runs for ten years, a long enough period, it is hoped, to make the fund self-financing. The support price each year is set at 75 per cent of the cash costs of producing beets, plus 20 per cent of the average price received by growers during the previous fifteen years. Walter Boras, in his last president's report before retiring in 1987, wrote: "The tripartite solution for sugar beet production was not our way of solving the problems of marketing, but we take it with satisfaction that it will and can sustain us for the immediate years ahead."[13]

The contract revisions, which the growers believed shifted as much as $10 million in revenue to the company, also restored the sugar factories to profitable operation. "They've got to stay in business," conceded grower Brian Anderson. "If your partner is not making anything, your future is not very good."[14]

26

The Whole Chemicals Business

THE COMPANY MAKES A BOLD DIVERSIFICATION.

In August 1984 William Ashman, whose Seattle firm the Clarion Group had been hired to seek capital to help reopen a mothballed chemical plant in the Vancouver suburb of Delta, invited a small number of prospective investors for a plant tour and then lunch at the University Club downtown. The party included Peter Cherniavsky and William Brown, at that time BC Sugar's vice-president. The luncheon was chaired by Arnold F. C. Hean, a Vancouver lawyer who headed the newly incorporated Chatterton Petrochemical Corporation,[1] which was hoping to buy the plant. Hean told the luncheon that Chatterton preferred not to surrender control to a new investor. After lunch, Cherniavsky took Hean aside and asked whether, in fact, controlling interest might be available. Hean replied: "If it is to BC Sugar, you've got a deal."[2] Two years later BC Sugar seized the opportunity to invest in Kalama Chemicals Inc., a Seattle firm whose plant in Kalama, Washington, is a sister to the Chatterton plant. By 1988 chemical sales generated $109 million for BC Sugar compared to $153 in sugar sales.

The imperative behind this move into chemicals is the same as that which took BC Sugar into packaging in 1970 and energy in 1975: the flattening of sugar consumption. The company's growth from sugar depends almost entirely on population growth in Western Canada. Although this is a market in which the company can describe itself as the sole supplier, BC Sugar can never take its sales for granted. Refined sugar from suppliers in Europe, the United States and even South Korea periodically make inroads into the market.[3]

Dow Chemical Canada opened the Delta plant in 1961; the Kalama plant was opened the following year by Dow's American parent. Both produce phenol, used as a base for adhesives in the plywood and particle board industries of British Columbia and the Pacific Northwest. Dow sold Kalama in 1971 when it began planning a large facility in Texas, and Dow Canada decided to sell the Delta plant in the early 1980s. When Dow first began looking for a buyer for the Delta plant, a vice-president at Reichhold Chemicals named Frederic Shelton recommended that his New York headquartered company take it over. When neither Reichhold nor any other potential operator stepped forward, Dow simply closed the Delta plant in May of 1982. A Seattle native with a master's degree in engineering, Shelton was intimately acquainted with the chemical industry in Western Canada. In 1971 he left Reichhold and, with Hean and an American chemist named John Stephan, bought Monsanto's chemical plants in Vancouver and Edmonton. After this business was restructured successfully and sold to Borden Chemicals, Shelton rejoined Reichhold. However, a 1983 change in control of that company swept out a number of senior executives, including Shelton.

Meanwhile, Stephan, a co-inventor of phenolic resin adhesives, learned that the Delta plant was to be dismantled. At Stephan's urging in April 1983, Hean initiated what was to be eighteen months of negotiation with Dow Canada. Although Dow gradually came down from its $12 million initial asking price, the partners still needed considerable capital beyond their own modest resources and had trouble finding it since the plant already was closed.[4]

Hean was well-connected. Besides practising law, he had established one of Canada's first waferboard plants in the 1960s in Saskatchewan; he had been a charter member of the high-powered Pacific Basin Economic Council; and he had headed the Majority Movement, a business-based political movement that contributed to the 1975 defeat of David Barrett's New Democratic government in British Columbia. But in 1983 Hean's contacts were not coming forward to invest in the chemical plant. British Columbia—particularly its forest industry, the major potential customer for phenol—was in a deep recession. The partners turned to Ashman, then a Seattle venture capital consultant. He canvassed about fifteen potential investors in British Columbia, narrowed the list to five and identified BC Sugar as the most likely investor. Ashman even sold himself on the chemical venture. After finding BC Sugar, he took a portion of his finders' fee in Chatterton shares and in 1987 joined the chemical company as its vice-president of sales.

BC Sugar's initial investment of $3 million for 60 per cent of Chatterton enabled Hean's group to clinch the deal with Dow. The chemical giant assisted the new owners by financing, interest-free for two years, the initial supplies of toluene, the plant's raw material. As well, Dow agreed to purchase a significant portion of the plant's phenol during the first two years after it restarted. And it guaranteed a $1 million bank loan for the original Chatterton partners. When the purchase of the Delta plant from Dow was completed on 21 December 1984, BC Sugar believed it had a bargain. Cherniavsky put the replacement value at $40 million.[5]

In Ashman's view, the sugar company's diversification into chemicals was commercially logical. "The sugar business really is a chemical business," Ashman says. Peter Cherniavsky, William Brown and Forrest Rogers all had university degrees in either chemistry or engineering and understood what went on in the Chatterton plant. Bruce Levelton, who had acquired Stephan's interest in Chatterton and became executive vice-president, recalls Forrest Rogers saying, during a plant tour, "I don't know why we didn't get into this type of thing twenty years ago."

Levelton himself was a major reason for BC Sugar's interest in Chatterton. "We were impressed by the people," Brown says. "The aura of respectability was due to Bruce Levelton being there." Before he founded his own firm, Levelton had been a senior scientist with B.C. Research, an organization BC Sugar had retained for various technical assignments. Although, as Brown noted, the other members of Chatterton were strangers to BC Sugar, Levelton "was known to our engineering people and to us and we knew he was a very clever and honest guy. If he was associated with this from a technical point of view, then maybe it did make some sense."

BC Sugar named William Brown and John G. Cochrane, its vice-president of finance, to be directors of Chatterton. A chartered accountant with a law degree, Cochrane had come to BC Sugar in 1973 from the accounting firm of Thorne Riddell. He became Chatterton's chairman when ill health forced Hean to step down in early 1986. Brown's position on the Chatterton board identifies him with this important new direction in BC Sugar's business. He counts his role in helping get "the whole chemicals business off the ground" as a career highlight. Born in 1938 near Peticodiac, N.B., Brown graduated in chemistry from the University of New Brunswick and went to work in the laboratory of the Atlantic Sugar refinery in Saint John. By 1965 he was chief chemist; in 1972 he was transferred to the refinery's Montreal headquarters as assistant to president W.J.R. Paton, who was then beginning to diversify Atlantic into businesses besides sugar. Brown was Atlantic's officer in the Canadian Sugar Institute where he impressed William Hetherington, BC Sugar's representative. On Hetherington's recommendation, BC Sugar recruited Brown in May 1976 as a vice-president; a dozen years later, Brown became president.

Dow had not mothballed the Delta plant with the intention of resuming operations. Frederic Shelton recalls: "When I first looked at it [the plant] I just threw up my hands in despair." Some piping was corroded; other piping had been cut open with a saw, rather than unbolted, to facilitate cleaning chemicals from the lines; and instruments had been dismantled carelessly. But after a detailed study, Shelton concluded that his pessimistic first impression was wrong. The equipment turned out to be in better repair than had at first seemed and, because so many former operators rejoined the company, Chatterton was restarted within five months, on 1 May 1984.

The timing was not fortuitous. With the forest industry still in recession, the demand for phenol was poor and a large surplus had depressed prices. "We had a pretty bad year and a half," Shelton says. "BC Sugar very bravely said, 'Well, we are going to stick with you.' " The sugar company ploughed more money into Chatterton (ultimately securing complete ownership) to keep the chemical company in business until markets turned around. A sharp recovery in the demand for phenol began in mid-1987.

By then BC Sugar also had invested in Kalama Chemicals. By coincidence, Hean and Stephan had tried to buy this chemical company in the early 1970s but were unable to make a deal. When Hean learned from an American banker in 1985 that Kalama might again be available he urged Chatterton's board to investigate. The smallest of Dow's American plants, in the 1970s Kalama no longer fit into the large company's scheme of operations. Ted Palmer, general manager of Dow's organic chemicals division, was given the assignment of selling it. "On the lookout for something of an entrepreneurial nature," this long-time employee talked Dow's board of directors into selling him the plant for US$2.2 million.[6]

Palmer found partners—one was Kalama president Robert Kirchner—and a banker to back him. In February 1971 he took charge of a plant with twenty-six employees and annual sales of about US$4 million. Like the Delta plant, Kalama's output of phenol was sold primarily to the adhesive industry. Under Palmer's direction, Kalama broadened its range of products, acquired a chemical plant in Philadelphia, another in South Carolina and, in 1982, Tenneco's fine chemicals plant in New Jersey. Its sales reached US$120 million in 1984; even after selling two subsidiaries that year, Kalama remained a profitable $60 million-a-year company.

In 1986 Palmer was looking for an outside investor because some of his original backers or their heirs wanted to sell their Kalama shares. To BC Sugar, the opportunity was highly attractive. Kalama was a profitable going concern producing chemicals similar to Chatterton's line. "There was a synergistic effect," William Brown says. The sugar company paid US$8 million for forty-nine per cent of Kalama, with the right to buy the remaining interest by 1996. When Palmer left Kalama in 1988, BC Sugar bought his shares and raised its stake to seventy-five per cent. Robert Kirchner remains the only other shareholder.

Both Kalama and Chatterton have developed a substantial menu of products in addition to phenol. Like sugar, some of the products are basic to everyday consumption: salicylic acid used in headache tablets; sodium benzoate, a ubiquitous food preservative; chemicals used in food flavourings and insect repellents. The two plants, besides developing their respective markets for these products, are exploring related opportunities. Chatterton's choice 180-acre industrial site on the Fraser and its feedstocks are intended as a base for a future joint venture in petrochemical manufacturing, possibly with an international company.

The chemical subsidiaries not only are reshaping BC Sugar dramatically but are confirming the corporate direction that began with the investment in Belkin in 1970. There have been few opportunities to expand by acquisition in the Canadian sugar industry since Forrest Rogers was unable to come to terms with St. Lawrence Sugar in the 1960s. While there were opportunities in the American sugar industry during the 1970s, BC Sugar chose not to invest in an industry whose prosperity is largely dependent on the U.S. government's policy to support its domestic sugar beet industry. "The chemical business on the other hand is entirely different," Brown says. "There are a huge number of chemical manufacturers in the United States that are of the Chatterton or Kalama size. There is a niche to be found in these specialty chemical manufacturing areas." Among those would be successful private companies where, as with Kalama, the founding ownership is ready to sell. "That" asserts Brown, "is where we have some potential for expansion."

Epilogue

In 1916, when BC Sugar was twenty-five years old, B. T. Rogers penned triumphant letters to several of his major shareholders, celebrating the company's success. The asset value of the company was $7,500,000; the refinery was the best equipped in Canada, having had its capacity increased thirtyfold; and the shareholders had received in dividends an average of 49 per cent a year on their original investments.

"Those results have been accomplished without my asking shareholders for one cent beyond their original subscription," Rogers boasted to shareholder Sir Edmund P. Osler. "I think therefore I am entitled to be proud of what I have been able to do. I was 25 years old when the refinery started operations, so that I am only 50 now. Given a continuance of good health I think I can safely promise even better results for the future."

He was to live only two years and two months longer but, even without his aggressive hand on its destiny, the company thrived, run through much of its 100 years by members of the founding family. Indeed, by many members: because of a series of tragedies, each of B. T.'s four sons served for a time as president. The eldest son, Blythe, was prevented by ill health from making much of a mark on the company, aside from his courageous defence of BC Sugar when it first came under political attack.

The other sons each made substantial contributions, and the youngest, Forrest, handed control to Peter Cherniavsky, the grandson with B. T.'s entrepreneurial instinct, whose mark has been protecting the company's sugar franchise while diversifying to secure growth for the second century.

Throughout its history, BC Sugar has contended with the unsavoury perception that it owes its success to being a monopoly. Ernest Rogers, when he was president during the 1930s, once had a sharp exchange of letters on this matter with the publisher of the *Vancouver Sun,* who alleged that monopoly explained why BC Sugar spent so little on advertising. Rogers had to point out that sugar is a generic commodity; producers of such commodities seldom advertised much. That publisher was not alone in his notion. BC Sugar has been through a number of inquiries, including the 1960 Anti-Combines prosecution, and has emerged with honour from all. For 100 years, the company generally has been the sole supplier of sugar in its market area, a position held not by virtue of monopoly but by managing its affairs well enough to retain the market and keep competitors at bay. Indeed, in his judgement of the 1960 case, Justice E.K. Williams wrote that the Western Canadian market for sugar was open to any competitor that wanted to enter.

The dividend record of which Rogers was proud, a visible measure of a company's success, became a record of continuity seldom matched in business. The first dividend was declared in 1893, after only two years of operation and after Rogers had overcome severe competition. A loss in 1895 and a small profit in 1896 prevented the company from paying a dividend in 1896. But in every year since, the shareholders have received dividends. Perhaps the most remarkable period was the decade of the Depression in the 1930s, when the stability of the company's business demonstrated the fundamental importance of sugar in diet. Not only did the dividends continue generously and without interruption but also the company laid off no employees and invested heavily in the Alberta sugar beet factories, expanding the production of a product for which there was then no suitable substitute. Dividends, that measure of effective business operation, have continued even though sugar has been challenged by alternative sweeteners and attacked by critics whom the sugar industry considers food faddists.

What of the future? The company is on a course of diversifying beyond sugar but by no means of withdrawing from sugar. It has been clear for several decades that the growth in the consumption of sugar is slowing. The company no longer is the sole supplier of sugar in its market, even though it has a commanding share of that market and has the ability to defend its share. Other natural sweeteners, notably one made from corn, have captured some market, as have artificial sweeteners, even though the latter are medically controversial. To remain competitive, BC Sugar has made the necessary adjustments, including the difficult restructuring of revenue-sharing with the sugar beet growers. The strategy that served B. T. Rogers best is the same one that President William Brown enunciated at the company's 99th annual meeting: "to be the lowest cost seller of sugar in Western Canada."

Chapter Notes

Chapter 1

Much of the source material for this book comes from the BC Sugar company's extensive archives and is referrred to in these notes by the abbreviation **BCSA**. References to the private papers of B. T. Rogers, also found in the company archives, are listed under **BTR papers**.

1. BTR papers, box 1.
2. This episode is recounted by Mary Isabella Rogers in *The Story of the B.C. Sugar Refinery,* (hereafter referred to as *B.C. Sugar*), p.5.
3. Rogers toyed briefly with the notion of building a Portland refinery in 1896 when a merchant there showed interest in buying large quantities of refined sugar.
4. Daniel Catlin, Jr. *Good Work Well Done: The Sugar Business Career of Horace Havemeyer, 1903–1956,* p.358.
5. Palmer, on 10 Jan. 1890, wrote William Stevenson, the Canadian Pacific agent in New York, who passed along Palmer's letter of introduction. Palmer described Rogers "as a man who can be relied upon in all respects." Canadian Pacific, Corporate Archives.
6. Vancouver *News-Advertiser,* 13 Dec. 1890.
7. In a reorganization of the capital some years later, B.C. Sugar Refining Company, the operating company, was made a wholly-owned subsidiary of B.C. Sugar Refinery Limited. This remains the shareholder-owned holding company today. But since the 1970s, the company styles itself simply as BC Sugar in all but technically legal references.

8. BCSA, Gutleben file; *see also* Letterbook p.131 for acknowledgement of so-called resignation.
9. *B.C. Sugar,* p.13.
10. Vancouver City Archives, Correspondence in City Clerk's files, RG 2-A1, vols. 2–70, p.3232.
11. Ibid, pp.3227–8.

Chapter 2

1. Canadian Pacific, Corporate Archives, 30711.
2. Ibid.
3. "The sugar was sent up there to be sold for what it would bring," the Vancouver *World* wrote on 19 June 1891. "That simply meant that the Vancouver refinery could not sell its output."
4. BCSA, Minutebook, p.37.
5. Ibid, p.43.
6. Rogers wrote to Van Horne, 5 July 1892: "The new stock was bought—and then the prices went down in Winnipeg, steadily month by month, until some three months ago when sugar was selling there below the parity of New York. As there is no prospect of a better market . . . I decided to drop Manitoba as soon as possible and confine our business to B.C."
7. BCSA, Letterbook, 1892–1918, pp.1–5.
8. Ibid.
9. Letter to William Van Horne, 5 July 1892, in Canadian Pacific, Corporate Archives, 72193.
10. BCSA, Letterbook, 1892–1918, p.32.
11. Ibid., p.35.

Chapter 3

1. F. W. Howay, and E. O. S. Scholefield, *British Columbia from the Earliest Times to the Present,* vol.4, pp.1134–36.
2. Harry Gregson, *A History of Victoria 1842–1970,* p.105.
3. *B.C. Sugar,* p.18.
4. BCSA, Minutebook, pp.45–47.
5. BCSA, Letterbook 1892–1918, p.57.
6. Canadian Pacific, Corporate Archives, 76930.
7. Ibid.
8. BCSA, Letterbook 1892–1918, p.150.
9. BCSA, Minutebook, p.93.
10. Canadian Pacific, Corporate Archives, 78897.
11. BCSA, Letterbook 1892–1918, p.167.
12. Ibid. p.189.
13. BCSA, Minutebook, p.107.

14. On 24 November 1896 Rogers assured Forrest Angus in Victoria that he was not plunging "recklessly" into the Japanese market but only with the intention of selling surplus refined sugar and keeping the refinery running at an efficient capacity. Letter in BCSA, Letterbook 1892–1918, p.235.
15. Canadian Pacific, Corporate Archives, 82365.
16. Chinese sugars were troublesome again in the spring of 1914. When they were dumped cheaply into the Vancouver market, BC Sugar responded with some remarkable advertising. "Would you relish a meal cooked by a half-naked, unwashed, perspiring Chinese Coolie whose bath consisted of nothing more than a shower of rain—where rain is rare?" shrieked one advertisement. "Then imagine a horde of unwashed Coolies in the steaming heat of an Oriental sugar refinery preparing the sugar you use on your table." By contrast, the advertisement ran, "British Columbia White labour Refined Sugar" was made in a refinery "every inch" of which is "spotlessly clean." The tightening of sugar supplies after the European war began that autumn ended the problem with Chinese sugars.

Chapter 4

(The principal sources for this chapter are the records and annual reports of the Vancouver-Fiji Sugar Company in the BC Sugar archives.)

1. Brodziak reported that there were 4750 acres planted to cane, 4970 acres fallow and another 3000 acres ready to develop.
2. E .B. Osler, a leading Toronto financier and broker, took 700 preferred shares; Wilmot D. Matthews, another Toronto financier, took 500. B. T. himself subscribed for 400 shares while 300 were purchased by T. G. Brough, who was general manager of the Dominion Bank in Toronto. Donald Forbes Angus in Montreal, a descendant of R. B. Angus, bought 250 shares. Van Horne, now Sir William, declined to subscribe, but another early investor in BC Sugar, Ernst Gerbracht, bought 250 shares for himself and his wife. Finally, 50 preferred shares each were taken by BC Sugar's secretary, William Prentice, and by a vice-president of the company, Harry Abbott.
3. BCSA, Minutebook, pp.167–70.
4. BCSA, Letterbook 1892–1918, pp.437, 439.
5. Ibid., p.480.
6. BTR papers, box 42, Misc. Correspondence.
7. BCSA, Annual Reports of Vancouver-Fiji Sugar Company.
8. BCSA, Letterbook 1918–1940, p.57.
9. BCSA, Letterbook 1915–1925, p.282.
10. Johnson in a letter on 4 June 1923 to W. D. Matthews in Toronto; BCSA, Letterbook 1918–1940, p.112.

Chapter 5

1. Canadian historian Charles Lipton wrote in *The Trade Union Movement of Canada 1827–1959* (p.59): "Between 1900 and 1913 union membership [in Canada] increased from about 50,000 members in about 1,000 locals in 1900, to 175,000 members in 2,017 locals in 1913. The rising struggle for conditions is reflected in strike statistics. Between 1900 and 1915, 377,234 workers were involved in 1,519 strikes."
2. Ibid., p.105.
3. Melvyn Dubofsky, *We Shall Be All: A History of the IWW,* p.350.
4. BCSA, file box on 1917 strike.
5. BCSA, Blythe Rogers's diary, pp.3–7 in file on 1917 strike.
6. BCSA, Blythe Rogers's diary, p.11.
7. Copies of these reports are in BCSA, file box on 1917 strike.
8. BCSA, clipping from *British Columbia Federationist,* 27 April 1917; in file box on 1917 strike.
9. BCSA, Blythe Rogers's diary, p.36.
10. Ibid, p.41.

Chapter 6

1. Susan Schroeder, *Cuba: A Handbook of Statistics,* p.260.
2. *Louisiana Planter,* 17 Jan. 1920, p.40.
3. Reported in the *Vancouver Daily Province,* 10 Feb. 1917.
4. BCSA, file box BCSR 1.
5. BTR papers, file box 1, letter to Matthews, 8 Sept. 1917.
6. BTR papers, file box 1.
7. BCSA, file box BCSR 2, Federal Government Indictment file.
8. BTR papers, file box 1; also Letterbook 1892–1918, p.541.
9. *Daily News-Advertiser,* 12 Feb. 1917.
10. Government of Canada, House of Commons sessional paper no. 189, Report on Sugar 1917, p.36.
11. BCSA, Letterbook 1929–33, p.288.

Chapter 7

1. See BCSA, Minutebook for a discussion of BTR's salary and its progression.
2. Michael Kluckner, *M. I. Rogers,* p.28.
3. BTR papers, box 2.
4. *Vancouver Daily Province,* 25 March 1905, p.1.
5. Michael Kluckner, *M. I. Rogers,* writes that this car was destroyed in a 1911 garage fire at Gabriola.
6. Howay and Scholefield, *British Columbia from Earliest Times,* vol. 4, p.1064.
7. BCSA, Letterbook 1891–1918, pp.334, 339.
8. The logbook of the *Aquilo,* in BCSA, indicates that the yacht was seconded to the navy from 5 August to 29 August 1914, based in Esquimalt. For her

first patrol, 7–9 August, with B. T. Rogers on board, the yacht also carried an armed military party of eleven. Rogers returned to the refinery on 9 August, but the yacht spent much of the next three weeks patrolling off Cape Flattery or escorting the submarines.

9. Bentall's biographer, Shirley F. Bentall (*The Charles Bentall Story,* p.86), described how Rogers awarded the Shannon contract: "One day B. T. Rogers invited Charles to go for a drive with him. They proceeded southward from the centre of the city, through the encroaching forest, along a plank or skid road, until they came to the ten-acre property. . . . [Rogers's] plan was to build a stately new mansion. . . . He asked Charles to build it for him."
10. Correspondence regarding Shannon is in BTR papers, box 3.
11. Shirley Bentall, p.102.
12. BTR papers, box 1, W.D. Matthews file, 6 July 1910 letter.
13. BCSA, Letterbook 1892–1918, p.528.
14. Ibid., p.535.
15. Van Horne was then building a railway across Cuba.
16. BTR papers, box 1, D.W. Matthews file.
17. *Saturday Chinook,* 28 June 1918.
18. BCSA, Letterbook 1918–1940, p.73.
19. BCSA, Letterbook 1892–1918, p.549.

Chapter 8

1. BCSA, Letterbook 1918–1940, p.56.
2. Vancouver *World,* 21 Feb. 1917.
3. Rogers complained privately to W. D. Matthews on 30 Nov. 1917: "I have chartered a wooden schooner to bring up to 2,000 tons more of our own sugar and that is *all.* . . . I can assure you—with politics added to my other troubles—it is most unpleasant to run a business these days." The politics referred to his outrage at new income taxes levied by both the dominion and the province. BTR papers, box 1, W. D. Matthews file.
4. Dr H. C. Prinsen Geerligs in the *Louisiana Planter and Sugar Manufacturer,* 3 July 1920.
5. *Louisiana Planter,* 18 Sept. 1920, p.181.
6. Reported in the Victoria *Daily Colonist,* 4 March 1920.
7. Pablo de la Llama, president, Banco Espanol, quoted in *Louisiana Planter,* 17 July 1920.
8. Luis A. Aquilar, *Cuba 1933: Prologue to Revolution,* p.43.
9. Reported in the *Vancouver Sun,* 27 Feb. 1920.
10. Blythe Rogers's letters to his parents during this period can be found in the BTR papers.
11. BTR papers, box 1, W. D. Matthews file.
12. *B.C. Sugar,* p.36.

13. Reported in the *Victoria Daily Times,* 16 March 1920.
14. Quoted in the *Financial Times,* 27 March 1920.
15. British Columbia, Legislature, Votes & Proceedings, 9 April 1920, p.191.
16. BCSA, Letterbook 1918–1940, p.62; letter to W. D. Matthews.
17. BCSA, Letterbook 1918–1930, p.79.
18. *Vancouver Sun,* 14 October 1920.
19. BCSA, Letterbook 1918–1940, p.91.
20. *Vancouver Daily Province,* 15 October 1920.

Chapter 9

1. BCSA tapes; 1975 interview by Nicholas Dykes.
2. Author interview with Mrs. Beatrice Wood.
3. Ibid.
4. Letter in Mrs. Beatrice Wood's possession.
5. Helen Wood diary, in Mrs. Beatrice Wood's possession.
6. Author interview with Mrs. Beatrice Wood.
7. BCSA, Minutebook, pp.288, 293.
8. BCSA tapes; interviews by Nicholas Dykes.
9. BCSA, Letterbook 1925–1929, p.159.
10. BCSA tapes; 1975 interview by Nicholas Dykes.
11. BCSA, Letterbook, 1929–33, pp.100–162 passim.
12. BCSA, Letterbook 1925–29, p.414.
13. Ibid, p.432.
14. *Vancouver Sun,* 6 Dec. 1924.
15. BCSA, Letterbook 5, p.2.
16. BCSA, A. M. Robertson files.
17. BCSA tapes; 1975 Wilfred Kenyon interview by Nicholas Dykes.
18. Author interview with Mrs. Beatrice Wood.
19. Victoria *Daily Colonist,* 28 July 1931.

Chapter 10

1. Correspondence in BCSA
2. Vancouver *News-Advertiser*, 12 Dec. 1905.
3. BTR papers.
4. The Knight factory had produced 4.6 million pounds of sugar in 1906 from 18,000 tons of beets. When beet production declined in 1908, the factory imported about 500 tons of beet sugar from Germany, an obviously uneconomic attempt to retain a position in the Alberta sugar market. Ellison next talked the Alberta government into paying beet farmers a subsidy over five years which totalled $250,000. Nothing worked. In 1914 farmers delivered only enough beets for two days of processing, and the factory had to be closed. Will Knight, some years later, stated: "The Raymond Sugar Factory was not built as a commercial enterprise so much as a benefit for the settlers

of the surrounding country. According to the contract, it was to be in operation for 12 years. This was done although the factory did not prove to be as great a success as had been hoped, for various reasons." The processing machinery was reassembled in 1917 in a plant at Cornish, Utah, and when that company closed, it was put into a plant at Missoula, Montana, which operated until the early 1960s. BCSA, Knight Sugar Company files.

5. BCSA, Letterbook, 1929–33, p.468.
6. BCSA, BC Sugar's submission to the Dominion government, 15 March 1932. Copy in BCSR 3; statement of BCSR regarding future of Alberta sugar beet industry.
7. F. G. Taylor, *Saga of Sugar,* (Utah-Idaho Sugar Co., 1944), p.126.
8. BCSA, Letterbook, 1929–33, p.147.
9. BC Sugar submission, BCSR 3.
10. Author interview with Forrest Rogers.
11. BC Sugar submission, BCSR 3.
12. Report in BCSA.
13. Author interview with Arledge Hill.
14. Wood's close attention to spending was shown after the 1937 audit at Raymond by Helliwell, Maclachan & Co., B.C. Sugar's accountants from Vancouver. For its work that year, the firm's auditor billed Canadian Sugar Factories $844.35 compared with $643.60 in 1936 and $514.45 in 1935. Wood complained to Robert Adamson, BC Sugar's secretary, that the fee was excessive, in particular the $94.35 charged for expenses when "the auditor is furnished with board and room at our Club House without any expense."
15. BCSA, Ernest Rogers private papers.
16. BCSA, Letterbook 1929–33, p.300.
17. BCSA, Letterbook 1933–39, p.41.
18. Alberta Sugar Beet Growers Association 1935 annual report. Copy in BCSA.
19. BCSA, Raymond Letterbook, Oct. 1934–Nov. 1935, p.224.
20. BCSA Letterbook 1933–39, p.242.
21. Canada, Restrictive Trade Practices Commission Report, 1957, p.44.
22. BCSA, Letterbook 1933–39, pp.194–97.

Chapter 11

1. This description is based on contemporary newspaper accounts.
2. Michael Kluckner, M. *I. Rogers,* p.115.
3. BCSA, Ernest Rogers private papers, letters. Vancouver *Province,* 27 July 1939, p.4.
4. Author interview with Forrest Rogers.
5. BCSA tapes; 1975 interview by Nicholas Dykes.
6. Kluckner, p.113.

7. Author interview with Margaret (Rogers) Clark.
8. BCSA, BCSR 2, Christmas Speeches by ETR, 1927–37.
9. BCSA, Letterbook 1933–39, p.220.
10. Author interview with H. Allan Dunlop.
11. BCSA, Letterbook 1933–39, p.71.
12. Six voluminous letterbooks of correspondence to the Raymond factory, each containing about 500 pages, as well as additional letters to Wood covering the period are in BCSA.

Chapter 12

1. Author interview with Forrest Rogers.
2. Michael Kluckner, *M. I. Rogers,* p.119.
3. Anecdote related by Margaret (Rogers) Clark in an interview with the author.
4. Public Archives of Canada [PAC], Sugar Administration files, RG 64, vol. 1393.
5. Feb. 1941 letter in PAC, RG 64, vol. 1390.
6. PAC, RG 64, vol. 1390.
7. BCSA, Distribution Report, Fourth Quarter 1948.
8. BCSA, A.M. Robertson files.
9. BCSA, Robert Boyd letter, 7 Oct. 1948.

Chapter 13

(The primary source material for this chapter is in BCSA, A. M. Robertson files.)

1. Author interviews with Royce Craig, Lincoln Wood, William Hetherington and Peter Cherniavsky.
2. BTR papers, letter to W. D. Matthews, 26 Oct. 1911.
3. BCSA, Letterbook, Johnson correspondence.
4. Author interview with W. A. Davies.
5. BCSA tapes; 1975 interview by Nicholas Dykes.
6. Author interviews with Royce Craig, Lincoln Wood, William Hetherington and Peter Cherniavsky.
7. Blankenbach believed he was behind an incident that led to the formation of the Operating Committee. Some time earlier he had been made editor of the weekly review of operations, a no-hold's-barred critique which Boyd had initiated in 1928. It had been designed to highlight any problems so that quick and co-operative action could be taken. One week early in 1944, Blankenbach recalled, "Boyd had encouraged me to write this rather critical comment about this particular incident. Ballou was mad as hell about it." After that eruption, Philip Rogers formed the committee.
8. Wood thought the factory could start 16 Nov. 1949. "Well, I am not quite

so optimistic as that now," Rogers told him. "I mean, it could be quite easily ready the 15th of November but it could quite easily be the 15th of January." A transcript of this telephone conversation is among many from this era in BCSA.

Chapter 14

1. BCSA, Ozama Sugar Company files.
2. Author interview with William Hetherington.
3. BCSA, unpublished memoir of the company's Ozama experience by Forrest Rogers.
4. Author interview with Forrest Rogers.
5. BCSA, Philip T. Rogers memorandum.
6. Taxes consumed 98 per cent of the company's 1952 profit, 99 per cent in 1953 and 92.5 per cent in 1954.
7. Ian Bell, *The Dominican Republic*, p.71.
8. Author interview with William Hetherington.
9. Author interview with Frank and Alice Low.
10. This is one of many tales in the unpublished "Anecdotes of Ozama," a collection of employee memories put together at Forrest Rogers's suggestion. Copies are in the BCSA.
11. William Hetherington in "Anecdotes of Ozama."
12. Author interview with Frank Low.
13. Forrest Rogers, "Ozama Sugar Company," p.28.
14. Ibid., p.19.
15. Author interview with Forrest Rogers.
16. Ian Angus quoted in "Anecdotes of Ozama," p.25.
17. Author interview with William Hetherington.
18. Author interview with Ian Angus.
19. Forrest Rogers, "Ozama Sugar Company," p.47.
20. Ibid.
21. Author interview with William Hetherington.
22. Author interview with Ian Angus.
23. "Ozama Sugar Company," p.47.
24. BCSA, Forrest Rogers correspondence.
25. Ibid.
26. BCSA, Robertson correspondence.
27. "Ozama Sugar Company," p.55.
28. BCSA, Forrest Rogers correspondence.
29. The insurance value was estimated for BC Sugar in 1951 by B. L. Johnson, Walton Company, insurance brokers.
30. BCSA, Forrest Rogers correspondence.
31. Author interview with Ian Angus.

Chapter 15

1. Heather Robertson, *Sugar Farmers of Manitoba,* p.49.
2. J. H. Ellis, "Historical Sketch of Sugar Beets in Manitoba," an unpublished Paper. Copies in BCSA.
3. Robertson, *Sugar Farmers,* p.60.
4. BCSA, Letterbook 1929–33, p.466.
5. Author correspondence with Ernest Flegenheimer.
6. Flegenheimer paid the German company in advance 1,650,000 Reichsmarks, the equivalent of Cdn$660,000, and established a letter of credit with the Bank of Montreal for $375,000 (the balance to be $100,000 in Manitoba Sugar debentures).
7. Author interview with John Hecht.
8. Government of Canada, Restrictive Trade Practices Commission Report, 1957, p.133.
9. Robertson, *Sugar Farmers,* p.67.
10. Author interview with John Hecht.
11. Harold Aikins, Manitoba Sugar's new president, pressed Flegenheimer to invest $100,000. "I have pointed out to Colonel Aikins repeatedly . . . that I am not in a position to pay $100,000 as I have not got that amount here or in the States, but that my fortune amounting to ten to fifteen million lira is in Italy in shares and cash and a portion of my fortune is in Germany," Flegenheimer said in a later memorandum. (BCSA, Flegenheimer papers.) He tried to get some capital transferred from Europe through a bank in Brussels, only to have that attempt blocked when the Germans invaded Belgium.
12. Author correspondence with Ernest Flegenheimer.
13. Author interview with John Hecht.
14. BCSA, Report on the Manitoba Sugar Co., 20 Nov. 1940.
15. Author interview with Ted Zacharkow.
16. BCSA, A. M. Robertson files, transcript.
17. Author interview with William Hetherington.
18. Author interview with William Hetherington.
19. "There was an awful lot of infighting," recalled Zacharkow. "There always appeared to be a rift between all of them. Abras and Kramer never saw eye-to-eye. Everyone was sort of spying on one another, to report back. You didn't dare to say something that might have been overheard." Kramer was to complain to a bemused Forrest Rogers that all Abras did was "send French letters to Kronacher."

    Hetherington, transferred from BC Sugar's recently sold Ozama plantation, was appalled at the divisions. "When I got there I found funny things," he said in an interview with the author. "The master mechanic was a French Canadian called Charlie Pelletier, but a lot of other people working there were of Mennonite background, German speaking. Abras would go out and he would talk to Charlie Pelletier in French and get all kinds of stuff going in French. Kramer would go out and speak German to the German fellows. When I got there and saw this hassle, splits in the factory, I said 'I don't care, we are going to work in English from here on, period.!' "

20. Author interview with Ted Zacharkow.

Chapter 16

1. BCSA, Forrest Rogers memorandum, 1983.
2. Ottawa, Dept. of Justice, Restrictive Trade Practices Commission [RTPC]: Sugar Industry in Western Canada, 1957, p. 164.
3. BCSA, Forrest Rogers correspondence.
4. BCSA, Forrest Rogers memorandum, 1983.
5. Author interview with William Hetherington.
6. Ibid.
7. RTPC, p. 183.
8. Author interview with William Hetherington.
9. Horace Havemeyer Sr. was considering bidding for control of Canada & Dominion Sugar when he died in 1956. His sons turned their interest to BC Sugar, accumulating 68,000 common shares by 1962. They sold most of their holdings by the end of that decade, in part because Forrest Rogers expressed unease with the level of non-Canadian ownership in the company. However, in 1988 Horace Havemeyer Jr., by then retired from the sugar business, still owned 6000 BC Sugar shares. "Maybe I am emotional about the fact that B. T. Rogers worked for my great uncle," he wrote Peter Cherniavsky.
10. BCSA, Forrest Rogers correspondence.
11. BCSA, legal file in Secretary's files.
12. BCSA, Forrest Rogers memorandum, 1983.
13. BCSA, Forrest Rogers correspondence.
14. BCSA, Forrest Rogers memorandum, 1983.
15. J. J. Robinette letter to author.
16. Chief Justice E. K. Williams judgement, p. 72; copy in BCSA.
17. Ibid., pp. 128–29.
18. Heather Robertson, *Sugar Farmers,* p. 123.
19. Author interview with William Hetherington.

Chapter 17

1. BCSA, Forrest Rogers correspondence.
2. Author interview with William Hetherington.
3. Heather Robertson, *Sugar Farmers of Manitoba,* p. 108.
4. Author interview with William Hetherington.
5. Robertson, *Sugar Farmers,* p. 121.

6. Ibid., p. 133.
7. Hopper noted in the 1967 Manitoba Beet Growers Association, annual report: "The effort to increase the use of Manitoba sugar in Winnipeg homes has been successful. Investigation was made of the homes represented by some 487 Grade VI pupils in schools visited in the fall term 1966. Out of these 487 homes fewer than two per cent were users of cane sugar other than cube or brown sugar." The factory made neither of these.
8. Author interview with William Willison.
9. BCSA, Manitoba Sugar files, memoranda and correspondence.
10. Author interview with William Willison.
11. Author interview with William Hetherington.
12. BCSA, Forrest Rogers memorandum to William Hetherington.
13. Anecdote related by William Willison in an interview with the author.

Chapter 18

1. BCSA, H. A. Dunlop memorandum to Forrest Rogers, 21 May 1959.
2. BCSA, Canadian Sugar Factories operating reports.
3. BCSA, Taylor memorandum on Raymond factory, 2 May 1959.
4. Ibid.
5. BCSA, T. George Wood letter, 26 Oct. 1960. Wood added a poignant footnote to his letter: "Your courageous Mother & brothers, have influenced my own life. She is a contemporary, with the inspired President of our church—David McKay, now 87 years old. I Quote 'No blessing is truly ours, till we are aware, that God has blessed someone else with it, through us.' In this present issue, you can bless our people, and all the people of Southern Alberta."
6. Reported in the *Lethbridge Herald*.
7. Ironically, the old factory and its employees set records. The average daily slice of 1626 tons was the highest average in any campaign in the factory's history. On 18 October the factory set its all-time single-day record by slicing 1759 tons.
8. BCSA, Forrest Rogers correspondence.
9. BCSA, correspondence between BC Sugar and the Alberta government.
10. Author interview with William Hetherington.
11. Incident recalled by William Willison in an interview with the author.
12. BCSA, Peter Cherniavsky correspondence.

Chapter 19

1. Author interview with Peter Bergen.
2. In his privately printed memoir, *Jus' Ramblin'*, Snow said that beet growing was "dependent on the labour of many hands and strong backs which resulted in a stigma being attached to the industry."
3. Author interview with J. Gerald Snow.

4. Baker's comments appeared in Alberta Sugar Beet Growers Association annual reports of the period.
5. Forrest E. La Violette, *The Canadian Japanese and World War II*, p. 125.
6. Author interview with Arledge Hill.
7. BCSA, memorandum in H. A. Dunlop files re CSF Beet Sugar Subsidy.
8. Alberta Sugar Beet Growers Association annual reports detail labour recruitment.
9. Author interview with Peter Bergen.
10. Alberta Sugar Beet Growers Association annual report, 1967.
11. Author interview with Frank Low.

Chapter 20

1. BCSA, memorandum in World Seeds file.
2. BCSA, Cherniavsky memorandum.
3. The Jenkins affair intruded into a late January meeting in Vancouver between Cherniavsky and Dr. A. E. Hannah, who ran the Canada Department of Agriculture's rust laboratory in Winnipeg. Cherniavsky, in a memo to Peto, reported: "In Hannah's eyes when a man leaves an institution of any kind all his breeding materials belong to the institution and if he wishes to take some, he must apply in writing—this Jenkins did not do, and furthermore, Hannah is quite sure that Jenkins made off with some materials that even today the University doesn't know about."
4. BCSA, Forrest Rogers files, letter dated 25 May 1967.
5. Ibid.
6. BCSA, memorandum in World Seeds files.
7. BCSA, brief in World Seeds files.
8. BC Sugar had sunk more than US$750,000 into World Seeds, financing its operations during 1967 and 1968.
9. The company's investment in the seed company now totalled $1,021,159, which included $230,453 (US$214,000) for 50,000 shares (or 50 per cent interest) and $790,706 advanced to World Seeds as interest-bearing notes.

Chapter 21

1. This story was told to the author by Geoffrey Tullidge, a retired business partner in Western Plywood, whose father-in-law was the manager of the Bank of Montreal branch where the introduction was made.
2. BCSA, Western Plywood files.
3. Author interview with Geoffrey Tullidge.
4. BCSA, Western Plywood files, letters.
5. The company began 1957 owing $2.8 million to the bank, another $519,000 in a mortgage debt and $279,000 to the former owner of Murray Plywoods.
6. BCSA, Forrest Rogers correspondence, July 1966.

7. References to the cooperage can be found in BC Sugar's original minutebook and B. T. Rogers's letterbook in BCSA.
8. Author interview with H. Allan Dunlop.
9. Author interview with Peter Cherniavsky.
10. Anecdote recalled by Stuart Belkin, son of Morris Belkin, in an interview with the author.
11. Its personnel manager was a young social worker named David Barrett, a future premier of British Columbia. A social democrat distrusted by business, Barrett as premier relied on Belkin as a bridge to the business community.
12. In 1979 the sugar operations earned $6,725,000 million while the packaging business earned only $430,000. Even the oil and gas activities in which BC Sugar invested in 1976 generated $309,000 in profits.
13. Author interview with Peter Cherniavsky.
14. BCSA, letter in P. A. Cherniavsky files.

Chapter 22

1. Author interview with J. C. Anderson.
2. Author interview with Richard Whittall.
3. BCSA, B.C. Sugar annual report, 1976.
4. Potential investors in the petroleum industry were extremely negative to the National Energy Policy because it introduced higher taxes, attracted drilling incentives away from Alberta to the Arctic, and set as an objective a higher level of Canadian ownership in the industry.
5. BC Sugar invested $37.2 million cash and 455,000 of its own shares for a 53 per cent interest.
6. In this private placement, Kerr Addison bought $85 million Anderson shares and BC Sugar bought another $25 million.

Chapter 23

1. This spike disrupted a lucrative postwar export business B.C. Sugar had developed to Japan and Guam. Selling through San Francisco broker Kelley-Clarke & Company, BC Sugar exported to this market 1.7 million pounds of sugar in 1949 and 20 million in 1950. The company cut back sharply in 1951 to 2.1 million pounds because the Korean spike made it difficult to buy reasonably priced raws. When prices stabilized, the company sold Japan 10 million pounds in 1953 and 5 million in 1954. The market dried up as Japan's own refiners, who had suffered damage during the war, resumed production.
2. M. I. Rogers was a founder and long-time patron of the Vancouver Symphony, and Jan Cherniavsky became a frequent concert soloist with the orchestra.
3. Author interview with Peter Cherniavsky.

4. Correspondence in Peter Cherniavsky's private files.
5. BCSA tapes; interview by Nicholas Dykes.
6. The sugar companies were acquitted.
7. Letters from Horsey in Peter Cherniavsky files, BCSA.
8. BCSA, BC Sugar 1976 annual report.

Chapter 24

1. Author interview with Dave Ritchie, Dec. 1987.
2. As reported by James Clifford of Clifford & Associates, Vancouver, who was a Council employee at the time.
3. Author interview with G. B. Murdoch, Jan. 1988.
4. Author interview with Ray Haynes, Dec. 1987.
5. Collective agreements on file at BC Sugar. Initially, collective bargaining for the company was handled by Robert Boyd, its granite-willed general superintendent. After his death in 1951, the responsibility was given to Reginald Clark, the husband of B. T. Rogers's youngest daughter, Margaret. Clark, the son of a stock broker and a teenage sailing companion of Philip Rogers, was a distinguished colonel in the Princess Patricia's Canadian Light Infantry who returned home after the war with no job. His wife suggested that he talk with her brother Philip at the refinery; "Reggie had always been good with men," Margaret maintained. William Hetherington, who relied on Clark to help establish personnel policies at the beet factories, remembered him as a strong and forthright administrator. But because Clark was the negotiator of so many often generous contracts, Forrest Rogers teasingly called him "giveaway Clark." Ray Haynes characterized Clark as a "big, heavy, tough guy" who could be goaded to anger. At the end of one grievance committee meeting in mid-1952, a member of the union's committee, Joe Dockwray, snapped that Clark was "a better soldier than a negotiator." On another occasion, Clark pounded the table so strenuously that a sheaf of flimsy papers became airborne, and the negotiators dissolved into laughter at the sight of Clark swatting papers from the air.
6. The company, worried that employees would object to compulsory check-off, negotiated a clause in 1952 reading: "The Union agrees to indemnify the Company in the event any legal proceedings are commenced against the Company in connection with the payment of compulsory Union dues by any employee."
7. BC Sugar kept minutes of the bargaining meetings and these are filed in the company archives.
8. Anecdote recounted by Gib Murdoch in an interview with the author.
9. "They [the employees] weren't irresponsible," said Stanley George in an interview with the author, Dec. 1987.

10. Recounted in BC Sugar minutes of negotiation meetings; see BCSA, Labour file (restricted).
11. Ruling by BC Labour Relations Board, 14 July 1978.

Chapter 25

1. This characterization is by J. Gerald Snow, a former CSF agricultural superintendent.
2. Ernest Rogers wrote to T. George Wood: "Drastic interference with private enterprise is not, as a rule, practised by normal Governments, but the present Government in Alberta can hardly be considered normal." BCSA, Raymond Letterbook.
3. Author interview with Arledge Hill, May 1988.
4. This trait was singled out by G. M. Guccione, the general manager of Alberta Sugar.
5. Jensen told this anecdote on himself when he retired in 1975.
6. Alberta growers received $47.10 a ton for beets in 1973 and a record $51.34 in 1974.
7. BCSA, study by Bryon Karren. Karren's father, Fred, was superintendent at Picture Butte when it closed.
8. From the Alberta Sugar Beet Growers Marketing Board annual report, 1985.
9. *Lethbridge Herald,* 16 April 1985.
10. Author interview with G. M. Guccione, May 1988.
11. This position is recounted by Paul Thibodeau, writing in the 1985 annual report of the Alberta Sugar Beet Growers Marketing Board.
12. Author interview with G. C. Guccione, May 1988.
13. Alberta Sugar Beet Growers Marketing Board annual report, 1987.
14. Author interview with Brian Anderson.

Chapter 26

1. Chatterton is Hean's third given name.
2. Anecdote recalled by Hean in interview with author, August 1988.
3. Equally significant, sugar has been under assault for more than a quarter of a century from nutritionists and from makers of artificial sweeteners. BC Sugar was a founding member in 1965 of the Canadian Sugar Institute which has addressed sugar issues ranging from tariffs to nutrition. There has been a persistent danger that sugar's place in the diet would be undermined if mythology about sugar became conventional wisdom. For example, in 1975 the Food Prices Review Board, a federal agency, declared without any substantiation: "Sugar cannot be considered an essential food commodity from the point of view of nutrition and health." In June 1977, Marc Lalonde, then the federal minister of health, linked sugar consumption and heart disease in a speech to the Canadian Public Health Association in

Vancouver. That fall, despite three letters from Peter Cherniavsky to the minister, Lalonde's deputy repeated the assertion. Cherniavsky cited a long list of scientific authorities debunking the linkage since it had been first suggested in the 1950s. But he also realized that the attacks on sugar had gone beyond science to polemicism. In a letter late in 1977 to Lalonde's successor, Monique Begin, Cherniavsky lamented: "For twenty years or more food faddists have been propagating unfounded and often ridiculous ideas about sugar. Knowing these ideas to be nonsensical, and seeing them win no support from the scientific community, we have always assumed they would die away as such fad notions usually do. We were evidently mistaken, for a prejudice against sugar seems to have taken root in North America."

4. The partnership had expanded in July 1983 to include Tacoma businessman Alvin G. Ash and Vancouver consulting engineer Dr. Bruce Levelton.
5. Cherniavsky gave this valuation in remarks at BC Sugar's annual meeting six weeks after the acquisition closed.
6. Interview with author, June 1988.

ADDITIONAL SOURCES

Agnew, Netta
Anderson, Brian G.
Anderson, J.C.
Angus, Ian
Ashman, William
Belkin, Stuart
Bell-Irving, Mrs. Robin
Bentley, Peter
Bergen, Peter
Blankenbach, William
Bridge, D.J. (Dave)
Brown, William
Cherniavsky, Peter A.
Clark, Margaret
Craig, W. Royce
Davies, W.A.
Dunlop, H. Allan
Elliott, David
Faviell, Malcolm
Ferrier, Harry
Flegenheimer, Ernest
George, Stanley
Guccione, G.M.
Haynes, Ray
Hean, Arnold F.C.
Hecht, John
Hetherington, William
Hewitt, R.E.
Hill, Arledge
Hranac, Edward M.
Levelton, Dr. Bruce H.
Low, Alice
Low, Frank
Mowers, Cleo
Murdoch, G.B.
O'Brien, Richard S.
Palmer, Ted
Purdy, Dwight
Ritchie, David
Rogers, Brian
Rogers, Forrest
Rogers, Martin
Scales, MacCabe
Shelton, Frederic J.
Snow, J. Gerald
Stipkala, E. J. (Ed)
Thibodeau, Paul
Tullidge, Geoffrey
Willison, W.A.
Whittall, Richard
Wood, Mrs. F.G.H.
Wood, Lincoln A.
Zacharkow, Ted
Zeinstra, John

Appendix A

HOW SUGAR IS PROCESSED

A sugar refinery starts its refinery process with raw sugar—which in fact is already semi-processed, having been extracted from sugar cane in mills at the cane plantations. Sugar cane, a hardy grass, thrives in semi-tropical and tropical regions. (BC Sugar's plant in Vancouver is always called a refinery while the plants at Taber in Alberta and Fort Garry in Manitoba are referred to as factories. This usage is long-established in the sugar industry. A factory converts a raw material, the sugar beet, into the final product, sugar. Refined cane sugar is chemically indistinguishable from refined beet sugar.)

When B. T. Rogers began refining in 1890, the raw sugar he received was dark brown. Cut sugar cane and the syrup pressed from it are subject to browning when exposed too long to air, not unlike a sliced apple. In Rogers's day, the mills on the plantations were slow and somewhat primitive, typically producing dark and very sticky raw sugar. Refining this product into crisp white granulated sugar was a difficult technical challenge but one which Rogers mastered. Not all of his competitors were as skilled. Rogers once commented that a rival's imported sugar "stank," very likely because bacterial action had begun in poorly refined sugar.

Today's plantation sugar mills are highly efficient: the Vancouver refinery now receives tawny-coloured crystals of raw sugar already processed to 98.5 per cent purity. Easy to store in dry form, the raw sugar is warehoused and refined as required. Originally, it was shipped in baskets and then, for many years, in jute bags; it now arrives at the refinery in large bulk-carrying ocean vessels, each of which carries about 20 000 tonnes.

Refining begins in what is called the melt house, where the raws are blended with a warm sugar syrup. This mixture is spun in a centrifuge, which separates the tawny-coloured syrup from the raw sugar crystals. The raws then receive one more washing, after which the syrup and the wash water are combined and mixed with a fresh batch of raw sugar, starting the cycle again.

Meanwhile, the washed crystals are dissolved (or melted) with hot water. This raw liquor, as the solution is called, passes through screens to remove any foreign matter that may have entered the raw sugar in transit and then put through either a filter or a clarifier. The washed raw liquor, though still retaining some slight colour, is now almost pure sucrose. At this stage it enters the filter house and passes through bone charcoal filters. These are massive three-storey high cisterns (BC Sugar's refinery has forty-five) filled with charcoal. The carbon in the charcoal decolourizes the liquor, which drains from the bottom of the cisterns. The white liquor, as it is now called, is filtered to remove bacteria, concentrated and then introduced to the vacuum pan—perhaps the heart of the refinery. About five pounds of icing sugar is added to the vacuum pan with each fresh batch of white liquor. This fine sugar serves as the seed around which crystals form when the liquor is boiled under a vacuum. Slightly less than two hours is required to boil a forty-ton "strike," or lot, of white granulated sugar. Spun once again in a centrifugal to remove remaining traces of syrup, the sugar is then dried. After another two or three days of "conditioning"—a final drying to ensure that it does not go lumpy in its consumer packages—the sugar is ready for market.

The form most familiar to consumers is white granulated sugar of which there are special grades such as confectioners' sugar with small crystals that dissolve more rapidly. These grades are made by passing granulated sugar through sieves to segregate the crystal size. Icing sugar, the finest grade, is made by grinding granulated sugar. During the last thirty years, such food processors as soft drink bottlers, bakeries and wineries have found it more convenient to buy liquid sugar—granulated sugar dissolved in water.

One rare specialty sugar, Crystal Diamonds, has been discontinued by BC Sugar because its processing caused production delays in the refinery. The sugar was boiled for more than a day until each crystal was the size of a small gemstone. This luxury product was packed in purple presentation cartons and was popular for gift-giving or for special dining occasions. The story is told that Peter Cherniavsky, BC Sugar's chairman, was once a luncheon guest at a Tate & Lyle refinery in London, England, when its version of Crystal Diamonds was on the table. One of his hosts said proudly: "We only make this for Tate & Lyle and the Royal Family." Cherniavsky replied puckishly: "We make it too—and we make it only for *our* family."

The coloured syrups separated during the refining process go through another series of refining steps to make dark sugars or various syrups. BC Sugar makes a dark-brown Demerara sugar, which has relatively large, hard crystals, and two soft-textured coloured sugars, Best Brown and Yellow. The best-known of the refinery's syrups is, of course, Rogers' Golden Syrup, on the market since 1912; a thinner version, offered as a pancake syrup, has been made since the 1960s, while maple-flavoured and butter-flavoured pancake syrups were introduced recently.

In a sugar beet factory, the procedure varies somewhat. Beets, which look like large turnips and grow in temperate climates, are processed as soon as possible after harvesting since they deteriorate fairly quickly. Thus, the campaign, as this processing of beets is called, seldom lasts more than four months. As beets enter the factory, they are first washed of any earth clinging to them and then sliced into "cossettes"; next the cosettes are introduced into a unit called a diffuser, a massive drum in which they are mixed with hot water which extracts the sugar from the beets. The resulting juice is then treated much like the syrups in a cane refinery. The coloured syrup or molasses derived from sugar beet processing is not generally palatable to humans. However, it is an excellent supplemental feed for livestock, either on its own or, as is more common, incorporated in dried beet pulp made from the dried, de-sugared cossettes. The sale of beet pulp itself is a significant source of revenue for sugar beet factories. BC Sugar has exported beet pulp as far afield as Japan.

This description of sugar-making glosses over the considerable skill that is required to make sugar whose high quality and consistency is taken for granted by users. It is not taken for granted in either BC Sugar's refinery or its beet factories. B. T. Rogers was a perfectionist who, when the business expanded beyond the scope of his personal technical supervision, established around 1900 what likely was one of Vancouver's earliest commercial laboratories. It has remained a centre for quality control and technical innovation ever since, and is one reason why BC Sugar's refinery, in good times and bad, has operated efficiently and profitably.

Appendix B

A BRIEF CHRONOLOGY OF BC SUGAR (1890–1988)

1890
March 27: BC Sugar is incorporated with J. M. Browning as president. B. T. Rogers signs contract as managing director for $5,000 a year.

October: Shares with a par value of $100 are issued.

1891
January: Refinery produces its first sugar.

1892
May: Browning resigns as president.

June: B. T. Rogers and Mary Isabella Angus are married.

August: Forrest Angus is elected president. Rogers gets $20,000 bonus.

November 30: Company's first dividend is paid: $7.50 a share; total payout, $18,750.

1895
Company reports a $29,582 loss for the twelve months ended 31 March, the result of fierce competition and a wild swing in the price of raw sugar.

1897
June: B. T. Rogers succeeds Angus as president.

1898
Klondike gold rush causes business to improve dramatically. Company begins paying regular quarterly dividends.

1899
October: The original shares of BC Sugar are split four for one. A holding company, B. C. Sugar Refinery Ltd., is formed, and B. C. Sugar Refining Company Ltd. becomes the operating company. The shareholders have shares in the holding company, whose only income is dividends from the operating company. Thus, only dividend income has to be disclosed. The operating company's finances remained a closed book to shareholders until after World War II.

1905
Vancouver-Fiji Sugar Company is formed.

1907
Company pays a 100 per cent stock dividend, in effect splitting shares two for one.

1910
Company registers its trademark: B.C. Sugar Refinery–Rogers. The signature in the oval is that of B. T. Rogers.

1913
Rogers' Golden Syrup is introduced.

1914
BC Sugar switches from the Canadian Bank of Commerce to Bank of Montreal because of its superior branch network in the West.

1915
Blythe Rogers becomes vice-president and is appointed to the board of directors.

1916
BC Sugar pays special $400,000 dividend (a 160 per cent bonus on capital stock).

1917
Company pays special 120 per cent dividend in April and a 160 per cent dividend in December.

Company is accused of price-fixing; prosecution is dropped and company is exonerated.

April: Refinery workers strike and stay out for four months.

1918
June 17: B. T. Rogers dies.

Blythe Rogers becomes president.

1920
BC Sugar, previously provincially chartered, re-incorporates with a Dominion charter. This is done to safeguard the company from being entangled by the wide powers of a new provincial Public Utilities Act, which empowered the B.C. government to declare any business a public utility.

February: B.C. Legislature investigates an allegation that BC Sugar is manipulating sugar supply. Company is exonerated.

May 6: Blythe Rogers dies.

May 11: J. W. F. Johnson becomes president.

November 20: Ernest Rogers is named vice-president.

1921
Dramatic rise and fall of world sugar price cause the company to lose $321,000, one of only four losses suffered during the company's history.

1923
Vancouver-Fiji Sugar Company is closed.

1924
Company pays special $800,000 dividend, sharing a windfall gain on foreign exchange.

1930
J. W. F. Johnson resigns from presidency; Ernest Rogers succeeds him in May.

1931
Canadian Sugar Factories Ltd., Raymond, Alberta, is purchased.

1936
Picture Butte, Alberta, beet sugar factory is constructed.

1939
July 25: Ernest Rogers drowns while on a yachting holiday with his family.

Philip Rogers becomes president.

December 19: J. W. F. Johnson dies.

1944
BC Sugar acquires Ozama Sugar Company in the Dominican Republic.

Sugar Workers' Union is certified in the refinery.

BC Sugar invests in Western Plywood Company, Vancouver.

BC Sugar takes over the Buckerfield's beet seed operation in Ladner, B.C.

1950
September: Taber (sugar beet) factory is opened by Mrs. B.T. Rogers.

1953
November: Philip T. Rogers is succeeded by his brother Forrest as president and managing director.

1955
Ozama Sugar Company is sold.

BC Sugar acquires a block of shares in Manitoba Sugar Company.

1956
Restrictive Trade Practices Commission launches investigation into BC Sugar's control of Manitoba Sugar.

1957
BC Sugar completes takeover of Manitoba Sugar.

1958
Federal Minister of Justice launches Combines prosecution against BC Sugar.

1959
Western Plywood is taken over by U.S. Plywood.

1960
August: BC Sugar wins Combines case.

1961
June 9: Philip T. Rogers dies.

Company lists its shares on the Vancouver and Toronto Stock Exchanges. Company issues a tax-free dividend of one $20 preferred share for each common share outstanding.

1962
Head office of Canadian Sugar Factories is moved from Raymond to Lethbridge.

1963
Raymond factory is closed.

Refinery installs facilities to make and sell liquid sugar for its industrial customers.

1967
BC Sugar acquires 50 per cent of World Seeds.

1969
World Seeds interest is sold to its American officers. BC Sugar takes a $550,000 write-off on its investment.

1970
Fifty per cent interest in Belkin Packaging is acquired 30 June 1970. A bond issue of $9.5 million is made, the first time in the company's history that long-term debt is used to finance an expansion.

1973
Peter Cherniavsky succeeds Forrest Rogers as president.

1975
June 2: Second strike in company's history begins and lasts ten months.

1976
BC Sugar invests $5 million, as an initial investment of a planned $15 million over five years, in a joint venture called Fairweather Gas, with Anderson Exploration Ltd., Calgary.

1977
Belkin Packaging buys Somerville Industries and becomes a national force in packaging.

Forrest Rogers retires as chairman.

BC Sugar decides to close the Picture Butte factory and concentrate beet processing at Taber.

1978
Canadian Sugar Factories changes its name to Alberta Sugar Company.

Ladner beet seed plant is sold to Canada Beta Seed.

Picture Butte factory closes.

1979
Employee share purchase plan is started with 82 per cent of eligible employees buying shares.

1980
BC Sugar sells its interest in Belkin Packaging to Keycorp Industries for $18,040,000, realizing a gain of $11,063,000 on the investment.

1981
BC Sugar buys 24 per cent of Anderson Oil & Gas for $17.2 million and 455,000 shares. Subsequently, BC Sugar buys another 27 per cent for $31 million.

1983
BC Sugar invests $25 million in Anderson Exploration.

1984
BC Sugar raises $23 million in sale of one million common shares (with 500,000 warrants attached)—the company's first public equity issue.

BC Sugar acquires controlling interest in Chatterton Petrochemical Corp.

1985
Taber beet factory suspends processing; no sugar beets are grown in Alberta because of a dispute between the company and the growers on sharing returns.

1986
BC Sugar acquires control of Kalama Chemicals, Seattle.

Taber resumes production.

Head office of Alberta Sugar Company moves from Lethbridge to Taber.

1988
May: William Brown is named president and chief operating officer, with Peter Cherniavsky as chairman.

BC Sugar pays its biggest dividend in history, distributing shares of Anderson Exploration, worth about $44 million, to BC Sugar shareholders.

Appendix C

DIRECTORS OF BC SUGAR—1890 TO PRESENT

J. M. Browning	1890–1892
Harry B. Abbott	1890–1915
Forrest Angus	1890–1920
James C. Keith	1890–1894
B. T. Rogers	1890–1918
John Hendry	1892–1900
Ernest E. Evans	1894–1899
Cesare J. Marani	1898–1902
George Coleman	1899–1906
Osborne Plunkett	1902–1910
William Prentice	1906–1907
J. W. F. Johnson	1907–1938
L. G. McPhillips	1910–1913
Mrs. B. T. Rogers	1913–1960
Blythe D. Rogers	1915–1920
Robert Adamson	1916–1946
Mrs. B. D. Rogers	1920–
E. T. Rogers	1920–1939
D. Forbes Angus	1920–1940
Mrs. E. T. Rogers	1925–1965
P. T. Rogers	1938–1961
Forrest Rogers	1939–1982
(Director Emeritus 1982–87)	
Dr. Henry F. Angus	1940–1969
George Pierson	1942–1951
Alan Robertson	1944–1969
Arthur C. Law	1946–1970
Reginald H. Tupper	1951–1972
P. A. Cherniavsky	1960–Present
H. A. Dunlop	1961–1981
H. R. Whittall	1965–Present
John W. Pitts	1969–Present
Ian Angus	1969–1986
F. C. Wilkinson	1970–Present
W. R. C. Patrick	1971–1978
W. R. Hetherington	1978–1988
W. C. Brown	1981–Present
J. G. Cochrane	1981–Present
J. C. Anderson	1982–Present
R. Stuart Angus	1988–Present
Ms. Pat Carney	1989–Present

ORIGINAL SUBSCRIBERS

The following thirty-seven people subscribed for the original capital ($250,000) of BC Sugar. Thirty per cent of the stock was held in the United States, forty-five per cent in Eastern Canada and the remaining twenty-five per cent in British Columbia.

Harry Abbott, Vancouver
D. Forbes Angus, Montreal
Forrest Angus, Victoria
John M. Browning, Vancouver
Louise J. Casamajor, Brooklyn, N.Y.
George W. Cummings, New York City
Charles T. Dunbar, Vancouver
Ernest W. Gerbracht, Brooklyn, N.Y.
Caledon F. Gilder, Montreal
Mrs. Henriette Hamilton, Montreal
Charles F. Havemeyer, New York City
Edmund P. Hemenway, Vancouver
John Hendry, Vancouver
A. R. G. Heward, Montreal
E. H. Heward, St. John, P.Q.
E. Stuart Johnson, Vancouver
J. C. Keith, Vancouver
George A. Kirkpatrick, Kingston, Ont.
J. M. Lefevre, Vancouver
Andrew Little, New York City
Duncan McIntyre, Montreal
George G. McKay, Vancouver
W. D. Matthews, Toronto
George Olds, Montreal
David Oppenheimer, Vancouver
E. B. Osler, Toronto
B. T. Rogers, Vancouver
Harry Rhodes, Vancouver
Otto Semisch, Vancouver
Charles H. Senff, Queens, N.Y.
Donald A. Smith, Montreal
Thomas W. Stephens, Montclair, N.J.
Elihu Thomson, Swamscott, Mass.
James P. Townley, Vancouver
W. C. VanHorne, Montreal
Paul Wilcox, New York City
Johann Wulffsohn, Vancouver

Appendix D

LONG-SERVICE EMPLOYEES

A remarkable number of individuals have worked nearly all their working lives for BC Sugar or its subsidiaries. In some instances, several members of the same families have had careers with the company. It is a comment on the satisfaction that these people derived from their work.

The most exceptional are those who have worked more than forty years. The following list notes such individuals who have retired, as well as others still in the company's employ, including chairman Peter Cherniavsky.

BC SUGAR

Name	*Occupation*	*Service Years*
ANDERSON, *Monty*	Packing House Foreman	1925–1967
BANKS, *William*	Shift Superintendent	1927–1974
BLANKENBACH, *William*	General Chemist	1929–1970
BOOTH, *Leslie*	Costing—Main Office	1911–1957
BORRIE, *Violet*	Packing House	1909–1950
BRUCE, *William*	Purchasing Agent	1890–1932
BURNEY, *Edward*	Machine Shop	1929–1972
BYFORD, *Harry* G.	Bag Room Foreman	1915–1962

Name	*Occupation*	*Service Years*
CHALMERS, *Thomas*	No. 2 Man	1926–1967
CHERNIAVSKY, *Peter A.*	Chairman of Board	1948–Active
COLQUHOUN, *Thomas*	Pipefitter	1934–1980
COOKE, *Carleton*	Foreman	1896–1940
COPP, *Kay*	Packaging	1948–Active
CORBIERG, *Arthur*	Crane Operator	1906–1949
CORRADO, *Kenneth*	Instrument Engineer	1938–1981
CORRADO, *Vernon*	Sub-Foreman-Packing	1940–1985
COULTER, *John*	Sweetland Presses	1936–1978
CRAIG, *Douglas*	Chief Draftsman	1945–1987
CUMMIFORD, *Al*	Mechanic, Garage	1946–1987
DAVEY, *Kathleen M.*	Executive Secretary	1946–Active
DAVIES, *William A.*	General Sales Manager	1939–1983
DICKENSON, *Edward*	Electrician	1930–1980
DUFRESNE, *George*	Labour	1929–1971
DUKE, *Lionel*	Material Receiver	1928–1973
EDMONDS, *Arthur*	Sales Department	1906–1950
ELMS, *Arthur*	Master Mechanic	1925–1974
FARREL, *Percy*	Constable	1918–1966
FERGUSON, *Peter*	Mechanic	1927–1968
FROST, *Austin T.*	Pipefitter	1919–1959
FROST, *Wilfred*	Pipefitter	1920–1963
FULLER, *Marshall*	Foreman	1907–1960
GLOVER, *Agnes*	Restaurant	1923–1963
HADDON, *Robert*	Assistant Sales Manager	1897–1944
HAKE, *Joffre*	Welder	1939–1985
HAMILTON, *Frank*	Pipefitter	1920–1962
HARRIS, *Henry A.*	No. 2 Laboratory	1929–1970
HAWTHORNE, *William*	Machinist, Leading Hand	1940–1986
HENDERSON, *Thomas B.*	Watchman	1920–1965
HENNEY, *Gordon*	Machine Shop Foreman	1935–1978
HENNEY, *John T.*	Foreman	1911–1954
HETHERINGTON, *Robina*	Sewing Room	1920–1960
HEWITT, *Ronald E.*	Office Manager	1930–1974
HILL, *George*	Foreman	1920–1961
HITCHENS, *Edward F.*	Superintendent-Packing & Warehouse	1936–1980
HOLTON, *John*	Refined Centrifugals	1946–1987
HOPE, *Kenneth*	Accounting	1934–1974
KENYON, *Wilfred*	Plant Superintendent	1921–1966
LEWIS, *Gordon*	Power House	1920–1970

Name	*Occupation*	*Service Years*
LIVINGSTONE, *Harriet (Jo)*	Packaging-Envelopes	1946–Active
McGLASHAN, *George*	Office Manager	1910–1957
McINTYRE, *Thomas*	Draftsman	1925–1972
McKENZIE, *Elsie R.*	Restaurant	1927–1971
McKILLOP, *J.F.*	Mechanic	1926–1967
McKILLOP, *William*	Mechanic	1947–Active
McKINNON, *Alexander*	Oiler	1890–1937
McLELLAN, *Jack*	Sweetland Liquor Operator	1947–1987
McLEOD, *Donald*	Electrician	1939–1981
MAITLAND, *Adam*	Tank Floor	1947–1987
MILLAR, *John*	Shipping Foreman	1923–1966
MILLER, *William R.*	Labour	1927–1973
MILLS, *Reginald*	Electrician	1925–1973
MITCHELL, *John C.*	Machine Shop Foreman	1931–1973
MOROPITO, *Frank*	Labour	1937–1980
MORRIS, *Donald*	Filter House Foreman	1919–1969
MURDOCH, *Gilbert*	Warehouse & Packing Supt.	1937–1985
MURDOCH, *William*	Superintendent	1929–1978
NEVILL, *Ralph J.*	Electrician	1918–1958
NIELSON, *Alan*	Chemical Engineer	1947–1987
NORDIN, *Joel A.*	Pipefitter	1926–1969
NORTH, *John S.*	Personnel Manager	1942–1983
PAVEY, *Harry W.*	Electrician, Lead	1902–1943
PERRY, *Albert*	Mechanical Superintendent	1942–1987
PERRY, *H. William*	Superintendent	1915–1958
PERRY, *John R.*	Shift Superintendent	1928–1968
PILLING, *Jack*	Raw Sugar Warehouse	1946–1987
PLUMBLEY, *Oswald (Ozzie)*	Carpenter	1935–1975
PURCHAS, *William*	Coppersmith	1923–1973
RAINS, *Frank*	Sugar Boiler	1928–1973
REID, *George*	Process Shift Supt.	1947–1989
REID, *John*	Purchasing Agent	1920–1970
REID, *W.C.*	Icing Station	1934–1975
RIPPON, *Harold*	Bench Chemist	1925–1974
ROGERS, *Forrest*	President	1935–1977
SANDERSON, *Charles*	Painter	1927–1969
SCOTT, *Arthur*	Storekeeper	1930–1977
SCOTT, *Flora M.*	Shipping Checker	1922–1966
SHAW, *John H.*	Clarification System	1949–Active
SHOOVE, *E. Frank*	Plant Superintendent	1918–1965
SKATCH, *Eris*	Packaging	1946–Active

Name	*Occupation*	*Service Years*
STOBBART, *Hugh M.*	Labour	1927–1968
STOBBART, *Richard*	Warehouse & Packaging Supt.	1943–1987
TACK, *Simon R.*	Carpenter	1927–1968
TUDGE, *G. Cecil*	Sugar Boiler	1920–1968
TUDGE, *Percy A.*	Container Recorder	1924–1972
TURNBULL, *Ernest*	Refined Centrifugals	1946–1988
VALACH, *Vincent*	Material Receiver	1949–Active
WAKLIN, *Nelson*	Material Receiver	1933–1977
WATRET, *Robert*	Storekeeper	1912–1955
WEBSTER, *Ernest*	Superintendent	1895–1944
WHYTE, *James*	Labour	1918–1958
WOOD, *Lincoln A.*	Purchasing Manager (1936–1970 CSF) (1970–1980 BC Sugar)	1936–1980
YOUNG, *Geraldine*	Purchasing Stenographer	1945–1988
YOURCHEK, *Joseph*	Packing House Foreman	1926–1973

ALBERTA SUGAR COMPANY

Name	*Occupation*	*Service Years*
BENNETT, *C. Rich*	Chief Electrician	1939–1980
DEWSBERRY, *Francis J.*	Sugar End Foreman	1926–1969
ERICKSON, *Lawrence M.*	Master Mechanic	1936–1978
FINLEY, *Andrew*	Master Mechanic	1930–1976
FINLEY, *Clifford M.*	Shift Superintendent	1936–1980
FINLEY, *John Ray*	Fieldman	1935–1980
GIBB, *Roscoe F.*	Engineering Assistant	1927–1972
GILL, *Harold*	Shift superintendent	1943–1985
HAGUE, *Albert E.*	Plant Supervisor	1928–1976
HAGUE, *Wilfred*	Superintendent	1927–1972
HEDLEY, *William R.*	Head mechanic	1947–1987
HILL, *Arledge W.*	Agricultural Supt.	1945–1985
KARREN, *Clinton H.*	Shift Superintendent	1937–1983
KARREN, *Fred H.*	Superintendent	1937–1983
McLEAN, *Joseph A.*	Superintendent	1925–1966
O'BRIEN, *Richard S.*	Office Manager	1928–1974
PILLING, *Harold*	Lead Mechanic	1931–1976
PILLING, *Keith E.*	Sales Supervisor	1931–1977
PRICE, *Darwin H.*	Head Mechanic	1939–1983
QUINTON, *Frank*	Shift Superintendent	1929–1974

Name	*Occupation*	*Service Years*
ROLFSON, *Brownie*	Chief Electrician	1931–1972
SHAW, *Kenneth W.*	Purchasing Clerk	1939–1985
SNOW, *J. Gerald*	Agricultural Supt.	1935–1977
STONE, *Allwyn Y.*	Fieldman	1932–1977
STRONG, *Joseph P.*	Beet End Foreman	1927–1973
TURNER, *Fred H.*	Credit Manager	1934–1978
WATSON, *Leonard D.*	Chief Accountant	1936–1981
WEST, *Clifford D.*	Superintendent of Op.	1929–1976
WEST, *Russell J.*	Shift Superintendent	1941–1985

MANITOBA SUGAR COMPANY

BATTEY, *Richard H.*	Warehouse Supervisor	1941–1981
COMEAU, *George J.*	Chief Powerhouse Engineer	1948–1989
NEUFELD, *Dietrich A.*	Beet Accountant	1948–1988
YEATES, *G. Russel*	Accountant	1946–Active
ZACHARKOW, *Ted P.*	Chief Accountant	1944–Active

References

Adachi, Ken. *The Enemy That Never Was: A History of the Japanese Canadians.* Toronto: McClelland & Stewart, 1976.

Aguilar, Luis E. *Cuba 1933: Prologue to Revolution.* Ithica, N.Y.: Cornell University Press, 1972.

Barman, Jean. *Growing Up in British Columbia: Boys in Private School.* Vancouver: University of British Columbia Press, 1984.

Batten, Jack. *Robinette: The Dean of Canadian Lawyers.* Toronto: Macmillan of Canada, 1984.

Bell, Ian. *The Dominican Republic.* Boulder, Colo: Westview Press, 1981.

Bentall, Shirley F. *The Charles Bentall Story: A Man of Industry and Integrity.* Vancouver: The Bentall Group, 1986.

Broadfoot, Barry. *Years of Sorrow, Years of Shame: The Story of the Japanese Canadians in World War II.* Toronto: Doubleday Canada, 1977.

Canada. Restrictive Trade Practices Commission. Report concerning the sugar industry in western Canada and a proposed merger of sugar companies. Ottawa: Queen's Printer, 1957.

———. St. Mary and Milk River Water Development Committee: Report. Ottawa: King's Printer, 1942.

———. Tariff Board. Report Relative to the Investigation Ordered by the Minister of Finance Respecting Sugar. Ottawa: Information Canada, 1971.

Catlin, Daniel Jr. *Good Work Well Done: The Sugar Business Career of Horace*

Havemeyer, 1903–1956. Privately printed (New York, 1988).

Crassweller, Robert D. *Trujillo: The Life and Times of a Caribbean Dictator.* New York: Macmillan, 1966.

Foster, Peter. *The Blue-Eyed Sheiks.* Toronto: Collins, 1979.

Gregson, Harry. *A History of Victoria 1842–1970.* Vancouver: J.J.Douglas, 1977.

Hugill, Antony. *Sugar and All That. . . ; A History of Tate & Lyle.* London, Eng.: Gentry Books, 1978.

Kerr, G.J.A., and Donnelly, J.A. *Fiji in the Pacific.* Milton, Qld., Australia: Jacaranda Press, 1969.

Kluckner, Michael. *M.I.Rogers 1869–1965.* Privately published memoir of Mary Isabella Rogers. (Vancouver, 1988.)

———. *Vancouver: The Way It Was.* North Vancouver: Whitecap Books, 1984.

Janes, Hurford, and Sayers, H.J. *The Story of Czarnikow.* London, Eng.: Harley Publishing Co., 1963.

La Violette, Forrest E. *The Canadian Japanese and World War II.* Toronto: University of Toronto Press, 1948.

Lipton, Charles. *The Trade Union Movement of Canada 1827–1959.* Montreal: Canadian Social Publications, 1967.

Myers, Gustavus. *History of the Great American Fortunes.* New York: Random House, 1909.

Ormsby, Margaret A. *British Columbia: A History.* Macmillan, 1958.

Redpath Centennial: One Hundred Years of Progress. Montreal: Canada & Dominion Sugar Co., 1954.

Robertson, Heather. *Sugar Farmers of Manitoba: The Manitoba Sugar Beet Industry in Story and Picture.* Winnipeg: Manitoba Sugar Beet Growers Association, 1968.

Rogers, M.I. *The Story of the B.C. Sugar Refinery.* Privately printed by BC Sugar. (Vancouver, 1958.)

Roy, Patricia E. *Vancouver: An Illustrated History.* Toronto: James M. Lorimer & Co., 1980.

Scholefield, E.O.S. and Howay, F.W. *British Columbia: From the Earliest Times to the Present.* 4 vols. Toronto: S.J. Clarke Publishing Co., 1914.

Schroeder, Susan. *Cuba: A Handbook of Historical Statistics.* Boston: G.K. Hall & Co., 1982.

Weitzenhoffer, Frances. *The Havemeyers: Impressionism Comes to North America.* New York: Harry N. Abrams, 1986.

Williams, Eric. *From Columbus to Castro, The History of the Caribbean 1492–1969.* London, Eng.: Andre Deutsch, 1970.

Wood, T. George. *Memories of My Life.* Privately published (Vancouver, 1961).

Index